Shirley, Goodness & Mercy

'...an authentic and important contribution to South African literature; it is also an entertaining social document of a specific community.'

Mail and Guardian

'Van Wyk is a man possessed with writing and transmitting a love of literature so that it makes a positive impact on people's lives.'

Sowetan

'*Shirley, Goodness & Mercy* with its fulsome homage to Es'kia Mphahlele's seminal *Down Second Avenue*, is unprecedented in South African literary narratives of the self. Well worth waiting for, this is a memoir not to miss.'

Sunday Independent

'A lovely book; well told and beautifully executed.'

Cape Times

'*Shirley, Goodness & Mercy* is a tale of optimism and hope – the kind of tale that South Africans tell best.'

Citizen

About the author

Chris van Wyk was born in Baragwanath Hospital, Soweto, in 1957. He was educated at Riverlea High School and still lives in Riverlea, Johannesburg, where he works as a full-time writer. He writes poetry (published in Denmark, Sweden, France, Turkey, the UK, the USA and Canada), books for children and teenagers, short stories and novels.

In 1979 he won the Olive Schreiner Award for his collection of poems, *It Is Time to Go Home* and in 1997 he was awarded the Sanlam Prize for the best South African short story, for a story entitled 'Magic'.

His novel, *The Year of the Tapeworm*, was published in 1998. In 2003 he published 'Freedom Fighters', a series of ten biographies for children and young teens including those of Nelson Mandela, Helen Joseph, Desmond Tutu, Thabo Mbeki and Steve Biko. The books are used extensively in schools.

A biography entitled *Now Listen Here – The Life and Times of Bill Jardine* was also published in 2003. *Shirley, Goodness & Mercy* is his latest work.

By the same author

It Is Time to Go Home
The Year of the Tapeworm
Now Listen Here: The Life and Times of Bill Jardine

CHRIS VAN WYK

Shirley, Goodness & Mercy

A childhood memoir

PICADOR AFRICA

First published 2004 by Picador Africa

This edition published 2005 by Picador Africa an imprint of
Pan Macmillan South Africa
PO Box 411717, Craighall
Johannesburg 2024
www.picadorafrica.co.za

ISBN 1 770 10021 0

Typeset in 10 on 12 point Palatino by The Setting Stick
Cover design by Donald Hill of Studio Five
Chris van Wyk and Cedric Nunn
Endpaper photograph by courtesy of Chris van Wyk

For Kathy

Disclaimer

The names and surnames of some characters have been changed to protect their privacy.

Contents

Prudence in Tomato Yard

TODAY IS THE DAY I SEE MAGIC.

We're living in Newclare, Johannesburg. It's 1961 and I'm four years old. There are dramas unfolding in the country, which are putting black faces on the front pages of newspapers on a daily basis. The Sharpeville massacre, the banning of the ANC and the PAC. The beginning of long prison terms for many.

But I know nothing of any of this. My world is a slum called Tomato Yard, which got its name from the blotches of rotting tomatoes and vegetable peels around the over-full dustbins.

But what do I know about slums and the struggle?

Tomato Yard is my home and I am happy here.

Four rows of tiny cemented-together cottages make up a square. We – me, Ma and Dad, live in one of these cottages. Everyone's back door looks on to the courtyard, the washing-lines and the shared outside toilets. In lots of places on outside walls paint is peeling away and rough brick is peeping through crumbling plaster. The front doors of the row of houses where I live open on to Southey Avenue. But it's in the courtyard, Tomato Yard, where life happens.

We live so close together that we could be one family.

Even at that young age I remember realising that I am a new arrival, gazing up at people who, by their sheer size and their confidence and their knowledge of where the butcher and the grocer are, have been around before me. Life is one huge magic show.

Two doors from us live the Sacks brothers, Allan and Irwin. They are so big and tall that they could be adults if they wanted to. All they need is a wife each, because that seems to be what makes people adults. Allan is in his final year of primary school. Irwin is doing his first year at high school. They're always writing in books with pencils – and then rubbing some of it out again.

Today finds me playing outside our door when one of them calls me over.

'Hey, Chris!' It's Allan. 'Come over here quickly, I wanna show you something.'

Allan and Irwin are sitting at their kitchen table where, as usual, their books are spread out. It's a hot afternoon and the generous sun warms their kitchen, glancing off glasses and shiny doorknobs.

'You wanna see magic?'

Of course I do.

They push their books aside and place a teaspoon, the metal top of a medicine bottle, a hairclip and a yellow tin mug on the kitchen table. Allan slides his hand underneath the table. I follow his hand but he says:

'Don't worry about my hands, just watch the stuff on the table.'

The things on the table begin to move about – without any help from anywhere. My face has such a stunned look on it that the brothers fling their heads back laughing.

A new couple, the Jacobses, moves into the Yard, keeping me in thrall almost from the moment they arrive. His name is Nicholas. This is exactly the same name as my father's. Why? How could that be? And she has the biggest stomach in the world. I would have been even more enthralled – no, disbelieving – if someone had told me there was a baby growing inside there.

One day Uncle Nicholas, sitting in the shade of a peach tree, calls me over. He's fixing his scooter, which is leaning unhappily against a wall. A tool-box squats at his feet and he has smears of grease on his face and hands.

A tool-box is a strange thing. I've seen many in my life since that day. They have compartments, shelves and sub-shelves, which rise up and present themselves when you open the lid as if they're saying: 'Look at me, look at me.' They are all full of nuts, bolts, screws, wire, screwdrivers, pliers, things with such strange shapes that you wouldn't believe they had names. But here's the thing: very seldom have I seen a man put his hand into his tool-box and come out with what he wants. They are forever pushing aside cascades of screws, digging into strata of greasy ball-bearings and bolts. Usually they are all after one thing: the twin of 'this one' that they've got in the other hand – and which they hardly ever find.

Uncle Nick is digging and poking around in his tool-box. Out comes a pinkie-sized Eveready battery, a piece of electric wire, a tiny light bulb.

'Watch here,' he says. He rigs all these things together and the bulb shines brightly in the shade of the peach tree, like a distant planet on which life has been discovered. It's so cute and I wonder if he would find it in his heart to give it to me.

As it turns out there's no need to worry: it had been meant for me even before the light went on. This is electricity. In our home we have candles that drip long streaks of wax all evening and make our shadows dance and bounce about on the walls, lamps that hiss and a primus stove that Ma pricks and pumps into life.

Another of our neighbours are husband and wife, Hansie and Maureen Pyos. Hansie is a short man with a perpetual grin on his face – which increases fivefold whenever he has a drink in him. His wife is even shorter than he is, with a voice that has a high pitch whether she's happy or sad. They have no children.

One sunny Sunday afternoon, I stand on our front stoep, unaware of the discovery I am about to make. A black teenage boy pedals down the street past me on his bicycle, ringing his bell and calling out his wares. Except that he has no wares because all I see is a bunch of green sticks stuck into his carrier like broomless broomsticks, and he's shouting down an already noisy street: 'Sootreek! Sootreek! One penny. One penny!'

Uncle Hansie materialises in the street, stops the boy and buys two sticks from him. He calls me and gives me one.

'What must I do with this?'

'Eat it.' I can't say he grinned because that was a fixed feature of his face.

'I don't eat sticks,' I tell him.

This time he really does do a sort of extra grin. He peels away some green bark and gives the stick back to me. 'Suck there,' he says.

I'm suspicious and suck tentatively. Sweet heaven!

Uncle Hansie laughs. I turn on the heels of my Jumping Jacks and run home.

In our two-roomed house I run into the room where my mother and father are lying on the bed.

'Sootreek!' I announce breathlessly, making asterisks in the air with my treasure. 'Uncle Hansie bought it for me. Sootreek! Taste.'

My mother takes a quick suck, but my father refuses. Instead he says to me, 'What's this?' I tell him again.

'*Soet riet,*' he says the words slowly. 'It's two Afrikaans words: sweet and reed ...'

My mother is so pretty and life is good. Even after the accident.

I am my parents' firstborn and I have a little brother, Derek, who the aeroplane has dropped off at our house ... I don't know when. Either while I was out on my backyard wanderings or when I was asleep.

One evening Ma is making *vetkoek*. Derek and I are watching her. Watching her roll out the dough from a fat blob into a thick buttery eiderdown on the kitchen table. Watching her cut it into squares, sprinkle on flour. The blue panelyte table is white and powdery. The primus stove is hissing an angry blue flame. I am four years old and big enough to see all of this if I stand on my toes. Derek is two so he has to get on to a chair to see, and he's sucking his dummy since breasts are so close but oh so far away.

The pan is on the primus stove and into its hot oil Ma places the wads of dough. The pan greets each one with an excited sizzle ... *chishhh* ... *chishhh* ... then something goes wrong and it all turns into a poem that I would write a quarter of a century later.

Memory

Derek is dangling on the kitchen chair
while I'm shuffling about in a flutter of flour.
Mummy is making *vetkoek* on the primus.
Derek is too small to peer over the table,
that's why Mummy has perched him on the chair.
His dummy twitters so he's a bird.

I'm not that small; I was four in July.
I'm tall enough to see what's going on;
I'm a giraffe and the blotches of shadow
on the ceiling and the walls
from the flames of the primus and candle
are the patches on my back.

Daddy's coming home soon
from the factory where they're turning him into
a cupboard that creaks,
but the *vetkoek* are sizzling and growing
like bloated gold coins.
We're rich!

This is the first vivid memory of childhood.
Why have I never written it all down before?
Maybe because the pan falls with a clatter
and the oil swims towards the twittering bird.
Mummy flattens her forearm on the table
stopping the seething flood.

As she does so she pleads with the bird to fly
away, quietly, so as not to ruffle his feathers.
But my brother clambers off the chair
as if he has all the time in the world.
Sensing danger, the twittering gives way to a wail
and the giraffe's patches flare on the restive walls.
Mummy gives a savage scream that echoes across the
decades
and cauterises my childhood like a long scar.

But, remember, I mentioned an accident. What happened in the kitchen with the *vetkoek*, OK, that was an accident. But not a big one, not the one that no one will ever forget.

The Domingos live two doors away from us. They have two daughters, Prudence and Dorothy. Prudence is blonde with spark-ling green eyes. Dorothy has dark hair and deep blue eyes.

Dorothy is shy and soft-spoken. She keeps those blue eyes of hers inside her home mostly, where she does chores and pages through old magazines. Prudence is always outside, racing about, soaking up the sun and the smells and the gossip. She's wild, full of mischief and plans.

They both come into our lives when they're in their teens. Prudence is about nine years older than I am and about twelve years younger than Ma. So in a way she's my friend and my mother's buddy.

On Saturday mornings Prudence bursts into our kitchen, like a tornado, all dressed up in a clean white dress and a big bow in her golden hair.

'Is he ready, Shirley?' she says, out of breath as usual.

I look up at her in my own clean clothes: socks, shoes, shirt and shorts.

'Where are we going?' she asks me.

'Bioscope!' I shout out loud and proud.

'And what are we gonna see?'

I whip two imaginary guns from my invisible belt and fire them at her and Ma – '*dwa-dwa-dwa*'.

'But first you must pee-pee-pee,' Prudence says.

Then Prudence holds my hand and we walk down the bustling Saturday morning Southey Avenue to the bioscope four blocks away. It's called the Reno, but also 'Die Jood' because its owner is a Jew. I promise not to ask to pee until the interval and sit on her lap watching the antics of … whoever.

Prudence is a beauty – who greatly admires my mother's beauty.

'Shirley, Shirley,' she calls, breathless as usual, and excited, as she skips into our kitchen one Saturday morning. She is a girl with secrets flying out of her adolescent bosom.

'What, Prudie?'

'Alfie? The butcher?'

'What about him?'

'He asked me if you and I were sisters and I said yes, so if he asks you, just say yes, OK?'

'OK.' Ma smiles.

Saturday evenings are Prudence's favourite visiting times –

she pops in every day of the week but stays longest on Saturday evenings. She fills the kitchen with her breathless plans and her schemes and her life. She helps Ma bake a cake, they drink Milo together, she makes tea for my father who lies on the bed in the bedroom next door, sometimes listening to her prattle, sometimes getting lost in the newspaper or a book.

We have a tiny transistor radio, which stands on our kitchen dresser. It's in a brown leather case with lots of holes in it, like a square Marie biscuit. Connie Francis, Frank Sinatra and Nat King Cole sing songs about being in love, almost being in love and not being in love any more.

'Shirley, you know what?'

'What, Prudie?'

'When I'm big I'm going to wear lipstick, like you. And a little cream here' – on her cheeks – 'and let my hair grow long and comb it all back like yours.'

Ma is about to tell her about concentrating on her schoolwork first but, ag, it is Saturday evening after all, a time for magical moments.

There's a knock on the door. Prudence says, 'Come in.' It's her sister Dorothy.

She greets my mother and turns to her sister. 'Prudie, Ma wants to have a quick word with you.'

'What for? What does Ma want?' The magical moment is gone.

'Go quickly, Prudie,' my mother says, 'before your Milo gets cold.'

'OK, I'll be back now-now.'

Prudence is indeed back now-now, as promised – and a little annoyed.

'What's it now, Prudie?' Ma asks.

'Ag, you know this Dorothy. My Ma sent her to ask if Shirley doesn't have a few slices of bread for us, for supper. But instead of coming straight out and asking Shirley, she comes here and lies and says Ma wants to see me quickly.'

'Ah, but you know Dorothy is a little shy,' Ma says, taking out the bread, butter and liver polony. 'Take it home quickly and come back. I want to see what you look like with some of my lipstick on.'

'Really, Shirley?'

Ma nods. 'Plus we'll comb your hair back too.'

Saturday mornings are for settling accounts. They're money days. Days when mothers go to the butcher and give him the money for all that mince and those chops that they had bought during the week. The rent, the tinned food, the rice, the shoes bought on lay-bye, the dry-cleaning. Even that useless bric-a-brac, like wind chimes, that you now have to pay for and which have begun to irritate you.

'Come see me on Saturday morning,' is the motto from buyer to seller throughout the week.

David is a hawker who sells eggs during the week. He collects his money on Saturdays and he is in our house receiving his payment when you surely know by now who bursts in with more news than she can bear.

'Shirley, Shirley – oh hullo, Eggs ...'

David hates the nickname the silly girl has given him, but he's too dull to retaliate.

'Shirley, it's going to happen at last!'

'What, Prudie?'

'Nick's gonna give me a ride on the scooter – not tomorrow, not next week, today!'

Nick Jacobs, the man who had given me the little light bulb. She has been wearing him down with her pleas for a ride. And Nick has finally relented.

'See you just now,' she calls over her shoulder and charges out of the back door.

But there would be no 'just now'.

The next time somebody burst into our house, it would be Dorothy, this time not her usual subdued, shy self, but wringing her hands and screaming, 'Shirley! Nick and Prudence had an accident, up there at Corrie hospital!'

'Oh God! When?'

'Now!'

My mother drops everything and joins the neighbours running down the street towards the scene of the accident a kilometre away.

At the busy intersection outside Coronationville hospital, Nick had crossed over with the excited Prudie riding pillion. The car came and smashed into them, broadside, sending the two bodies and the machine all flying in different directions.

Nick ended up in the nearby hospital, and Prudie in its mortuary.

A few months later we move to Riverlea; but not before there is another death.

Ma is about to have another baby and, when the time comes for the aeroplane to make another landing, I am sent to live with my ouma (my mother's mother), two kilometres away in Coronationville, for a few days. One morning a boy comes to give my ouma the news. My mother has given birth but there have been complications and little Allister has died after living for only a few hours. I remember absolutely nothing about this. But many years later, my mother tells me the story. For years I think about it, about my ouma taking me to my mother, my mother in bed crying, me asking innocently where the new baby is. Then years later I write this poem:

The Road

I was four and living at my ouma's
when the news came as it
does to all four-year-olds
from the overhanging vines
of the adults, through the eaves
of the wise who suddenly
are not so wise.
Cooking stopped.
Panic shattered the eardrum
of the cup of peace.

All was not well
after that out-of-breath boy
had brought the news
in short telegram gasps.

Quickly Ouma wrapped me
in a blanket as cold as the flag
of a sad country, took me away
to my mother whose tears by
now were warmer, had more salt
than the dead child, brother, grandchild

Along the rough road
cobbled with the dirges of beer cans,
tremulous with stones
and filled with more people than children
born to the world that day,
my grandmother walked
and for her the road grew shorter.
For me, staring over her shoulder,
it grew longer and longer.

Soon after the death of our friend Prudence and my brother Allister, we pack up everything and come to live in Riverlea. It's a Coloured township to the south-west of Johannesburg. The first thing you see when you hit Riverlea is a mine dump that heaves hundreds of metres into the sky like a giant breast. This tells you that gold was once mined here.

Huddled around this breast are rows and rows of tiny, square houses. All the streets are named after rivers that flow somewhere in the world. We move into 13 Flinders Street. A few years later I look for Flinders in an atlas and find that it's in Australia.

We have two bedrooms, a bathroom/toilet, a kitchen and a lounge. And, for the first time, running water, right there in the house. While Ma and Dad are unpacking and arranging and heaving beds and wardrobes about, Derek and I flush the toilet – about ten times before Ma tells us to 'stop it now'.

We also have electric light!

The government calls Riverlea a sub-economic housing scheme. I didn't know what those words meant then, and still don't know now. But, compared with Newclare, it's luxury.

What happened to our chamber pots, the primus stove, the paraffin lamps? Who cares! Ma still cooks on a coal stove. And there is another, tiny stove in the kitchen attached to a geyser for hot water. But we can now boil water in an electric kettle for tea, and after a while Ma and Dad buy a radio/record player, the size of a coffin, which takes up an entire wall in our lounge.

Flinders Street, like all the other streets, is not tarred – and won't be for another ten years. On a dry, windy August day it's a dusty strip. On a rainy summer's day it turns to mud. The adults complain. If it were a white suburb, they say, it would have been tarred long ago. But we kids don't mind. It's perfect for football, spinning tops and skipping.

That mine dump. I would have to wait four or five years to conquer it. In the meantime I have to be content to listen to the stories of the bigger boys who go up and come down every week and live to tell their tale.

Most fascinating of these stories is the one about how they climb the mine dump in the evenings. Why in the evenings when it's scary enough in broad daylight? On top, the mine dump overlooks a drive-in cinema for whites only. The boys sit perched on top of the mine dump and steal into a prohibited world of white entertainment. That it is soundless and therefore makes no sense at all matters little to them.

This is apartheid into its second decade, its second phase if you like, with Mandela, Sobukwe, Sisulu and others safely locked up, thousands in exile, and the white people smirking and prospering.

But of all this I know nothing.

My father

My father was born in Adderley Street, in the shadow of Table Mountain. I'm not sure if that famous mountain actually stretches its shadow over my dad's birthplace, I've just said that because it sounds sort of poetic – though I suspect it's literally correct too.

My father was born in February 1936. When he was about two or three years old, the Van Wyk family, consisting of mother, father, Nicholas (my dad) and Stella (his sister, about two years younger than him) left that beautiful city forever and came to live in Johannesburg.

If they hadn't come up here he wouldn't have been my dad for one thing. And then he would probably have had that weird Cape Coloured accent and said things like orksin for auction, myawntin for mountain and feess for fish. He might also have had his two front teeth removed – a grotesque Cape Coloured fashion. But, of course, it wouldn't have mattered because he wouldn't have been my father. In fact I wouldn't have been around myself.

I don't know how long they were in Joburg. But one fateful day his mother decided that she had had enough of her husband, Frank, and her children, Nick and Stella, and she fled back to Cape Town.

Frank recovered from this setback quick enough and met and married Molly Campbell.

In 1939 war broke out and Frank enlisted. A white sergeant called him out from a bunch of Coloured men who were being put through their paces – Stand at ease! Attention! that soldier stuff – and told him he was sergeant of this lot. My oupa said:

'But, sir, *sersant*. I'm not an educated man, I didn't go far in school.'

He could also have told the white sergeant that he was probably the shortest man there, but the sergeant could see this. The sergeant said:

'I don't care what you are or are not, you're sergeant and that's an order!'

Sergeant van Wyk was probably in the army for two or three years. He had lots of adventures there, but one of them is especially worth telling. One day, somewhere in North Africa – Tobruk or Abyssinia – the German Messerschmitts came a-bombing and a-shooting. These planes could be heard five or six minutes before they actually appeared, like angry birds, to drop their bombs. All soldiers had to dive into trenches and stay put, face down until the danger had passed.

Apart from the trenches there was also a cesspit, where all the soldiers did their shitting.

One night, during a raid, Sergeant van Wyk dived into the cesspit by mistake and had to lie face down until the Messerschmitts flew away.

Sergeant van Wyk remained full of shit all his life. He was a mean, irritable, unfriendly and very stingy little man.

After Molly got married to Frank she seemed to spend all her free time beating up her stepson, Nick. For some minor misdemeanour she would snarl:

'Go to your room and take off all your clothes and wait for me.'

Later she would arrive with a long whip, position herself in the centre of the room and lash out at his bare body while he screamed out in pain, jumping from bed to floor to cupboard, begging her to stop.

Molly sometimes bought a packet of mixed sweets for her stepchildren, which she doled out to them at the rate of two per week – if she was in a good mood and Nick and Stella had been good.

Now, as you know, most kids would make a career out of filching the odd sweet every now and then when Ma wasn't looking. But this never happened with Molly's packet of sweets, oh no! because Molly had a very unorthodox security system. In the mornings, before she went to work, she called the two children to the dining-room table. In their presence she counted out the sweets and made them both say the number of sweets out loud.

'How many, Nick?'

'Eighteen, Ma.'

'Stella, how many?'

'Eighteen, Ma.'

She put the sweets back in the packet. Now mothers everywhere in the world would lock the sweets up in a wardrobe, hidden in the pocket of an old gown or tied into a scarf. But Molly did no such thing. She left the packet of sweets in the centre of the dining-room table and went to work.

In the afternoons when Nick and Stella came home from school, they did their chores, which included dusting that dining-room table with its tempting centrepiece, and doing their homework – at the dining-room table.

Molly's method worked all her life.

Nicholas got beatings for things he knew he shouldn't have done. But often also for something he didn't believe was wrong. One good example of this is:

The Van Wyks were members of the Anglican Church in Malay Camp, a township for Coloureds. When Nick was fourteen he joined, on his stepmother's instruction, the Church's Band of Hope. This was a youth group that kept kids off the streets and gave them moral guidance. Kids gathered in some hall on a Wednesday to do things like play table tennis and memorise bible verses.

One evening the priest took a group photo of the boys and girls in the Band of Hope. Being in a jovial mood, Nick van Wyk decided to strike a playful pose for the camera. He put up his fists as if daring anybody to enter the ring with him and gave a hearty laugh. Click.

A week or two later each child in the photo received a copy and took it home. Molly took one look at her stepson the pugilist, and reached for her whip, which was never far away.

'Embarrassing my good name in the Church with your pranks, you little swine!'

If Nick wasn't being whipped or slapped, the look on his stepmother's face told him another beating wasn't far off.

It's better, he told himself, to hang out at the corner café down the road. He could be with friends and not have to watch his every step and every word. And sometimes a boy or girl would put a tickey in the jukebox and he could listen to Ella Fitzgerald sing 'Cow Cow Boogie'.

Sergeant Van Wyk, who had dived into the shit in the army, had absolutely nothing to say about all these beatings his son was being subjected to.

Stella, for her part, was grateful that she wasn't getting half the hidings Nick was getting.

There was another side to Nick's mother. He loved the jazz that was swinging and stomping its way all the way from America. Duke Ellington and his band shaking it up, exhorting everyone who could to 'Take the A train'. Louis Armstrong's deep and gravelly 'Wonderful world'. Ella Fitzgerald and the Tympani Five seducing you to stay awhile longer because 'Baby it's cold outside' and of course Ol' Blue Eyes who crooned about 'That old black magic'.

Molly bought, for her stepson's listening pleasure, all these records. But in 1958 when Nick married my mother, Shirley, and started to pack his things, Molly pointed to the records and said, 'Those stay here.'

So Nick came to be my father and the father of five others with a history of silence. He had no music. He had no stories and the ones I know have been secretly whispered to me over many years by Ma. And he has nothing to tell me about the politics of the fifties. Not a word. Not once do I ever hear him say the word 'Mandela' out loud, or 'ANC' or 'Defiance Campaign' or 'Robben Island' or 'Treason Trial'. It's as if he has passed through an entire history blindfolded and deaf.

His friends are no different. When they get together for a drink they complain about the white man and how he underpays. But that's it.

My mother

WILLIAM AND RUBY VAN HEERDEN had a whopping eleven children. They had William junior, born in 1935, Shirley, my mother, in 1936, Susan, in 1937 …

They lived in a three-bedroomed house in a working-class suburb called Coronationville. This name had something to do with the queen of England putting in an appearance here in South Africa sometime in the forties shortly after she was crowned and declaring that this suburb be the exclusive residence of Coloured people.

Talking about names, Van Heerden is also interesting. Shirley's grandfather was a white man who married a Coloured woman. He saw no reason to go anywhere near his racist relations or the many privileges his skin colour allowed him, but on pension day he always chose the white queue.

'Why, Papa?' William and Shirley wanted to know.

'It's shorter and quicker, and I need a drink now!'

One day, when Shirley was about ten years old, she came home from school in the hot sun, dragging her schoolbag, her socks grubby and heaped on to her ankles. She was listless and tired.

Through the wire perimeter fence of their yard she spied her father. He was doing something so interesting that her listlessness suddenly gave way to a sudden surge of energy. Also watching Dad was her brother William.

'Afternoon, Daddy,' she said, climbing over the fence instead of taking the long way through the gate.

For the past three weeks a turkey had been strutting about in the Van Heerdens' yard. But today was the day when it went from pet to pot. The scene was set thus. Shirley's father in the yard. Shirley's brother, William, in the yard. A wooden block. A big carving knife on the block. The turkey still alive and well and resisting capture.

'Dad,' William said, with a nervous lick of the lips. 'Does he know what we're … what Da's gonna do to him?'

'Oh come on, Willieboy. *Vang die ding en laat ons klaar kry.*'

While William was still summoning up his courage, Shirley pounced on the turkey, caught it by the neck and took it to her father standing by the block. There was a wriggling, a scattering of feathers, a spattering of blood.

Shirley said: '*Jislaaik* it!'

Willieboy winced.

While her father was washing his hands under the tap, Shirley picked up the turkey's head and wobbled its vertebrae with her thumb. Its beak opened and closed. 'Hey, Willieboy, look,' she said, pleased by her discovery. 'I'll get you for killing me,' she said, in a squeaky birdlike voice.

'Shirley, don't do that!' her brother said, stepping back.

'You scared of this thing?' said Shirley with a mischievous smile.

'Just stop it, OK.'

'Scared, Willieboy? Now that I don't have my body. Huh, huh?' She brought the 'talking' head ever closer while her brother backed off. Then he turned and ran away, with Shirley giving chase.

Willie ran around the house and quickly slipped in through the front door and into his parents' room. He locked the door behind him and leaned against it panting. He was safe.

'Open up, you coward!' It was Shirley, and turkey-head, on the other side of the door.

Willie kept quiet, hoping they would leave him alone.

Shirley was about to give up and walk away … until she looked up and saw the small fanlight window above the door gaping open. She smiled a wicked little smile.

On the other side of the door, Willie suddenly felt the turkey head fly down past his face, so close that he swore it brushed against his nose, and he fainted clean away.

Shirley's mother cursed her long and hard but her father chuckled as he unscrewed the door handle to rescue his hapless son.

Ten years later, many things had changed in Shirley's life. She had dropped out of school and, like hundreds of Coloured girls in the townships, had become a factory worker earning no more than one pound a week.

South Africa was six years into apartheid: the 'Europeans Only' signs in public places were becoming an everyday feature. There was discrimination for every occasion: in the hospitals, the schools, public toilets and, of course, on the factory floor.

But Shirley was only eighteen; what did she know? A communist called Solly Sachs was fighting her factory floor battles for her. Besides, it was a Sunday afternoon, time to dress up and sashay down Hamilton Street with her best friend, the redheaded Rachel, and their friends, Bob and Edgar.

As the foursome strolled along the street in their Sunday best, a car pulled up alongside them. This was not good. There were two men in the car. The passenger rolled down the window and said: 'Hullo, can we have a word with you?'

Bob and Edgar became protective and took up their male positions in front of Shirley and Rachel.

'What d'you want?'

The two men in the car had plenty to say while the foursome listened. And it was a very interesting proposition they were making.

These two men wanted to start something that had never been seen in South Africa before: a picture-story magazine. It would work like, say, a Superman or Spider-man comic, but instead of drawings there would be photos. The magazine would come out once a month, then every fortnight. And, who knows, if the public liked it, every week.

The first story was to be a love story. David and Peter are friends. They both have girlfriends, Debbie and Jane. Peter is loyal to Debbie, but David likes to play the field. David's girlfriend is Jane but he soon enough seduces Debbie. Later David learns his lesson when he has a car accident.

'You are the perfect four for the photos in our first issue. For three or four hours' work we'll give you ten bob each.'

Ten bob! It took three full days at the buttonhole machine to earn that.

'When do you want us to start?'

'Now.' He showed them his camera.

They squeezed into the car and went to shoot the first-ever South African photo story.

A month later, Shirley came home from work one Friday evening, plonking handbag and parcels on the kitchen table. She said: 'Hullo, hullo, hullo,' because this was a family of many siblings.

But Shirley's mother had no time for hullo or for admiring the bananas and grapes that made up Shirley's Friday parcels.

'What's this?' Ruby wanted to know, shoving a magazine in Shirley's pretty face.

'What's what?' Shirley was taken by surprise.

This is being sold by the shops and people are buying it. And that's you kissing Bob and kissing Edgar in the veld, you little bitch. And this boy has had an accident and now he's in a wheelchair! You should be ashamed of yourself. I allow you to go to the football grounds and visit Rachel and this is what you do!'

Shirley's dad had to sit his wife down and explain that, 'it's only a story, Ruby. Can't you see!'

Before she met Nick van Wyk, Shirley had a boyfriend called James Volkwyn. He was a bright and serious young man, who was determined, despite apartheid, to carve out a career in music. He played the piano so beautifully that people who passed the Volkwyn's home believed that they had the most wonderful selection of imported classical records.

One day in the mid-fifties Yehudi Menuhin came to town. He performed at the City Hall for Europeans, but the City Council generously set aside one evening specially for non-Europeans. Volkwyn wasted no time. He bought two tickets, for himself and his new girlfriend, Shirley.

James sat in a swoon while the maestro, already bald even back then, charmed him with his music.

'Isn't it just beautiful, Shirl?' he whispered in her ear.

She shrugged and said, 'Hm, gimme Bobby Vinton and Jerry Lee Lewis any time.'

They never went out again.

That was the Van Heerdens. Or at least some of them.

I won't do it again

In Riverlea, every house has its own little yard and I'm sitting in ours.

This house is brand new, the yard is new. Four of us live here: Ma, Dad, me and Derek. But in the next fifteen years or so four more brothers and sisters will arrive. Shaun is in fact on his way as I speak, Allison and Nicolette will arrive in a few years, and Russel in the early seventies, when I'm in high school.

It's winter but it's warm and sunny in the late morning. The older children of the township have all gone to school. The radio is on and Springbok Radio is playing requests for people in hospital. It's always white people on the radio. Sometimes they speak English and sometimes they speak Afrikaans but the radio is definitely a white-people-only thing. White people have phones so they can phone in and win prizes. We listen to the radio, but like eavesdroppers, listening to white people talk and laugh and cry and win prizes and stuff like that.

It's so quiet in the backyard you can hear a fly buzzing around the dustbin. You can hear the neighbours' toilet flushing and you can hear how they open the toilet window to let the bad smell out.

Ma is not at work today because she had to go to the clinic. Maybe she went to order a new baby and ask for the aeroplane to deliver it for us.

Ma comes out with a kitchen chair and a book. She puts the chair in the sand right next to the door and begins to read her book. She's washed her hair and now she's come to sit in the sun to let it dry.

I'm in the far corner of the yard. I'm building a house out of one plank and four crooked nails, so if it comes out as something else that's OK. I knock the nails into my plank. Then I do what my dad does when he knocks in nails; I say, 'Ah fuck it', but not loud enough for Ma to hear, and I pretend the whole job is not going according to plan and I scratch my chin and shake my head. Then I prise the nails out with my tools.

'Hey!'

Even though I know Ma is there, I think she's reading, not watching me so I get a bit of a *skrik*.

I look up and Ma's looking at me. She says, 'What's that in your hand?'

'My plank.'

'Your *other* hand?'

'My other hand?' I can hear by the sharp intake of breath that Ma's getting irritated with me. I look at what's in my other hand as if it's the first time now that I see it. 'My nail taker-outer.'

'Your *nail taker-outer*. That happens to be my bladdy egg-lifter, you little shit.'

I look at it again. Even though it's stainless steel I've managed, in the construction of my house, to get a couple of scratches on it. It's part of a set that hangs on little spikes from the wall in the kitchen. There's a big fork, a kind of big blunt knife, a funny big thing for mashing potatoes … and this nifty little egg-lifter, which is perfect for removing nails.

'Bring it here!'

I don't know why, but I say, 'No.'

Both Ma and I realise instantly what a stupid answer this is. I know Ma's thinking this because of the way she looks at me.

'I said, bring it here!'

'No.' This No is not quite as stupid as the first No. The first No was really stupid because if I hadn't said it I might have got away with a warning. But this second No is an attempt to escape punishment. What I was in fact saying with the second No was: you are going to give me a hiding so the least you can do is fetch me yourself.

'I'm warning you!'

A nervous giggle escapes from my throat.

Ma flies off the chair. I jump up and make for the front gate, twenty metres away. If I can get through that I'm home and away (away is what I'm interested in right now). Mothers won't come into the street, they'll just shout from the gate: 'You have to come home sooner or later.' She won't catch me. I'm five and she's a twenty-six-year-old mother. She wears slippers and cooks food in the kitchen; she knows nothing about running.

I have about a metre to go when Ma's hand clamps my wrist

like a vice. In another swift move she yanks the egg-lifter out of my hand.

I look up at her and she bursts out laughing. The look on my face is such a mixture of humiliation and fear that it has neutralised her anger.

A few weeks later Ma and her friend, Maureen, go down to Uncle Roy's. Uncle Roy comes in his yellow van and parks it on a patch of grass at the end of our street and sells fruit and vegetables to the people of Riverlea.

Ma leaves me and Derek in the house. She says, 'Behave yourselves, we're coming back now-now.'

The minute they leave, there's an atmosphere in the house, like invisible devils, saying: behaving is boring; misbehaving, now that's the thing to do. And be quick, you only have about twenty minutes.

What's there to do in the way of misbehaving? Check out her wardrobe drawers? No, boring. Besides, Ma always knows you've had your grubby paws in there because it's impossible to leave a wardrobe as you found it. Jump up and down on her bed pretending it's a trampoline? The jumping itself is nice but then you have to leave it as you found it, sheets tucked in, pillows puffed up – it's not worth it for a couple of jumps. We could also steal sugar … and that's what we do. You put your forefinger in your mouth to wet it then you plunge it deep in the bowl to make a sweet and crunchy sucker.

While we're doing that I look around the kitchen and there's a pot on the stove. I lift the lid and take a peep inside. There's meat in it. I take out a chunk and eat it. I take out another piece and offer it to Derek. 'Here.'

'It's for tonight,' he says.

It's not, it's leftovers from last night. Here.'

'Mummy's gonna shout.'

'You just tell her I gave it to you.'

He takes it and nibbles away. We're not really hungry but this is a good way to pass the time while I'm thinking about some other mischief to do.

I'm into my third chunk of meat when I hear Ma and Auntie Maureen's voices on the stoep.

'Come!' I pull my little brother by the arm and drag him to the bedroom. We slide under the bed.

Ma and her friend are still chatting away about I don't know what: the price of tomatoes, husbands who said this and that, children who don't seem to have ears. From my place of safety among shoes and between cold floor and bedsprings, I hear Ma abruptly interrupt her sentence with: 'Those little shits!'

I hear her footsteps and the next thing I see her feet right here in the room. She says: 'Come out!'

She must surely be talking to somebody else, how does she know we're under the bed?

Little Derek can't stand the tension and he crawls out and surrenders. Ma takes off a shoe. She grips one of his hands and lays into him with the shoe.

'Whaa, whaa, whaa,' he screams, saying something stupid like, 'I won't do it again!'

I feel sorry for my brother. But I also feel that if I stick around here I'm going to get the same treatment. I crawl out and make a dash for it. But Ma lets go of Derek's arm and grips mine as easily as if we had been rehearsing this for weeks. Ma gives me the same and I go:

'Whaa whaa whaa, I won't do it again!'

A big mistake

I WANT TO GO TO SCHOOL, I want to read and write like Ma and Dad and my uncles and aunts and cousins. But I'm nervous.

'Will my teacher first show me how to write before she asks me to write something?' I ask Ma.

Ma buys me a little school case for my lunch and my crayons. Hundreds of kids have exactly the same case, made of dark brown cardboard with shiny silver latches. If you click open the lid, with your thumbs – and be careful not to get your thumbs knocked off your hands – you will see the owner's initials written on the inside of the lid.

I take the initiative and a Koki pen and decide to mark my own property. I write, in fat, giant letters:

K – F – V

Ma says, 'What does that stand for?'

Aw, isn't it obvious? 'Chris van Wyk.'

'That's not right,' Ma says and smiles. 'It should be C–V–W.'

This writing thing is going to be harder than I thought.

I go to T. C. Esterhuysen Primary School in Langlaagte, half an hour's walk from Riverlea. This school used to belong to white kids, but they built themselves a nicer one and gave this one – which was in perfect condition I'll tell you that – to us Coloureds.

The first thing my teacher tells us is to put our lunches in a pigeonhole at the front of the class.

'And remember where you put yours.'

She's crazy. You need to be a mathematics professor to know where your lunch is. If it wasn't in one of the corner holes, you were doomed. There are about forty of us and we almost all have lunch on that first day. I sit with my eyes glued to my lunch throughout the whole of the first lesson – until my teacher distracts me by asking me my name.

'Christopher van Wyk.'

That done, I look back at the pigeonholes – and of course I have no idea which one's mine.

A day or so later, I look more closely at my teacher, and fall in love with her. Miss Abrahams is the second prettiest woman in the whole world. My mother is the prettiest. I decide, then and there, to learn all my sums and words so that I can be clever and marry Miss Abrahams one day.

In the meantime, I'm quite sure that we are boyfriend and girlfriend.

When we get our writing right Miss Abrahams says: 'You boys and girls are so clever!' She obviously means me, but we have to keep our thing a secret because if you like a girl, your friends might tease you by chanting: 'Boyfriend and girlfriend kiss one another!' They don't mind saying this over and over more than a hundred times.

Miss Abrahams writes up and down patterns on the board and tells us to copy them into our books. Afterwards, she comes to all of us to see if we're doing it right. Most of us are doing it right but she stays by me the longest. She smells like flowers. She smiles and her teeth are as white as chalk. And she gives me a pinch on my cheek. She says, 'That's nice, Christopher.'

When my friend, Allan Walburgh, wants to leave the room, he says, 'Miss, I gotta piss!'

She says, 'That's not the way to say it, dear.' She tells him to say, 'May I leave the room please, madam.'

I wish I had had a pee before Allan. Then I would've said the right thing because my ma told me the right thing last year already.

Rowan Valentine doesn't have shoes in winter and Miss Abrahams buys him a pair, just like that: new Bata Toughies, guaranteed for six months.

It's cold at school in winter and we shiver. But there's a fireplace in the classroom. Miss Abrahams tells us to bring just one piece of wood and just one piece of coal each. Some get it wrong and bring either just a piece of wood or just a piece of coal. Trevor McKay brings three pieces of coal and no wood. What did he hear her say? But she just smiles and says it's OK.

We now have enough wood and coal to keep us nice and cosy for a whole week.

We sit in a semi-circle around the fire and Miss Abrahams gives us lessons. She asks us simple questions about things she's just told us minutes ago, but we don't know the answers, we just don't know.

Miss Abrahams gets very cross. 'It's this fire, she says. 'It's making you sleepy. No more fire.'

And she means it. So now we answer her questions, but we're shivering all over again.

But it's nice in summer.

Miss Abrahams has a pretty ladies' watch. It has a gold strap and the face is small and dainty. In the afternoons, when we've done our work for the day, she looks at her watch. She tells us to pack all our stuff away. Then she says, 'OK, there's still some time left. What shall we do?'

'Sing!' we shout.

She laughs so much that she has to wipe the tears out of her eyes. She says, 'On the stage!'

We all get on to our chairs and when she gives the cue, we burst into:

Oh dear
What can the matter be
Oh dear
What can the matter be
Oh dear
What can the matter be
Johnny's so long at the fair
He promised to buy me
A bunch of blue ribbons
He promised to buy me
a bunch of blue ribbons
He promised to buy me
a bunch of blue ribbons
To tie up my bonny brown hair.

Miss Abrahams tells us bible stories and fairy tales and stuff. She tells us about Samson. The longer his hair grows the stronger he gets. Some guys try to fight him and he takes the jawbone of an ass and beats them up. Then Delilah, his girlfriend, betrays him and his enemies get hold of him and cut all his hair off. Then the idiots forget about his hair making him strong and they let it grow again. One day they tie him to two pillars and laugh at him while they're having a party. That's their biggest mistake because, the next thing, Samson breaks the pillars and that whole place where the party is happening comes crashing down and kills everybody.

Then there's David. He's a shepherd and he loveth God very much. While his sheep are lying around in the veld he takes his harp – which is like an olden days guitar – and sings songs about how much he likes God. But don't think this David is a sissy just because he plays music and sings those songs. One day a big guy called Goliath gives David a hard time. David goes to a stream and picks up five pebbles. Not six, not four – just five. The next time Goliath comes and looks for trouble with him, David puts a pebble in his sling, swings it around and around and lets go. The pebble hits Goliath right in the middle of his fat head. Boom! Dead.

Miss Abrahams tells her stories so nicely. When a big, fat, ugly giant speaks she makes her voice big and fat and ugly, like this: 'I SMELL the BLOOD of an ENGLISH-min.' And when she says it she doesn't just stand there at her desk, she walks between us, between the rows of desks. When she goes like that I tell you, you're glad you're not an Englishman. And when Rapunzel shouts for help from that tower, then Miss Abrahams makes her voice like a pretty girl's who's in trouble: 'Help, help!'

One day Miss Abrahams tells us a story about herself. She says she went on holiday to the Kruger Park.

'The Kruger Park is almost as big as the whole of England.'

I don't know how big England is but I decide the Kruger Park must be big; far bigger than Riverlea.

'It took us the whole day to drive from one end to the other. We saw elephants, lions and giraffes. And lots and lots of monkeys. They even jumped on to the roof of our car and put their hands in through the windows for food.'

I wish I could go to the Kruger Park. I'd give the monkeys some of my bread.

'They have bungalows there for people to sleep in. But we couldn't sleep in them because we're not white.' When she says this, her voice is neither like a giant's nor a pretty girl's; it's just her own voice.

Oh no! Couldn't these Kruger Park people see how pretty she is, don't they know how nice she smells? I'm sure they've made a big mistake.

One afternoon Ma gets home from work and she says, 'What did you do at school today?'

'Miss Abrahams told us ...'

'*Missis* Abrahams. She's *Missis* Abrahams.'

'But why can't I say Miss?' Everybody says Miss. Isn't it just short for 'Missis?'

'No, it's not.'

'What does Ma mean?'

'A miss is not married. A missis *is* married. Why d'you think people call me Missis van Wyk?'

Mrs Abrahams, I realise now, is just one big flirt. But I still like her.

Shirley, Goodness and Mercy

When Ma comes home from work, always at about five in the early evening, she puts on her slippers and starts cooking. For me this is the best part of the day. I stand in the back door watching her and I glance from time to time at the setting sun dropping in slow motion behind the mine dumps on the western side of Riverlea.

I watch my mother peel potatoes, one continuous peel on each potato, which swirls round and round until it plops on top of the piles of other peels. Or she dices an onion into hundreds of equally shaped, sparkling little diamonds. Or I marvel at her hands, damp and clean and clamped together as if in prayer as she turns mince into frikkadels.

'That's a waste of time,' I tell her.

'What is?'

'Making the frikkadels.'

'Why?' She's amused that I dare say such a thing.

'OK, look, this mince was once a whole piece of meat, right?'

'Mhm.'

'And then the man in the butcher shop put it into that machine and it came out broken up in little bits like this, right?'

Ma says, 'Right,' but by now she can see where I'm going with this and she begins to laugh.

'So now you're trying to put it back together again.'

Ma says, 'Oh get away,' but she laughs out loud and nods.

She gives me easy, pleasant little chores.

'Go and throw this in the dustbin for Ma,' she says, handing me vegetable peels wrapped in newspaper, like a neat parcel. Or she throws a few pieces of garlic, ginger and a chilli into the little brass pot and asks me to find a block of wood outside and stamp away. 'Just don't get the chilli in your eyes.'

While she cooks we talk about lots of things. Mostly I ask her questions. I always say:

'Ma, can I ask you something?'

'Ja.'

'My name is Christopher Clinton, right?'

'Right.'

'So why the 'Clinton'?'

'I liked that name as a middle name for you.'

'No, that's not what I mean.'

'What do you mean?'

'Why do we need middle names?'

'Uhm,' She puts some water in a pot to stop the onions from burning. 'Because one day you might forget your first name and then you can use your second name.'

'Really, Ma!'

'Oh yes.'

I'm ready to believe her, but then I see her trying to keep the smile from spreading and I know I've been tricked.

'Ma!'

Now she bursts out laughing and she says,

'We just all have middle names, I don't know why. Some people have three or four names. Just so they can have their mother's name, grandmother's name ...'

'I think it's just a waste of time.'

'Why?'

'Because nobody uses those names. Nobody says, "Christopher Clinton please come here a minute" you know what I mean?'

'I know what you mean.'

Ma asks me questions too. She always says, 'How was school today?'

'Nice.'

'Nice! That tells me nothing. Tell me something your teacher said. Something the principal said.'

One day I have some good news.

'I know Psalm 23.'

'The whole psalm?'

'The whole psalm,' I nod proudly.

'Well, what are you waiting for? Let's hear it.'

I stand facing her, hands clasped together in front of me, classroom style, and recite:

'Psalm 23 – a psalm of David
The Lord is my shepherd
I shall not want
He maketh me to lie down
In green pastures
He leadeth me beside the still waters
He restoreth my soul …'

I watch Ma listening to me and see her own soul being restoreth. She puts down her knife and her dishcloth, and stands watching me, a smile of pure pride lighting up her face. Then suddenly, as I reach the last two lines, Ma bursts into excited laughter.

I had expected some kind of approval, but nothing quite like this. David, Mrs Abrahams had told us, sang these psalms to God to the accompaniment of a harp. Well here I am doing a rendition without music and Ma is bowled over.

So bowled over in fact that when my father comes home from work, she makes me recite it all over again for him. I duly deliver, with much the same gusto as before – with the same effect. Ma smiles and bursts into laughter. Dad laughs too in the end and tells me that I am one 'helluva clever *laaitie*'.

My reputation as a reciter of Psalm 23 grows with every delivery. To quote another psalm from the good David, I 'make a joyful noise' – or at least cause one – whenever an uncle, aunt or neighbour comes visiting.

Then, one day, I discover the reason why I am causing so much laughter. My delivery is word-perfect – except when I come to the end where, instead of: 'surely goodness and mercy shall follow me all the days of my life' I am going for: 'Shirley, Goodness and Mercy …'

Despite this malapropism, I know that Ma and Dad are both proud of me. I think about David and Abraham, who was willing to sacrifice his son, and Daniel in the Lion's Den. I think about all these people and I say, 'These people really liked God and Jesus, hey Ma?'

Ma says, 'Actually Jews don't believe in Jesus.'

What crazy information is this! 'They don't believe in Jesus?'

Ma shakes her head. 'They don't.'

Jews, I tell myself, are taking one helluva chance. Everybody knows that you can't go to heaven unless you believe in Jesus. My teacher told us this, the preacher tells us this every Sunday in the Ebenezer Church. I think you can open the Bible on any page and it's right there in black and white. And now my mother tells me this – and goes on peeling potatoes as if she has just declared that it might rain tomorrow.

Well, I decide, if they want to go directly to hell, that's their problem.

'And the Muslims too,' Ma says.

'The Muslims too?'

'Oh yes.'

This is getting out of hand. The Jews, well, I don't know any of them on a personal basis. Ma's boss is a Jew. The man who owns the Reno movie house in Newclare is a Jew. Jews own clothing stores in town. All they ever say to you is: 'I'm telling you, you won't get this cheaper anywhere else.' They're white. They live far away, in places called suburbs that I don't even know how to get to. But Muslims, now that's a different story. Riverlea is chock-a-block with Muslims. In every street of thirty families, four or five are Muslim. We go to the same schools, play football together in the streets …

'Who do they follow?' I ask Ma.

She smiles at my choice of words. 'Who do they follow? They follow the prophet Mohammed.'

Mr and Mrs Lang are Muslims – we have a nickname for Muslims: 'slamsies', from 'Islam'. The Langs live at the bottom end of our street. They're an old couple, in their late sixties or early seventies. If you're not even near your tenth birthday then being over sixty is ancient.

Mr Lang is a perfect oval, an egg in braces … Moegamat Dumpty, I suppose, a strictly halaal egg. He has a bald spot surrounded by sparse grey hairs. Braces keep up his pants and thick glasses show him the way to town – where he goes once a week to buy spices for the *koeksisters* he and his wife sell on Sunday mornings. They also sell sweets (I especially like their nutty, brittle beetle nuts, which look like legless beetles), and popcorn in cones that they make out of quarter sheets of newspaper. A fair percentage of my pocket money ends up in a glass jar on the Langs' kitchen cupboard.

But the *koeksisters* are not for every day. Those are special and come, plaited and dipped in syrup and sprinkled with a confetti of coconut, on Sunday mornings.

Christian and Muslim kids all trudge, half-asleep, down to the Langs, dish in hand, for our half dozen or dozen. We sit on a little bench in their kitchen, yawning and staring at the Arabic holy script on the walls – always in green.

The Slamsies are our friends.

But there are kinds of inner circles that inevitably develop between the Muslims. They pray together and in the holy month of Ramadan you see children, *kufias* on their heads, taking little dishes of curry or pudding to Auntie Rashida or the Ali family. Ramadan is the fasting month and, to break their fast every evening, Muslim mothers cook special dishes, which they share amongst friends and family.

Every household has a 'Boeta'. Boeta Ibrahim or Boeta Gamat, usually the father or older brother. The Muslims greet each other with a *Salaam aleikum* (Peace be upon you), but when they greet us Christians it's a mere hullo. We're not part of the circle.

I find the Muslims a little weird. They seem to have only one song that they sing to God – and which wakes up the entire township around 4.30 a.m. on Friday mornings, when it blares out from a loudspeaker on the roof of the mosque. They like the colour green. From their hearse, which collects dead bodies, to clothes to the biscuits they bake on their holy days – all green, green, green. Many Muslim men quite like the green weed too.

The Christians too have their own religious customs and rituals that bind them. We almost all eat fish on Fridays, we could be pointed out on the football fields on Sundays by our white shirts (worn to church that morning) with their talismans of tomato sauce and brooches of beetroot from our almost identical Sunday lunches of chicken curry, with jelly and custard for dessert.

Then, within the Christian community there are the Catholics, the Anglicans, the Ebenezers, the Methodists, New Apostolic

Church, Dutch Reformed Church, Lutherans, Congregational Church ... These are called denominations. The first time I hear that word I take great pleasure in asking a friend:

'Which denomination do you belong to?'

'Huh?'

The Catholics are by far the strongest denomination in Riverlea. This is thanks to one Father Patrick McCullagh or Father Mac. Everybody knows him; he stands out like a sunburnt white Irish thumb on account of being the only white person in a sea of darker-skinned people. But it's not his skin colour that has made him famous in these parts. When I first hear about Father Mac I am both in awe of him and happy that I am not a Catholic.

Every day of the week, I straggle home from school with all the boys: Kurt, Ivan, Neil, Allan, Toolbag, Keith. We peer down mineshafts, pop in at the shops to buy sherbet and bubblegum, play 'Ollie' along the way. But on Wednesdays half the *chommies* are missing, running home past all of us.

'Aw, gents. Why yous in a hurry? Here's some sherbet.'

'No thanks. Can't stop now. I'm late for catties. Father Mac's gonna *moer* me if I'm late again.' Catties? Catechism.

Ask Ivan Johnson about Father Mac. One day he's in the confessional and he's going: 'Forgive *chew-chew* me Father *chew-chew* for I have *chew-chew* sinned *chew-chew* ...' Father Mac yanks him out of the confessional and delivers two hot smacks to his cheeks.

'Chewing gum while asking God for forgiveness, you feckin' stupid boy!'

It's not only the boys and girls who are scared of Father Mac. He scares the holy shit out of their parents too.

Mr Peffer beats up his poor wife from time to time ... until Father Mac comes to hear about it. One Friday Father Mac storms into the Peffer home in Potomac Street just as Mr Peffer, steamed up by a few brandies, is piling into Mrs Peffer. The priest takes off his dog collar and his cassock and tosses them over a dining-room chair.

'Father, what are you doing?'

'That,' Father Mac says, pointing at the things he has taken off, 'is *Father* MacCullagh.' Then, pointing a thumb at himself. 'And this is *Mr* MacCullagh. I see that you hit women, so I want to see how you'll fare with Mr Mac.'

'No, Father, please.'

'Mr. And by the way, Ralph, I was Dublin Middleweight Boxing Champion, 1939.'

There's a wham and a bam and a boom and a doof and, the next thing, Ralph Peffer is out for the count. When he gets up he's cured of woman abuse for ever. No prayers, no mass, no lighting a candle – just a good whack from Father Mac.

Riverlea still has a severe drinking problem. But Father Mac single-handedly reduces it by two or three per cent. Almost all the Catholic men go about with little green badges proclaiming that they are Pioneers. Shame, they look a little like babies deprived of their milk bottles. But their wives are so happy because now Ralphie or Eric or James comes straight home from work on Friday evenings and puts that pay envelope, sealed and stapled as it should be, into wifey's ever-loving hands. So instead of filling the coffers of the shebeens, the pay now buys bread and milk and tea and mealie meal and pays the rent. Will all this abstinence last? Nobody knows, but for the moment it's Father Mac's miracle.

There are exceptions though. But these are exceptions at their own peril. One of them is Boy Brown.

Boy Brown scoffs at this 'pioneer shit'.

'Sissies,' he calls these men. He takes centre stage in the backyard of Foxy's shebeen, where he debates the issue with the other regulars – who all seem to be on his side. 'All week long, I have to put up with a white man telling me what to do. Then on Saturdays and Sundays when I wanna sit around with some friends, there's another white man trying to tell me what to do.'

'Tell them, ou Boy Brown!'

'You got a point there.'

Someone puts a double brandy and water into his hands and asks him to act out his version of the mass, just one last time.

Boy Brown leaps into action and the circle of drinkers goes quiet. This is a sketch they've all seen before but it's worth seeing a hundred times more.

Boy Brown takes a hat off somebody's head and presses it down on his own head. He does a wide-brim charade with his hands: he's wearing a sombrero. He slaps his pockets: he's packing two colts. He strides a few paces into the sunlight: he's gonna fetch his horse.

Then suddenly Boy Brown swings around, faces his audience, makes the sign of the cross and announces:

'Mea culpa, mea culpa, me a Mexican cowboy.'

Foxy's backyard explodes into laughter and somebody passes Boy Brown another drink.

The story doesn't end there.

Boy Brown's wife is a devout Catholic. Meisie is one of a group of women who spend almost all their free time in the house of the Lord. They make tea for Father Mac, clean the church and make sure there are always fresh flowers in the many vases in the church.

One day Boy Brown is very short of cash for a drink and so badly in debt at the shebeen that there is no hope of getting even a nip on the book. As he swallows the last of his brandy, he suddenly remembers where he's seen a stash.

'I'll be here now-now, gents,' he says. 'With cash.'

'No problem, Boy Brown. But you seem very sure.'

'I am. Rinse those glasses so long.'

He goes home, and heads straight for his bedroom and his wife's wardrobe. There's an old black handbag from the 1940s. It used to be for going out into town but now it's used for hiding money from hubby. And, it seems, that use has now also had its day. Boy Brown snaps it open and there's the money!

'Boy!'

He gets a bit of a *skrik*; he didn't hear Meisie come in.

'What are you doing with my money?'

'Oh fuck off, this is our money ...'

'It's the church's money. For flowers.'

'Fuck the church.'

'Boy! How can you say that?'

He brushes past her and arrives back at the shebeen, waving the five-rand note for all to see.

Things are going well at the shebeen, but not so well down the road at the Catholic Church.

Meisie stumbles into the church sobbing. Father Mac is sipping tea in his room, humming one of those many Irish songs. He hears the sobbing and comes out to see.

'Meisie, what's the matter?'

She tells him.

'The money for the flowers?'

'Y-yes, F-father.'

Boy Brown is doing his skit for the boys when he sees the black cassock sweep into the dusty backyard of the shebeen. The Mexican cowboy has nowhere to run.

Father Mac flings off his cassock with his familiar fighting words: 'That's Father MacCullagh, this is Mr MacCullagh.'

Mea culpa, mea culpa, mea maxima culpa.

We belong to the Ebenezer Church. The services are mostly in Afrikaans, very rarely in English. We call the preacher *Meneer* (Sir). Mr Conley, our *Meneer*, unsettles me one Easter Sunday morning. Whilst telling us about how Christ had died for us on the cross, he bursts into uncontrollable sobs, dragging out the service an hour longer than scheduled. He is putting on such a performance, as if Jesus was his very own brother and had died that very morning.

We Ebenezers are like one family. Not as close as the Catholics – and not half as big. But a family nevertheless.

A few months, maybe a year, after Ma's religious revelations to me, she's sick in bed, groaning and moaning in pain. She has a headache, backache, a fever.

She calls me to her bedroom and tries to sit up to talk to me.

'Go to Mr Fortune,' she says, leaving long painful pauses between each word. 'Ask him if I can please have a jar of menthol camphor. Tell him I don't have the money now but I'll pay him … next week Friday.'

'Yes, Ma.' I nod. This is one chore I'm eager to do. If menthol camphor is going to take away Ma's pain, then I would go and fetch it in Cape Town let alone three streets down from where we live.

'And don't forget to say …'

'Please and thank you – I know, Ma.'

I run out the front door into a Saturday afternoon that is turning into evening. The sun is going down behind the mine dumps and clouds of smoke are billowing out of chimneys as coal stoves are lit all over Riverlea to prepare the evening supper.

The Fortunes are Ebenezers like us. Cyril and Cecil, handsome twins, are my classmates and among my best friends. I spend a lot of time at their home. Every Friday afternoon they buy *True Africa,* a photo comic about the adventures of a muscular African hero called Samson, who goes about rural villages and urban towns fighting crime with his ever-present monkey, Jacko, on his shoulder. What the twins have in looks they sort of lack in reading skills so they call on me to do the honours. Every Friday afternoon after school about four or five boys make their way to the Fortunes'. We sit down in the sand on the shady side of their house. Somebody hands me the latest *True Africa* and I become the centre of our informal reading club.

I begin to read: 'The Leopard Men had been harassing these peace-loving villagers for far too long now and Samson decided to do something about it. Jacko hopped on to his master's shoulder and they set off for the distant village of Taung.'

There are also the speech bubbles, which go like this: 'Take that, you thug!' (in a serrated bubble to show us just how angry Samson is).

Mr Fortune has a regular job like most fathers. But in order to earn extra money he is also an agent for Watkins Products, the cosmetics company that manufactures salves, deodorants, facial creams and that kind of stuff. During the week Mr Fortune goes from door to door taking orders for this cream and that spray. Then on Friday evening and Saturday morning he comes delivering his products and collecting his money.

The Watkins Menthol Camphor is a heady, pungent ointment that comes in a flat green tin. Once, when I had a cold, Ma rubbed it on my chest so that I could have a good night's sleep. I stayed awake half the night trying to avert my nostrils – until I called Ma to wipe it off my chest.

In about eight minutes flat I'm knocking at the Fortunes' door, a little out of breath. A voice inside says, 'Come in'. I open the door and, sitting at the dining-room table, is the man himself. He has a ballpoint pen in his hand and is surrounded by receipt books and invoice books with carbon sheets sticking out of them.

Actually I know it's Mr Fortune even before I open the door because it's the same voice I hear on Sunday mornings in church singing, 'What a friend we have in Jeee-zus ...'

I say good evening, Mr Fortune. He says yes.

'Mr Fortune,' I begin – I had done a quick rehearsal on my way here – 'my mother asks if she can please have a tin of menthol camphor. She says she will definitely pay you next week Friday.'

He looks me up and down once or twice, with disapproval. He sits back in his chair and enlarges his eyes. 'Tell your mother that I don't give Watkins products on credit to people who have changed their agents, who don't ... who can't make up their minds who they want to buy from. Tell her to go to the new agent when she's in trouble, not the one she refuses to buy anything from any more.'

Now here is a man who's been waiting to get something off his own chest too. I'm stunned.

'Off you go,' he says.

'Good night, Mr Fortune.'

He doesn't bother to respond to that. I leave, making sure to close the door softly; I don't want to be called back and told to *close* the door and not *slam* it.

At home I report to Ma. Through her pain she frowns, trying hard to make sense of what I'm telling her. It's all a misunderstanding. She had once bought something from another agent, not believing that this would be taken as a slight by Mr Fortune. And another time she had been in such financial difficulties that Mr Fortune's wonderful products, stuff like Body Mist deodorant and hand cream, just had to wait.

Ma's still in pain and I'm standing by her bed not knowing what to do. She twitches and makes little gasping noises and I'm at a loss.

'Listen,' Ma says, 'be a good boy and go to Mrs Lang for me. Tell her I've got backache and ask her for some *kruie*.'

'Krayer? What's that, Ma?'

This was the Afrikaans word for herbs. But, even if I spoke to Mrs Lang in English, which I planned to do, I was to use the word *kruie*.

'And tell Mrs Lang it's for my back.'

The trip to the Langs takes half the time it takes to get to Mr Fortune. I knock on the door and Mr Lang opens, in his usual braces and slippers. I greet him. He says, 'Hullo, little van Wyk,' smiles at me and waits for my order: popcorn, beetle nuts, Ice Kwenchies. But tonight I'm not here for sweets. I'm on a serious mission.

'My mother sent me to Mrs Lang, please Mr Lang.'

'Oh,' he says, 'Oh.' This has never happened before and he's thrown for a few seconds. He calls his wife and she comes waddling to the kitchen door, wearing long white socks, slippers, a long dress, a jersey and a scarf – even though it's a summer evening. I greet her.

'Hullo, my child.' She smiles.

'Mrs Lang, my mother sent me to ask you if you please don't have some *kruie* for her, for her sore back.'

'Oh shame, oh shame,' they chant a duet. Then they both bustle about in the kitchen. From the dresser drawer they haul out a bunch of what looks to me like dried out twigs. They wrap it in a sheet of newspaper; both pairs of old wrinkled hands trying to do the same work.

They hand it to me, shuffling in the doorway.

'Thank you ...'

'Don't say thank you!' they both chorus, almost aggressively.

I step back, a little alarmed.

'Do you understand me?' Mr Lang says.

'Yes, Mr Lang.' I take the parcel of brittle herbs from him, and almost say thank you again – it's such habit.

I run up the road wondering what's happening to me this evening. Everywhere I go adults are trying to bite my head off, no matter how polite I am.

At home I present Ma with the bouquet of *kruie* and tell her about my strange encounter.

'They sounded almost angry just because I said thank you.'

Ma nods. 'You're not supposed to say thank you for medicine. They feel it's their duty to give medicine.' She sits up in bed, and, for the first time that evening, I see her smile.

Grannies and gifts

MY FATHER'S PARENTS LIVE IN COLORADO DRIVE, in the same township as us. They are Molly, the one who beat my father when he was little, and Frank van Wyk, who fell in the shit in World War Two and remained full of shit to the end of his days. They have a dry cleaner's shop in Newclare, Sandy's Same Day Service.

One day when I'm about fifteen years old my grandpa will let me and my brother Derek spend our entire school holidays working in his dry cleaners. For which he will give us not a cent.

They are fairly well-to-do if you ask me – or anyone else in Riverlea. The house is the same size as ours but it's always spick and span – because there are no children to mess the place up. There are always chocolates in drawers and fruit in bowls. They own a Volvo. And three years down the line, if it gives trouble, they'll just buy another Volvo. I know nothing about cars but people tell me it's the only Volvo in Riverlea. Many years later, when I know a little more about apartheid, I learn that the Swedes were among the first countries to disinvest, way back in the early sixties, in protest against apartheid. But of course some of their Volvos stayed behind. For the driving comfort of the prosperous Molly and Frank van Wyk.

From an early age my paternal grandparents give me a lot of trouble. And the odd present on my birthday. The first gift I recall is a pair of binoculars when I'm about five years old. It's fascinating looking through them: a man far away on a bicycle is suddenly up close and I can actually see the effort he's making as he's struggling up a hill.

All I can say, staring through the lenses, is, 'Jô!'

My grandpa stands beside me on a rock, sucking on his pipe and puffing rum and maple flavoured smoke into the air. He stares into the distance, so far away I know no binoculars will bring what he sees closer. For years I remember this moment and have the sense that my grandpa is a kind of philosopher. But actually he's just a mean illiterate who once fell into shit and never got rid of the smell.

Years after the binoculars Gran van Wyk is still giving me and my brothers and sisters gifts on our birthdays. The day before my birthday she sends word, usually through my father who often goes to visit her, that she wants me to come up to her house the next day so that she can wish me happy birthday. I know there will be a gift waiting for me on her dressing-table.

On my birthday I walk up to the house where she lives with my grandfather and my father's sister, Stella.

'Are you working hard at school?' she asks me.

'Yes, Gran.'

How many kids answer no to such a question, like: 'Actually, I'm doing so badly at school, don't expect me to pass this year.'

'Have you been behaving yourself?'

This is a tricky one. At age seven it's not easy to be good every single day from one birthday to the next. Once or twice I really didn't feel like going to the shop for Ma and I said, 'Why don't you send Derek for a change?' But I think I've had more well-behaved days than rude and naughty ones put together.

Sometimes I try to be a really good boy. I get up in the morning and I decide, OK today I start being good … for ever. I will listen to my parents, I won't swear, I will do my homework, I won't go around with Vickie and them because they're older than me and make rude signs to girls with thumb between fingers … and then an hour later I say to a dog or someone who trips me in a soccer game, 'Fuck you!' And then I say, 'Oh shit, sorry, God, I'll start tomorrow.'

'Have you?'

'Yes, Gran.'

'Sometimes you are rude to your parents, I know.'

Now I don't know what to say.

'Am I right, Christopher?'

'Yes, Gran,' I admit softly.

My gran sighs deeply, like one about to commit herself with great reluctance to a cause.

'There's something in my room for you. On the dressing-table. Go and fetch it.'

I enter her clean room with its sweet fragrance of rum and maple. It's always dark because she keeps the curtains drawn.

This room is usually out of bounds for me. I'm curious to explore, but I daren't because in the lounge my gran is sitting, waiting for me to re-emerge. She has an invisible stopwatch in her head; I know she's timing me and my time in her room is almost up.

I thank her for the gift, a little speech that I've rehearsed dozens of times. She smiles, but when she smiles her fierce eyes don't go away, they stay there like two dogs on guard while the owner is relaxing.

I get home and show everyone my new football boots. The next day I wear them when we play football in the street and all my friends say, 'jô!'. Most play in old, worn out shoes and some play barefoot. I'm not one of the best players in Flinders Street. I'm not as fast as Rodney 'Rotakop' Jardine, as tricky as Melvin Langridge or as elusive as Gerome 'Gong' Alexander. But in these boots I get passed the ball more often than is warranted. And throughout the entire match the chant is, 'Give to ou Kuller, give to ou Kuller!'

But I don't wear the boots often and, I don't know what it is, but I don't really look forward to getting the next gift from Gran van Wyk. In fact I don't look forward to going up there at all.

My gran smokes cigarettes. Courtleigh. They come in a blood-red box and each one has a gold ring around it near the filter. Because she drives a Volvo and owns a dry cleaners and always has fruit in bowls on the sideboard, I assume that her cigarettes are more expensive than the other brands.

Sometimes my grandparents play cards with two or four friends. They all sit around the dining-room table with tea, biscuits and brandy by their elbows. Their faces are all serious as they concentrate, picking cards from a pack in the centre, sighing, looking around at the other faces, making the new card part of the fan, taking out a card from the fan and discarding it.

I try hard to work out the logic of the game, but I can't. Then there's the fact that I'm not allowed to make any remarks, say anything funny, ask something. I have to shut up. I'm in the heart of 'speak-when-you're-spoken-to' country.

And neither my grandparents nor their visitors show any

signs of passing me a biscuit or a chocolate from the table – though I live in hope, which is probably one of the reasons I've stuck around so long.

At some point one of the players shows everyone that he is the one who in fact has the ten of diamonds. Somebody says, 'I knew it!' My grandpa removes his pipe from his mouth to give his strange soft hissing laugh.

At this point I disappear.

Sometimes, when I go to their house, there is my Auntie Stella, her face in a swoon, recording Peaches and Herb, Diana Ross and Shirley Bassey records from her turntable on to her big reel-to-reel tape recorder. Then I have to do more shutting up.

Auntie Stella isn't married even though she's almost thirty. One day my brother Shaun, who was about three at the time, asked her when she was going to get married. She burst into tears and went to tell my gran, who summoned Shaun and gave him one of her tongue-lashings.

The way my auntie looks at us when we come to visit it seems to me she thinks we're going to ask her that question again and again.

One day my mother sends me up there to borrow the shoe-stretcher, a strange device you put into a shoe and then screw it so that it stretches shoes that are too tight.

I collect my friend Gregory 'Hippie' Johnson, who lives two doors away from us, and together we make our way up Colorado Drive to the other Van Wyks, Gran, Granpa and Auntie Stella. When we get there, who do we find but Sandy and Jenny. They're my father's cousins but they're about my age – Sandy's a year younger and Jenny a year older than me – and so I think of them as my cousins too.

We're happy to see each other and we sit around the kitchen table and chat about school, ask each other riddles, and page through my aunt's magazines, *Personality* and *Keur* and *Woman's Value*, which have film stars in them. While we're doing this Sandy turns to Auntie Stella and says:

'Stella, may we have some cooldrink, please.' Very polite girls, Sandy and Jenny.

'We don't have any, Sandy,' Auntie Stella says.

Sandy looks a little puzzled, but only for a moment before she turns back to the beautiful stars, Gina Lollobrigida, Faye Dunawaye, Elke Sommer. We carry on chatting and laughing. After an hour Hippie and I say our goodbyes and leave.

We make our way back down Colorado Drive, but after two or three minutes I turn to Hippie and say, 'Hey, we forgot the shoe-stretcher!'

What a silly thing! We went all the way to the other Van Wyks for the shoe-stretcher and we're halfway home without it. We turn back. The Van Wyks' front door is wide open and we walk right in. And find Auntie Stella, Jenny and Sandy happily sipping away on Fanta Orange – which my dear aunt claimed they didn't have.

When I get home Ma says, 'So what did the Van Wyks have to say?'

'Nothing, Ma.'

Seven years old and already I know what kind of news will hurt my mother.

A few weeks later I'm back there again with Sandy and Jenny, and Auntie Stella slouching about as usual in her slippers, saying not much. At one point I take a break to go to the toilet. Fifteen minutes later I come back to the kitchen. My aunt says:

'Did you wash your hands?'

Jenny and Sandy are watching this and I'm so humiliated that I almost burst into tears.

'Yes, Auntie Stella.' In this house you can't say, 'Of course I did, what do you think!' because then your gran might come after you for being rude.

'Hold them up let me smell them.'

Not only does she believe that I don't wash my hands, she also thinks I'm a liar.

I hold them up and she smells them and gives me one of her little spooky grins.

After that I go up there only when I really have to. And I don't stick around for too long.

Words and music

THE ONLY THINGS THE LOCAL SHOPS EVER GIVE AWAY are the following year's calendars at the end of the year. In December Ma sends me to the shops for bread and liver polony and the shopkeeper hands me a calendar, rolled into a tube. When I give it to Ma, she puts it away until the new year. On January 1 she takes out the calendar and unrolls it, and rolls it the other way so it will flatten out. Then she hooks it on a nail on the kitchen wall. Usually we have more than one, from the butcher, the café, OK Bazaars in town. So there are enough calendars for our bedroom, my parents' room and for the kitchen.

All the calendars say the same thing: With the compliments of … followed by the name of the shop: Adams Restaurant and Café, Sam's Fish 'n' Chips … They all have pictures of healthy looking white children romping through fields bursting with flowers, a pair of the cutest cats or dogs (probably owned by white people), or Jesus looking … well, before I learned the word 'solemn' I believed that he had this look of immense disappointment in us.

At around this time of my life I hear at every turn – school, Sunday school – how the Lord Jesus had died for us. Well, I wondered, it could not possibly have been for me as I wasn't even born then.

The Le Roux family own one of the shops in Riverlea and one December they too hand out a free calendar to each of their customers. I read mine as I walk home from the shop with a loaf of bread stuck under my arm. It says: Le Roux's Grocery Store.

I've heard their surname but never seen it written down before and the strange spelling fascinates me.

Three weeks into January, the Christmas and New Year festivities are over and it's back to school.

Mr Alexander, our new teacher, hands out our reader, a book that contains about half a dozen short stories. He tells us to shut up and keep ourselves busy by reading the first story in the book and we do so eagerly. The enthusiasm would wane so quickly that by the second or third week many kids would have great difficulty prising open this dreaded book.

The first story begins: Mr and Mrs Le Roux … Except that my desk neighbour, Trevor, pronounces it Lirowx – saying the x as he would in box or fox.

'It's Le Roo,' I correct him.

'It's what?' He shifts in his chair so that he can give me a full-frontal stare.

'Mr and Mrs Le Roo.'

He's shocked by my stupidity. 'Sonny, can't you see the x there,' he says, pointing.

'I can see it but you don't say it.'

'Then why the fuck did they put it there?'

I wish I could have told him: that it was French and the French had this funny way of pronouncing their words. But I knew nothing about the French and their language. All I knew was that it was the surname of Coloured people who owned a shop in Riverlea.

Trevor taps the two kids in front of him and asks them to pronounce the word. 'Le Rowx,' they both say. He turns to the two boys behind us. 'Le Rowx.' Of course he has to tell them: 'This *laaitie* (me) says it's Le Roo.'

They laugh, and want me to say it so that they can laugh some more.

When Mr Alexander comes back into the classroom, Trevor has gone through an entire row of respondents and is about to cross over to another row. (Who says democracy did not exist in South Africa in the sixties?)

Mr Alexander asks a girl, Dianne Fonseca, to get up and start reading aloud. She begins:

'Mr and Mrs Le Rowx …'

'Le Roo,' Mr Alexander corrects her. 'It's pronounced Le Roo.'

I give my neighbour a sidelong glance, in time to see him bury his head deeper into his reader. I chance a look around at a few of the others but they too seem to have forgotten the laughs they had enjoyed at my expense mere minutes ago.

When the bell rings for our first break, I tap Trevor on the shoulder and ask, 'So what do you say now?'

'Hey, fuck you, sonny,' he says and skips off … to the loux, perhaps?

Throughout my school career I continue to have strange adventures with words.

I am about eight years old and my uncle Edward (who I call Eddie) is living with us. He is in his first year at high school, Standard 6 and I'm in Standard 1.

In the afternoons he sits at our dining-room table doing his homework in his shirtsleeves and shorts. He puts the radio on LM Radio. The station beams all the way from Lourenco Marques. It's on short wave and crackles a lot no matter how big the aerial on your roof is. But Eddie is not deterred, and sings along as he does his homework: the Beatles, the Rolling Stones, Paul Anka, the Lovin' Spoonful, Elvis, Manfred Mann, Cliff Richard and the Shadows, Mungo Jerry, the Dave Clark Five, Diana Ross and the Supremes. He knows the words to almost all the songs and when he doesn't know the words, he just makes things up: 'It's not really doobee, deebee, a butterfly's life, so debee dee beee.' And for those instrumental parts full of guitars and drums, he goes: dang dang *dang* dang' when the Shadows play 'Apache' or Booker T and the MGs play 'Time is tight'. For this routine he puts down his pen and strums furiously on an imaginary guitar.

It's not with happiness that I remember his shorts. One day our domestic worker inadvertently makes me put on a pair of Eddie's shorts. I protest but I'm late for school so she shoos me out of the door and on my way.

All day at school a crowd of kids follows me everywhere I go, like the Pied Piper, shouting: '*Sambal broek*! *Sambal broek*!'

Sundays are always pleasant days: church (only sometimes – the Van Wyks are not very religious); *koeksisters* from Mrs Lang down the road; reading the Sunday newspapers in the dining-room or outside in the yard if the weather is warm and sunny (which is almost all year round). In the meantime, Ma would be cooking in the kitchen, curry, crispy roast potatoes and chicken, custard and jelly for dessert or bread pudding in winter.

Dad always buys three newspapers, The *Sunday Times*, *Post* and *Sunday Express*. The *Sunday Times* and *Express* are for white readers mainly, with an Extra section in the *Sunday Times* for Coloureds, Indians and Africans. The *Post* is for black readers only – those same Indians, Africans and Coloureds catered for in the Extra section of the *Sunday Times*.

Dad doesn't really want me to read the *Post*. When I ask him why, he says it's filthy. I sort of know what he means because every Sunday you open it and everywhere you look it says, 'Girl raped', 'Girl outraged' or the girl herself says in the headline: 'I was attacked and raped by Mamelodi rapist'. One story, which you can read like a weekly serial, is about the 'Panty Slitter'. This man lurks near the washing-lines in township yards with scissors and cuts up panties. Doesn't take them off the lines, just cuts them up right there. Don't ask me why.

I sneak a read of the *Post* on Mondays when Ma and Dad go to work, folding it back the way it was and putting it back exactly where I found it.

So, on Sundays, no matter what you want to read – black sport, white politics, white crime, black crime, black society news, comics – you can take your section and find a place somewhere in the house. And hope Ma does not suddenly run out of danja or cinnamon sticks and want to send you to the shop or to a neighbour to borrow some.

One Sunday morning finds me and Eddie doing a word puzzle together. There's a sketch of a weather-beaten old sea captain and a little boy chatting. The captain says to the boy: 'I've been to all four corners of the world.' The boy's reply is scrambled up and reads: 'Het orlwd sha on nercors, sit ounrd.'

Eddie fetches a pen and a sheet of paper from his schoolbag to start unravelling the puzzle. But before he can even start, I've thought what the most logical reply to the captain must surely be, and I shout it out triumphantly to Eddie: 'The world has no corners, it's round.'

'How did you know?' Eddie asks.

'I just *knew*. It's so easy. Couldn't you work it out? Why

couldn't you work it out?' I grab the newspaper from him and run to the kitchen. 'Look at this, Ma, Eddie was gonna take an hour to work this out but ...'

'Shut up,' she says. 'Just shut up, OK.'

I shut up, and as I do so I begin to think. And suddenly I understand. I had been humiliating my uncle, and from the kitchen, well within earshot, Ma had been listening to every word.

This facility with language comes about through my voracious appetite for books and the written word. Teachers were forever encouraging us to read. Open books, they'd urge. You will discover places and people, whole worlds you never knew existed. And reading will give you knowledge, and knowledge will give you confidence to go into that big wide world waiting for you. You'll have power. Almost throughout my school career we are called upon to read aloud. And almost all students read badly, turning a dramatic, exciting story into a mere list of meaningless syllables.

Pupil: 'Peter ... wall-ked ... in-to ... the room. (deep sigh) He tur ... ned' ...

Mrs Abrahams: 'Turned'.

Pupil: 'Turned ... on the ... the lig ... hit'.

Mrs Abrahams: 'Light'

Pupil: Light. 'The loon-ger ...'

Mrs Abrahams: 'Lounge ...'

My best friend, Allan Walburgh, sometimes takes the wrong cue from Mrs Abrahams.

Allan: Peter ... ran ... into ... the ... wood er woods ...'

Mrs Abrahams: 'Try not to pause between the ...'

Allan: 'Try not to pause between ...'

Mrs Abrahams never tires of stressing the value of reading. 'All the richest, most famous people in the world,' she says, 'are rich and famous because they read and read and read.'

To most of the class it sounds like too tiresome a path to fame and fortune. The rest just simply do not believe her, thinking that it's just another of those teacher tricks to get us to read.

Mrs Abrahams, ever patient, doesn't stop trying to raise the standard of reading aloud.

'Who listens to radio serials?' she wants to know.

Several hands fly into the air. I myself am a radio nut, my ears nightly glued to Mark Saxon and Sergei in *No Place to Hide*, the side-splitting comic duo *George and Rita*, and Friday night's cop series *Squad Cars*, which starts off with sirens and screeching cars and a no-nonsense voice which warns that: 'They prowl the empty streets at night, waiting in fast cars, on foot, living with crime and violence …'

'You know all that shooting and jumping and running and the car chases that you hear all the time? Well, it's really just a few actors sitting around a table and reading scripts with all those noises on a tape recorder.'

Allan seems not in the least bit interested.

My mother is an avid reader herself and encourages me to read in a way that no one else's mother ever does. I have never in my life heard her say, 'Reading is important. Don't sit around doing nothing, read.' I would just see her, curled up comfortably in an armchair or on her bed, reading and laughing out loud, gasping, shaking her head in disbelief. Soon enough I decided that I'd do it too. So, instead of saying: 'Read, read, read,' Ma read read read herself, and became my best ever role model.

'Have you been to the library yet?' she asks.

'Yes, Ma.'

'What did you get?'

I show her my two books. She takes one and I grab the other. We read them then swap around. And afterwards we sit at the kitchen table – or I sit there while she cooks – discussing the two stories. They're mostly boys' adventure stories about ancient gold coins on sunken ships, hidden panels in the rooms of old castles, cryptic notes, silhouetted figures crouching in the night, abducted girls being rescued by brave boys. What does Ma see in them, I wonder. But she seems to love every thrilling page.

My maternal grandmother, Ouma Ruby, also encourages me to read in her own sweet, wonderful way.

She still lives in Hamilton Street, Coronationville. Ouma Ruby's house is special to me and even though it's a mere four kilometres away from Riverlea, I spend much of my school holidays in Corrie, as we call Coronationville, because it feels like being in paradise. Maybe if I showed you a photo of the people who live in my Ouma's three-bedroomed house, you'd understand. Ouma Ruby has eleven children:

William: Born in 1935 and the eldest. I hear he was the fastest one-hundred-metre sprinter at school. But when he became an adult and it came to working, well, he was a little shy. There are things that maybe I shouldn't be telling you about him, but what the hell – why hide a good anecdote just because it's your uncle. I hear someone once saw him at the Tattersalls in town picking up the hundreds of losing tickets that the punters throw away, in the hope that one or two of them had made a mistake.

Shirley: That's my mother.

Susan: She's as pretty as my ma. She married Toy, a man who can sing exactly like Slim Whitman, which he does at all the family parties. 'I'll take you home again, Kathleen. To where your heart has never been.' The more brandy he downs, the more Whitman he sounds. One day I hear Slim Whitman on Radio Highveld and I rush into my parents' room and shout, 'Listen, there's Uncle Toy!'

Linda: Always smiling, always ready to listen to your troubles, even though she's had more than her fair share as far as men go.

Catherine: Auntie Katie, we call her. She bought me my first pen-and-pencil set when I was almost five years old. She's been poor all her life but whenever I visit her, 600 kilometres away in Durban, she takes something out of her display cabinet to give to my family – a saucer with a rickshaw painted on it, a small wooden hippo, sea shells from the beach.

Edward: I've already told you about him and how bad I felt when I out-thought him with that word puzzle. I'm glad Ma told me to shut up. Let me tell you something else about Eddie: When Eddie was in Standard 4 he was very unhappy. This is because of his teacher, Mr Holland, who was forever shouting at the class and beating the kids. But one day Eddie came home and he was happy. On that day the class went to visit the zoo and Mr Holland was as usual shouting and threatening everyone and making the outing miserable: 'Edward van Heerden, how many times do I have to tell you to stand in line?' 'Valencia Camhee, are you going to shut up or do I have to come there and shut you up myself?' 'Did we come here to show the Europeans what a bunch of barbarians we are?' So they go to see the lions and then the elephant and the giraffe. And all the time they have to shut up and just look. 'If you have any questions, raise your hand,' Mr Holland says. But nobody really wants to ask a question because they don't want to upset their teacher. Then they get to the monkey cages and here is where things get exciting. The monkeys are swinging about and finding lice in each other's hair and nibbling on chunks of pawpaw. And while all this is happening a big father monkey holds his hand under his bum and shits in it and then throws the shit smack into Mr Holland's face.

Venecia: She was born on exactly the same day as Princess Anne of Great Britain – 15 August 1950. I don't know why this is significant, but I've been told it hundreds of times. Venecia takes me to St John's Eye Hospital when Ma and Dad can't because they have to go to work. The day is long on those long brown benches as we shift up one bum per hour. But I make up funny stories about the other patients around us and it makes my aunt giggle and even laugh out loud. She feels embarrassed because the people glare at her and she begs me to stop. But of course I don't.

Mellvin: When his father died in the early sixties he was seven years old. The story goes that when the mortuary van came to fetch the corpse, Mellvin decided to follow the van. As you can imagine, the house had turned into a shambles of sympathisers and sobbing, so nobody noticed him go. A week or two after the funeral a woman who lived opposite the hospital looked out of her dining-room window and noticed something interesting. Every afternoon after school, a little boy walked up to the hospital fence and stared in at the mortuary. At first she thought nothing about it, but after the fourth or fifth day she became concerned and made some inquiries. It was Mellvin, staring in at the place where he had last seen his father taken.

Sharon: She always spoke with a lisp, but when she was about ten years old, her brother, Mellvin, decided that he had had enough of it. One day when my ouma was not at home, he locked Sharon up in the dark, dusty shed in the backyard, with spiders and other *goggas*, and told her he wouldn't let her out until she started talking properly. After a few hours she was cured. To make sure, he instructed her to say a sentence with lots of Rs in it. 'I run and I run on the roof, roof, roof!' After she had said it about twenty times, Mellvin unlocked the shed door and released her. She was angry and tearful, but also happy not to lisp any more.

Denzil: He showed me how to smoke before we were twelve, but we gave it up after Ouma Ruby threatened to kill us both. My mother tells me that when she was expecting me, her mother was pregnant with Denzil. It was most embarrassing, Ma says, to be walking down a street pregnant, with one's mother pregnant too. When Denzil turned eight nobody remembered that it was his birthday – until about a week later.

Neil: My ouma showed my mother that she would fall pregnant an eleventh time. So I have two uncles who are younger than I am.

Neil is the youngest, and the last. My oupa now has eleven children. One sunny Sunday morning, two years after Neil was born, Oupa goes outside to the fig tree and picks one or two ripe figs. He comes back into the house, sits down on the floor by the Kelvinator fridge and eats his figs. He feels a pain in his stomach and dies.

The next morning half the people in Hamilton Street are late for work. Why? Because, without fail, every morning, my oupa used to whistle as he walked down Hamilton on his way to work. And this whistling woke some people up and told others to finish up their coffee a little more quickly. But not on that Monday morning and so everybody was late for work. That's what they told my ouma anyway, when they came to sympathise. But all my ouma could think about was 'What now?' Like the old woman who lived in a shoe, she had so many children she didn't know what to do. My oupa had no insurance, no money in the bank, and about a week's wages paid to him posthumously. And the apartheid government was just flexing its newly acquired muscles and promising whites that they would be taken care of first.

Then there are also my cousins but I don't want to get into that because we'll have a list stretching to the end of the book. But whenever I visit my ouma's house it feels like I arrive in the middle of a festival.

Girls are playing 'doll house', by drawing out a patch on the ground and using bits of wood and bricks as furniture. Boys are singing rock 'n roll songs behind the shed, with upturned paint tins for drums and petrol cans for guitars. In the street and on the pavement there are games to choose from, *kirrebekke*, soccer, hopscotch, and *gatjie klip*. Take your pick and obey the rules. Hope to win but 'take a lose like a man, sonny'.

If you're brave enough you can fight in a real war. Go to the veld up the road from Ouma's house and just beyond the Anglican Church. The Coloured boys are always at war with the Afrikaner boys who live in Crosby, five or six hundred metres away on the other side of the veld. The white boys seem to win most times because they have pellet guns while the Coloureds only have catties. A skirmish usually ends with the cops packing all the boys, Coloureds and Afrikaners, into a *kwela-kwela* and driving around with them for a while.

Whenever I arrive at my ouma's house I'm treated like a prince returning from a distant place to his adoring subjects – and, of course, to the queen mother. If it's summer, Ouma gets my uncles, Denzil and Neil, to climb into the peach and mulberry and fig trees and pick for me the choicest fruit. Mellvin has a new *Tintin* comic – in hardback – which he has kept hidden just for me. Eddieboy tells me chilling stories about the notorious street gangs, the Spaldings, the Vikings and the Fast Guns, from neighbouring Western Coloured Township. The Spaldings stabbed a man in a street fight. He wasn't dead yet but was rushed to hospital. After an operation he was taken to a ward to recover, full of pipes and plaster and bandages. And that's when the Spaldings burst into the ward and finished him off.

My cousin Richard is my favourite because he's my age and we seem to have similar interests. When we were learning to talk, 'Christopher' was too much of a mouthful for Richard. He settled for the strange but simple 'Kuller', and that is my nickname to this day. On this particular day he has a brand new plastic pistol. He's so happy to see me that, with Ouma's help, he splits the gun magically into two and gives one half to me.

Between my last visit to Ouma and this one, my cousins and uncles and aunts have collected thousands of new jokes, riddles and stories.

Mellvin tells us all what happened to him at the scouts meeting last week.

'We did blindfold boxing.'

'What's that?' I think I know but I want to make sure.

'You pick two guys and you blindfold them with scarves. You put them in the ring and you tell them, right, box.'

'Jislaaik it!'

'They can't see each other with the blindfolds on so both boxers are swinging and missing all the time. All the scouts are standing up against the walls and they're shouting, 'To the left! To the right! Behind you! Behind you!'

When it's Mellvin's turn to be blindfolded they put him in the ring with Chris Cannel. Chris is two years younger than Mellvin so he's supposed to be easy meat. But he's not easy meat; he's a boxer and has been one since he was about nine years old.

'I protest. I tell them nay, not ou Chris. But they say don't be a coward. So what I do is I pull the scarf up a bit over one eye so that I can see the bastard. I pretended to hit a lot of misses, but then I hit him nicely.'

I wish I had been there to see it.

'How long is a Chinaman?' Denzil asks me this out of the blue.

'Huh?'

'How long is a Chinaman?'

'What do you mean how long is a Chinaman?'

'How long is a Chinaman?' he persists.

'Five and a half feet,' I say, just so that he'll stop it.

'How long is a Chinaman?' He says this about a dozen more times while everybody else is laughing. Eventually he explains: 'How Long is the name of a Chinaman.'

How witty are my uncles!

Even my ouma has a story for me, right there in the kitchen while she does some ironing. It's a story that happened in the 1930s, even before Cinderella was born and pumpkins could turn into carriages. I think ironing the clothes reminds her. The story goes like this:

I was so naughty when I was a little girl. We were only two children, me and my sister, Louisa, and we lived in Sophiatown. My mother did washing and ironing for a white woman in Newlands.

I was about sixteen and Louisa was eighteen. But you know this Louisa, she always went on as if she was ten years older than me.

So one day, it's a Saturday morning and Louisa and her friend, Rebecca, they're getting ready to go dancing at the Waldorf. It's nice dresses and high-heel shoes and lipstick and this and that and 'zip up my back' and 'does this hat go with this dress?'

I say to my sister, '*Saamgaan*? May I go too?'

She looks at me and looks at Rebecca and the two of them burst out laughing.

'Please!'

'You're too young and you know that, so don't nag, Ruby.'

I'm sixteen on my next birthday. I'm sure I can go dancing but, ah well, I leave them to get dressed. After a while a taxi comes to fetch them and away they go.

My mother finished doing the washing for this white woman and she asks me to help her with the ironing. So there I see this lovely white dress, broderie anglaise with nice satin here in front. I iron it, put it on. Size *pas* (a perfect fit).

I have a wash and put on the dress and off I go to the Waldorf. I step inside and there's Louisa and Rebecca sitting, and the couples are dancing on the floor and the band is playing very nice. Like Benny Goodman and them (but you won't know Benny Goodman). But nice.

They both get such a shock when they see me. Their mouths go wide open and they have to close them with their hands.

Louisa says, 'What are you doing here?'

'Same as yous.'

'Where did you get that dress?' I'm not in the mood for Louisa so I just say, 'Ask no questions and you'll hear no lies.'

At any rate, there I sit down by their table but I'm hardly in my chair and here comes a gentleman and he asks me to dance. I dance with him and I'm hardly back to my seat when here comes another gentleman and asks me for a dance. And after that another one. But, all the time, Louisa and Rebecca are sitting there and sitting there and no gentleman is coming to ask them for a dance.

So while I'm sitting with them, drinking a cooldrink, Lousa says to me:

'Ruby.'

'What?'

She whispers so that the people around us can't hear. She says:

'Listen here, if a gentleman comes and asks you for a dance you tell him no you're tired.'

'And why now?'

'So that they can ask us for a change.'

I don't say yes and I don't say no. But the next time a man comes and asks me would I like to dance I say:

'Of course, yes.'

I'm not always happy here at my ouma's. The last holidays I was here Mellvin made me cry.

Mellvin's got about thirty pigeons and he's built a *hok* for them, out of scraps of wood and wire mesh, at the side of the shed. There's lots of feathers there and blobs of white pigeon shit everywhere you look.

Me and my cousins and our friends watch the pigeons for about fifteen minutes or so until we get tired of it. When they're tired of flying around the skies of Corrie they come home in stages. First they fly on to the roof of the house, then the roof of the shed, then the roof of their own *hok*, then, voops, inside, with a flutter of feathers. They do that throaty noise all together and it sounds like they're all having a good gargle.

One day Mellvin makes an announcement. He takes out two

pigeons, holds them one in each hand and presents one to me and one to Richard.

He says, 'This one's for you and this one's for you.'

Richard and I say, 'Really?'

He sighs deeply as if he still has not made up his mind yet, and then he says, 'Yes. But look after them, OK?'

My pigeon doesn't know yet that I'm his new owner. He wriggles in my hands and wants to take flight, but I hold on to him and say, 'OK, boy, OK. Don't worry.' I don't really know what else to say without making a fool of myself.

Richard and I check out the markings of our birds. Mine's got purplish feathers around its neck, like a cheap necklace. I memorise it. I give it a final stroke and put it back in the *hok* among its dozens of brothers and sisters.

After that I don't know what to do about having a pigeon. My new pet knows where the seeds are, where the water is. I go and play football on the pavement with my dozens of cousins and friends.

Before the sun sets things start going wrong. It's five o'clock and I want to listen to Mark Saxon and Sergei on the radio in *No Place to Hide*. But I hear Mellvin in the yard calling the pigeons. 'Kiep-kiep-kiep,' he calls them. But he also calls 'Kuller!'

I jump up from the floor in the lounge and run outside.

'Aren't you gonna call your pigeon?'

I'm a little puzzled. I would've thought that if he called his 28 pigeons home, mine would come too. Surely it wouldn't stay behind on a neighbour's roof sulking and saying, 'Why didn't Chris call me? He doesn't love me.'

So I stand next to him and go kiep-kiep-kiep too. But I feel self-conscious doing it. It's really more fun watching my uncle do it.

The birds look down at us from the roof doing that claw dance of theirs.

'Come, boy,' I call out to my pigeon.

Mellvin turns and gives me a steely stare.

'What's wrong?'

Your pigeon,' he says, only managing two words at a time, 'is on … the roof … of the … shed.'

I turn around and he's right. My fellow is there on the shed.

Like Mark Saxon and Sergei, this is a serial, and the next instalment, actually the climactic end, happens tomorrow.

The next morning I arrive on the scene of scattered seed and down feathers to see that, like me, the birds have had their breakfast and are wandering about in the yard walking off their meal. I see my bird on the ground and pick him up to give him a couple of affectionate strokes.

Mellvin appears just then, sees me and stops dead in his tracks. I think he's shocked to see me there taking some interest for a change. Stroking my bird ever so smoothly, I say,

'He's a greedy one this bird of mine, he ate too much, didn't you, boykie?'

'That's a female and she's going to have babies!'

I drop her and she flies away, flapping indignant wings as she alights on the roof of the house.

The other uncles and cousins have, in the meantime, gathered to witness my latest humiliation.

'I'm taking that bird back,' Mellvin says. 'Because you're bladdy useless.'

I rush into the house to find my ouma. She's dusting the furniture in the lounge and singing along to a song on the radio, where a choir keeps saying: 'lace-covered windows'.

'Ouma, ouma.' It's hard to talk because I'm choking on my tears. 'What's wrong now?' She stops dusting and sits down and holds my hand.

'Mell-vin-Mellvin-took-took …' Somehow I manage to tell her how Mellvin gave me a bird and then took it back.'

'I'll sort him out,' she says and shouts, 'Mellvin!'

'No, Ouma,' I stop her,' I don't want his bird any more, I don't want it.'

'Ja, you're right. Let him keep his stupid bird. Let him kiep-kiep-kiep his bird.'

I am yet to learn the word 'pun' and my ouma will probably never know such a word. But there it is, a pun, and I laugh and my ouma laughs too and I feel a little silly because I'm laughing while I'm crying and it's like when it rains and the sun shines at the same time and we say, 'The monkeys are getting married.'

There is a serious lack of bed space at my ouma's house but that's not a problem at all. In the evenings, Ouma spills all the dirty washing from her washing box into a rough square on the lounge floor. She spreads two blankets over it and this is where I sleep with Richard, Denzil and Neil.

We tell jokes and giggle in bed and Ouma calls from her bedroom, 'OK, enough now you boys' but we don't stop ... but we do eventually, because the next thing it's morning and I can see sunshine lighting up the edges of the windows and I can smell coffee.

Because we're all so small and because there are only enough chairs for the adults, we sit on the floor and my aunties, Linda and Catherine, bring us two slices of bread each, and sweet black coffee. I dip my bread in the coffee and I think: all over the world thousands, millions of lucky boys and girls are sitting down and dipping their bread in their sweet black coffee. And I feel lucky to be part of it all.

Afterwards we all go out into the sunshine to play the many games on offer. If I'm feeling hungry later I go back inside and ask Ouma for a slice of bread. There's no butter or jam for it, but in her Kelvinator fridge she keeps something specially for such an emergency. Whenever she has fried meat or fish (a luxury which happens once or twice a week), she pours the leftover oil into a gigantic glass jar.

When she takes the bottle from the fridge you can see the layers of fat in their various shades of yellow and brown. She spreads some on to my bread and it's delicious, even though the fat sticks to my palate.

One afternoon, on one of my many visits, my ouma calls me from the street to her bedroom.

'Yes, Ouma?'

She says nothing, just shows me to follow her to her bedroom where she opens her wardrobe and points to a book.

'Take that down,' she says.

I heave it down from the shelf. I say heave because it's the biggest book I've ever seen. She tells me to sit on her bed. She lets me put the book on the bed, where it sinks in, and she sits next to it so that the book is between us. She takes my hand and places it on the book and puts her own hand on mine. It feels as if I am about to take an important oath. I giggle nervously as I sit there with bare feet and my shorts full of street stains, and Ouma smiles. But when she says, 'Your grandfather …' she wants us to be se-rious. So I shift higher up the bed and get serious and wish my T-shirt wasn't so dirty from playing in the sand.

'This was your oupa's favourite book. He bought it … ooh, I don't even know when he bought it because when we got married he already had it. He read it almost every day, sitting there by the kitchen table. But this book has stayed closed since the day he died. Eddie, Mellvin, Venecia, Sharon, Denzil and Neil, I've told all of them – read that book, see what your father was reading about. It might be important issues. But d'you think they'll listen? No, *gatjie klip* and football and hopscotch in the street! That's much more important to them. So I said to myself, this book I'm giving to my grandson …'

'To me, Ouma?' This is an important event and I want no misunderstandings – like those embarrassing moments when you say thank you for a gift only to be told, 'No, it's not for you, it's for him.'

The book is indeed for me. Mine. To keep. Forever. But would I want it? What would I find inside this big and serious-looking monster of a book?

My ouma leaves me to lie on her bed and get acquainted with the book. I dig an elbow into the candlewick bedspread and rest a cheek on my hand. The book is half the size of a pillow. It's a bit tatty and has those old-fashioned little cuticle-shaped things on the side to make it easier for you to find your place.

What will I find inside? Somewhere in the house I hear white people chatting away happily on the radio, in Afrikaans. It's Esme and Jan and they're talking about milk tart recipes and stuff like that. In the street I hear my cousins arguing about a goal, did so-and-so cross a line in a game or break a rule. I want to go back into the street where the action is. I know Ouma said things about how my cousins don't read and I do and she's proud of me, but there are nice things happening in the street and that's where I really want to be right now. But a few things – words and pictures – catch my eye as I flip through the book. I switch elbows and begin to page through it more slowly.

Well, without exaggerating, I can tell you this: think of anything and it's in that book. It shows you how to write a dozen different kinds of letters, from applying for a job to complaining to the City Council about street lights that don't work to condolences to birthday wishes. It has household tips by the hundred: how best to clean windows to how to get a stubborn nut loose. It's chock-a-block with card tricks, card games, matchstick puzzles, the words of old folk songs, what kinds of roots you can eat if ever you were stranded in the bush, how to treat a sore tooth in the middle of the night with stuff from your kitchen cupboard. There are riddles, anagrams, palindromes, jokes …

I can't believe my luck. And long after the games have ended in the streets I'm still locked up in the book on my ouma's bed.

When the holidays are over I take the book home with me and get lost in it for hours and hours every day, travelling up one column and down the next. I have no favourites; how to play a card game called pontoon is as interesting as how to change the washers on your bathroom taps (which they call faucets because this is an American book).

In our household, in the days before this book came into my life, we played a card game called patience, over and over again. This was a game you played on your own, when everybody else was too busy doing other things to play with you – or indeed when you were not in the mood for anybody. Everybody else – cousins, uncles and aunts, friends – all played this game.

One day, on my wanderings through the book, I find a dozen or more different kinds of card games you could play on your own – or solitaire, as I learn they are called. My eyes fall on the illustration of an intriguing game called pyramid and I can see immediately why it's been so named: One card is placed on the table. Two more are placed over it, covering it partially; in the third row are three cards, in the fourth four and so on and so forth. The eponymous pyramid.

I follow the instructions carefully and before I know it I'm playing the game like a champion. I teach my brother Derek and our friends Allan, Rodney, Norman and them. They teach their siblings and friends. And suddenly the whole of Riverlea is playing pyramid. One day I go visiting in Zone 2, the upper end of Riverlea, and come upon my friend's dad playing the game.

'D'you know this game?' he says. 'I'll teach you.'

It's a Saturday afternoon in early August. There is dust and wind and a lip-licking dryness in the air. The wind blows yellow dust off the mine dumps and coats you in it from head to toe, turns all Coloureds into yellows and makes them as dry as some of their jokes. I'm playing around in our yard when I hear our rickety gate squeak open. I look up and there's my uncle Willie with his wife Eunice in tow.

I greet them both, happy to see them.

They had taken a bus to get here. We had not been expecting them. Very few Coloureds have phones so friends and relatives often pop in unexpectedly.

'Is your mother in?'

'Yes, but she's sleeping, Uncle Willie.'

We're standing on our front stoep and our front door is open. He thinks about Ma, his sister, being asleep, for a while, his big curly coiff looking a little windswept and dusty from his trip from township to township. He peeps into the house. His eyes catch something on my bookshelf in the tiny passage facing the front door.

'Where did you get that?' He points to the big book.

'Ouma gave it to me.'

'*Ouma* gave it to you?'

'Yes, Uncle Willie.'

'*Gave* or *lent*?'

'She gave it, Uncle Willie.'

'Uhm.' He shakes his head. 'Bring it here.'

I heave it off the shelf, knowing that it's the last time I shall ever see my big, lovely book again. My uncle pages through the book as if there is some text there that will determine his next move.

'Can I borrow the book?'

I nod. I wish my mother would wake up. 'I'll wake my mother up.'

'No, don't wake her, let her sleep. We're not staying.'

He and Auntie Eunice walk back through our rickety gate and down the street. My uncle has a spring in his step despite the heavy load.

The mystery of the lots of nice books

ONE SUNDAY AFTERNOON MY OUMA COMES VISITING us in Riverlea. Before she leaves she calls me to her side.

'Hey, Kuller,' she says. 'I'm getting my pension on Wednesday.' She takes my hand in hers as she speaks. 'Meet me in town after school and we'll go and buy you some of those books that you like.'

I have a date with my ouma.

On Wednesday I'm there, in President Street, near the post office. My ouma comes up to me, materialising from the shoppers and passers-by. The city is not as busy as it is on Saturday mornings, when people stream in from suburb and township to 'shop where South Africa shops' – at stores like the OK Bazaars.

I saw my ouma only three days ago at our house but I'm so happy to see her that I laugh. She's wearing a hat and I think it's about a hundred years old. She's got a black bag slung over her arm. She once scolded me for clicking it open and closed, open and closed, about two dozen times. But the way she smiles at me now, and wipes the sweat off my nose with her crumpled tissue, I'm sure she's forgotten about that long ago.

Off we go, walking past shops where the white people sit and eat and talk. The bookshop in Diagonal Street is called Homes and Orphans. It has this name, I learn later, because it collects old books from the rich (who are white), sells them to the poor (who are Coloured and African), and gives the money to old-age homes and orphanages. I know I'm a Coloured boy because that's what you have to put on any kind of official forms – at school, in Church or when applying for an identity document – but right now I don't feel poor at all.

A second-hand bookshop must be the best place to visit anywhere in the world and the second-hand book is surely not a hand-me-down but a new creation in its own right. The books that line the shelves are old, slightly worn but proud to present themselves to another potential owner. They have grown in stature: from having started out with only one story, they now have two tales within their covers. They have the original story that you will read from cover to cover, written by a famous or favourite author. But they also have the other story, the one about their previous owner. This story is a mystery, never to be revealed to you, except in the merest of hints – if you're lucky.

Maybe it will be in the form of a dedication on the title page. It could say something like this: For Joshua. Take this on your journey together with our love. Auntie Ruth and Uncle David – August 1958.

Who is Joshua? you will ask. And if you're a South African growing up in the sixties you might think that he must be a white boy to have gone on a long journey. Coloured boys go to their grannies for the holidays over in the next township and maybe to the sea once in their lifetime. But as for leaving the country, oh no, they stay right where they are from birth to death. But white people, well every day they fill up the aeroplanes that fly over our homes, on their way to Cape Town, or far, far away, where they have a grandmother living in France or Holland or Spain or England. Or their parents are divorced and they go and live with Dad and his new wife in London. Or their parents are ambassadors so they go to Switzerland, Sweden, Denmark, Rome. Coloureds, well, they just roam from one ghetto to the next.

But in the end, no matter how old these books are, they take me on journeys to these 'Whites Only' places. There's no warning on page 13 or 48 that says: 'Stop reading. For 'Whites Only' like those signs I've begun to notice at post offices, bus stops, restaurants.

The bookshop has a bell that goes *ding-dong* for me and *ding-dong* for my ouma as we walk into the shop.

The white shopkeeper straightens himself up behind the counter where he has been reading a book. My ouma puts on her musical voice, reserved for white people and Coloureds who come to her door with pens and paper in their hands. It has a lilt in it and is, without being rude to my ouma, not unlike the bell we have just heard. I won't say my ouma is pretentious, it's just her way of showing politeness.

The man smiles at us. Ouma says, 'Tell the gentleman what you want.'

I tell him I want The Hardy Boys. He says, 'There you go,' pointing to a shelf behind me. I turn to the shelf and I can't believe my eyes. *The Clue in the Embers, The Sign of the Crooked Arrow, The Mystery of the Chinese Junk, The Sinister Signpost* ... There are so many of them it's The Mystery of the Lots of Nice Books!

These titles are not easy to come by. I have three in my collection, my friend, Robert Rhoda, has two, Cliffie Weideman has one and Keith Hendricks has two. And here is a whole row, all with the unmistakable embossed silhouette of the two sleuths (another word for 'detective', if you want to write compositions that impress your teacher) from Barmet Bay in the United States of America. Ouma says I can have two. I pull two off the shelf and bring them to the counter. Since it's Ouma's money – 25 cents each, from a widow's pension of about R15 per month, half that of a white pensioner – I want her to help me choose. She perches her glasses on her nose and pages through them, slowly, slowly.

'This one looks nice,' she says. 'And this one also looks nice, very nice.'

Good.

Ouma pays the gentleman. She says good afternoon. Usually I just say goodbye to people but now I also say good afternoon because it sounds posh. He nods and we're out of there.

My ouma takes me to the Riverlea bus stop and chats with me until the bus comes.

'Bye, Ouma.'

'Bye, son.'

I get on the bus and before we've reached home I'm ten pages into *The Flickering Torch Mystery*.

The story doesn't end there.

A few months later, my ouma turns fifty. We have one of those parties for her where every family brings something to eat and we all get together and eat and drink and joke and every room is packed with cousins jumping on the beds and the toilet is never vacant and two dozen adults are laughing and one dozen babies are crying.

Then somebody, I think Uncle Willie, calls us to order so that we can sing Happy Birthday for my ouma, who is sitting at the table blinking and beaming at all the goodies that have been cooked and baked and written up in icing in her honour.

This is my chance. While everybody else has bought birthday cards, I've written my ouma a letter. Birthday cards, those are somebody else's words, some man or woman who has never met my ouma but who tells her how much she is loved and to have a special day, all in lines that rhyme, so that if the last word on one line is 'mother' you know the last word in the next line would be 'another'. If you hit 'today' then you can be sure to run into 'in every special way'. And 'tears' always go with 'years' except when they sometimes surprise you with 'fears'.

Who am I fooling? I quite like the rhyming, and think the writers have great timing. My problem is simple: I had no cash, so I wrote my own birthday message to my ouma, in a letter. It doesn't rhyme. It goes like this:

> Dearest Ouma
>
> On this wonderful day as you turn fifty, I want you to know that I will always love you. You are special to me, buying me books and giving me money for the swimming pool. So enjoy your day and remember that I will love you for ever.
>
> Your grandson
> Christopher van Wyk

I step out from the jostling cousins and hand her my letter.

'Now what is this, my son?' she says, turning it over in her hand.

'It's a letter for you, Ouma. Birthday wishes. From me.'

'Oh, my child.'

'Read it, Ouma. Read it out loud so that everyone can hear.'

'Oh, but I don't have my glasses now.'

'I'll get them for you, just tell me where they are.'

'No, later ...'

A hand reaches out and pulls me away from my ouma's side, back into the crowd. It's my mother. Now, whenever we go out, the last instruction from my mother is always: 'And behave yourselves.' As far as I know I have behaved perfectly. So what is my mother's problem?

'Leave it,' she says, in a harsh, impatient whisper. 'Your ouma can't read.'

Can't read? That's impossible. I don't believe it. Surely all people my age and older can read. How? Well, they just pick up a book and read. Did I ever see my ouma read? I must've, surely ... But there's so much birthday noise around me I can't think straight.

About twenty years later, still intrigued by the mystery of the illiterate granny, I sit down and pen this poem:

Ouma

When I think of my ouma's house, I remember paradise
where the almighty was always broke
but kept puffing up the deflated clouds
and mending the flagging harp strings in the corner
of her room where the sun poured through the curtains
like the warm, weak black tea that she liked to sip
while she listened to our disputes, kissed our bloody
knees
felt our tired foreheads for fevers that sometimes
crept into our games and knocked us out for days.
In the mornings, holidaying at my ouma's,
all my cousins and I rose as one from beds and
makeshift beds among the shoes and mice and drifted to
the
warm kitchen where twenty cups stood like a fleet
of cracked steamboats waiting for us to dip
our buttered bread into the sweet black brew.

And my cousins knew all the film stars, all the pop songs
and some verses from the Bible that we learned

from the Salvation Army with their funny hats and
twangy voices and skins so white and frail that I did
believe
if we were all fitted with our wings one day their
shoulders
would never take the strain. They met us every Sunday
under
a tree in Hamilton Street where they dispensed
with endless tracts of verse.

And often all of these, the verses and the
film stars and the pop songs, came together
in one huge festival that brought every braided girl
and snot-nosed boy from Fuel Road
to Riversdale Street into my ouma's yard
so that my heart almost burst
with all the love and merriment.

And once upon a holiday I came
for my umpteenth – but almost last – time to ouma's
and there was my cousin Richard with a new gun
and without blinking, Ouma, the fastest gun alive
snapped the symmetric plastic pistol in two; one for me
and one for Rich, who didn't mind one bit. Then
we tamed the pillows into horses and shot each other
down until we both died laughing.

And once Ouma, the fastest draw alive,
took me to town to draw her pension. And
afterwards, at the second-hand bookshop,
bought me two books that she helped me choose
by flipping randomly through them.
Although much later I learned that the black words
on the white sheets that swept me across the seas
to adventures in faraway lands were to Granny
like coal strewn across a field of snow.

And now Ouma's hair is turning silver as the stars
drop their tears on her head begging her to come
and live among them in their own version of paradise.
Ouma has been resisting for so long now but soon
I know she'll give in as she always has to all of us whose
empty cups she fills with dreams and golden tea.

Supermen and superwoman

IT'S SCHOOL HOLIDAYS and Allan Walburgh and my brother Derek and me and Rodney 'Rathead' Jardine and Norman 'Nokker' Crowie and Gregory 'Hippie' Johnson are in the veld. We are dislodging and turning over logs and rocks that have been stuck in the sand a long time. Underneath you find worms that are so startled by the sudden disappearance of their roofs, they do a wriggly dance in their damp homes, like humans when we're caught naked. You also get scorpions. Allan points to one's tail and says, 'Sonny, if this bastard stings you, you're dead.'

There's also a *duisendpoot* – that's Afrikaans for thousand-legs. This is an ugly, black and red worm that likes curling itself up into three or four circles. I hear he's also supposed to be one helluva dangerous thing but some of the boys hold him in their hands. Not me, thank you very much.

If you're very, very lucky you find a snake.

We kill everything we find underneath the rocks – except maybe ants because we see them every day everywhere and there's so many of them it would be a waste of time to kill them. We don't think ants are dangerous but Norman says they are. He says: 'Say, for instance, you're on a picnic, right?'

'Right?'

'Now if you lie on your back and an ant crawls into your ear, right?'

'Right.'

'If he crawls out the other ear, you're dead.'

'What?'

'I'm telling you, you're dead.'

Somebody says, 'Don't talk *kak*, sonny.'

I'm not sure if I should believe Nokker's story, but I like it anyway. It makes me feel like we're all living one helluva dangerous and exciting life here in Riverlea. It's like we can go to bed and never wake up again. I also like the story that Gregory Johnson tells us. When we see a *streepie* darting under a rock, all those who have spotted the mouse with its stripe on the back shout 'Streepie!' and those who haven't shout: 'Where?' Then Hippie Johnson remembers his story:

'If your brother or sister pees in the bed, you know what you do?'

'What?'

'You come here to the veld, you catch a *streepie*, you cook it up, you give it to your brother to eat. He won't pee in the bed again.'

I don't believe this story either, but, like the ant story, I like it anyway.

It's a bit scary lifting rocks in the veld because you don't know what you're gonna get underneath, but if Allan is your friend, you've got nothing to worry about.

Allan is a warrior type of guy. He likes showing us his muscles and walking around their yard without his shirt on. We call it 'kaalbors' which is Afrikaans for 'barechested'. He says: 'Sonny, have you ever seen such big muscles?'

In the movies I've seen Samson with big muscles, and Reg Park and Charles Atlas in those body-building magazines that the white people throw away and we pick up. But not in real life, so to speak. So I shake my head.

Allan says in Albertsville, where they used to live before they came to Riverlea, he once fought a gang of lowlifes. It was an ongoing battle that lasted for a few weeks. One day they got hold of him as he was coming from the shop 'with a bottle of fish oil my ma sent me to buy'.

'I got away from them but they started throwing stones at me. I was ten metres away from them but instead of running away I hold the bottle of fish oil up in front of me. You know what happened, Christopher?' (He calls me Christopher when he's telling me something very serious.)

'What?'

'They threw a stone against the bottle, smashing it to bits, oil all over the place, my clothes, in the sand, everywhere.'

'And so?'

But there was no 'and so'. That was the end of Allan's story.

This had happened in Albertsville. Then the apartheid government came and turfed out the Walburghs and dozens of other Coloured families and replaced them with whites. But Allan never mentioned that story; it's something I found out years later.

The Walburghs live two doors away from us. Allan has two older sisters, Sylvia and Lorraine. One is short and chubby; the other is tall and thin. They are both about five or six years older than we are.

When Allan and I are in Grade 2, Sylvia is in Standard 5. She's one of the cleverest girls at T. C. Esterhuysen. But she is famous for something else. Sylvia and her best friend, Ruth, have an argument one day on the playground and they stop speaking to one another. Now this stop-talking thing happens everywhere and every day. We call it being bad friends. 'Hey have you heard, Errol and Rowan are bad friends'. 'For how long now?' 'Since day before yesterday.'

So at first there is nothing unusual about Sylvia and Ruth being bad friends. Until it does become unusual. Three or four months go by and still Sylvia and Ruth have not said as much as a howzit to each other. Best friends! In the same class!

Allan gives me an update every day. Yesterday the teacher asked the class a question and only Sylvia and Ruth's hands went up. It was weird. Ruth's mother asked why Sylvia doesn't come around there any more. In many ways it was like those radio soapies on Springbok Radio from 2.00 in the afternoons: *Die Banneling* or *Die Wildtemmer*. You had to wait a whole day to find out what happened next. But in those soapies the Afrikaners speak for fifteen minutes with the odd Surf or Ajax break in between. In this serial there are no words.

One day their class teacher decides that this has gone on long enough. Mrs Jacobs strides on to the playground and calls the two girls (who are on opposite sides of the playground) to her side. A circle forms. Mrs Jacobs tells them this is nonsense. It's gone far enough. Shake hands or I'll call the principal and we'll call in your parents and Father Ilett of the Anglican Church (where the Walburghs worship) and Father McCullagh of the Catholic Church (where Ruth is a Holy Angel).

The two girls shake hands, although Sylvia has a look on her face that says, 'I could have kept this up for ever.' The playground bursts into happy applause.

Afterwards, just to make sure they do become friends again, Mrs Jacobs sends them on errands together all over the school.

Me, I'm proud. Everybody at school is talking about this and all I say is, 'I know Sylvia, the Walburghs are our neighbours. They live two doors away and I go to their house any time I like.'

Allan says his father is the best wood-carver in the country.

'You mean the best Coloured wood-carver in the country?'

'Christopher, my father is the best woodcarver in the country. White, Coloured, Indian, anybody.'

Allan may be bragging, but if you look at Uncle Richard's wood-carvings, you too would be convinced that no human hand could do better. He works from home so I can go and watch him carve whenever I like. They live so close that I can actually hear the *doef doef doef* of his mallet tapping against his chisel, which is in turn cutting those grooves and patterns into the wood.

He hasn't got a workshop to work in so he has pushed his workbench right up against the bedroom window for maximum sunlight. This makes him look like an exhibition carver because you can stand in their yard at the bedroom window looking in and watch him.

He has about ninety to a hundred chisels packed in a perfect arc on the workbench, all in different shapes and sizes. Clamped in his vice is a dining-room table leg, which is very pale and plain. Uncle Richard gets to work on it, making grooves with this chisel, little ditches with that one, scallops with another. He picks up the chisels almost without looking. He's like a pianist who knows where all the keys are. As he works he breathes in short little gasps. He leaves cigarettes to burn into long grey worms in his ashtrays. He wipes the sweat from his face and his calloused palms with a towel.

As we watch, the table leg blooms into flowing roses. Headboards are transformed into a symmetry of leafy boughs.

We watch him until we get bored and go off to play or until he chases us away for asking him lots of stupid questions and distracting him.

Uncle Richard eats cheddar cheese while he works. He or Auntie Nita (her name is Anita but it's too much of a bother to put the 'A' there when we say her name), his wife, cuts the cheese into big pale yellow dice and leaves it on a plate at his side to eat. When he runs out of cheese he sends Allan to the shops for more and Allan fetches me – or Norman if he's available or Derek.

It's great to go to the shops with Allan. Where I get maybe five cents pocket money for sweets if I'm lucky, Allan's mum gives him twenty, twenty-five cents. We buy enough sweets to chew for a week, which we finish in an hour.

Three shops sell cheese and they all stock only sweetmilk (with the red wax jacket) and cheddar, which is crumbly and tangy. If Allan walks into the shop they reach for the cheddar. If they're out of cheddar they don't bother to even suggest sweetmilk.

Sometimes Allan gets into the mood for a fight but there's nobody to fight because nobody has provoked or offended him. Then he says to me, 'You know, that Vickie Johnson is just a piece of shit.'

Vickie Johnson is spinning his top down the road with a bunch of guys.

'Why, what's he done?'

'Ag, I just can't take him. He thinks he's somebody.'

Vickie Johnson is one of the big boys in our street. He's older than we are and in a higher standard. And when two boys have to pick a side each for a street game of football, Vickie is a picker.

If you greet Vickie: 'Heit, Vickie,' he says, 'Hoezit, my *laaitie*.' *Laaitie* means kid or youngster. You don't feel offended at being called a laaitie, you're actually glad that Vickie has taken notice of you.

Allan says, 'Christopher, do me a favour.'

'What?'

'Go up to Vickie and give him a smack.'

'For what, Allan?'

'Just do it. If he tries to smack you back, I'll be there to fuck him up.'

I don't know why boys want me to do stuff I know is stupid. The other day I was with my uncle Mellvin. A Zulu man walks past us with his earlobes so big they're hanging down on his shoulders. This is no exaggeration, it's a cultural thing. First the earlobes are pierced with a pin, then a few days later with a thicker pin, then gradually the hole is stretched until, eventually, the earlobes are hanging on the man's shoulders. Mellvin whispers to me, 'Say, "*Skaties glebe*".'

'Why?'

'Just say it, you'll see what happens.'

'Why don't you?' I don't know what it means but I do know that it would be a deep insult and that I would get that Zulu's knobkierie on my head.

(Mellvin tells me later that it means: What's the time on those two watches you have dangling from your ears?)

'But why?' I now ask Allan. 'He's done me nothing.'

'Ah shit, you scared? You think I can't fuck him up?'

It's neither of those things. It's just very illogical but Allan sees absolutely nothing wrong with this.

Even though Allan is a year or two older than I am, we're in the same class. One day our teacher, Mr Cannel, leaves the room and asks one of his favourites, Sharon Isaacs, to write down the names of the talkers. This is basically an informer job, but the informer considers it a great honour.

Sharon goes to the blackboard and draws a giant T in the middle of it, in white chalk. At the top of the board on the left of the T she writes a B and at the top on the right, a G. Then she turns to face us, the Bs and Gs, and watches and waits.

Aha! Sharon does not have to wait long. Barely three minutes into informer duty the initials A W appear, underneath the B column. All Allan has done is whisper to somebody to pass him an eraser.

'Oh shit!' says Allan, loud enough for us all to hear. Now I'm in the shit. Two cuts, three cuts, what the hell. I'll take it like a mouse-I-mean-a-man.'

'Quiet,' I whisper.

But Sharon is vigilant today. She points her chalk at me and swings around to scrawl C V W underneath A W.

'Aha!' Allan remarks as my initials come up. 'Is that you, Mr Christopher van Wyk? How many cuts would you like, two, three, four? Hand or bum?'

I've got the giggles now but I whisper from across the aisle, 'Shhh.'

'Ah, come on, Christopher. If you shut up now you're still gonna get a hiding, so talk.' To prove his point he rattles off a string of nonsense: 'My name is Allan ha ha ha. Jesus loves me this I know. Inky pinky ponky, daddy had a donkey.'

I get the point and I start talking too.

When Mr Cannel returns the only name that is not on the board is S I – Sharon the Informer.

'Oh, just rub it out,' says our teacher.

For once we don't get punished. Not that it would've bothered my friend Allan. He makes a vow one day after we get a beating.

'I make a vow, me, Chris,' he says as we're both trying to rub the pain from our bums.

'Wha-at!' I say, because that's how you say 'what' when your arse is on fire.

'No matter how many lashes these bastards give me, I'll never ever cry.'

Mid-term we get our reports and run home to show our mothers and to play, play, play, for the next three weeks.

I gobble down my lunch and minutes later I'm at Allan's house. His sisters Sylvia and Lorraine are reading his report.

'Allan if you don't pull up your socks, you're going to fail again,' Sylvia warns him.

'Fetch your report, Chris,' Lorraine says.

Minutes later I'm back. One sister takes my report, the other has Allan's. They begin calling out the marks, comparing the two reports, while I look on embarrassed.

'Jesus, Allan. Chris is two years younger than you and he's doing better.'

'Oh leave me alone!' Allan says, flouncing off.

Uncle Richard and I swap comics. This is strange; I should be swapping comics with Allan. But every now and then I knock on the Walburghs' door. Allan opens, he sees the stack of Marvels and DCs in my hands and he shouts, 'Dad, Chris is here!'

I have a stack of over two hundred comics and have become famous in Riverlea as a reader and collector of them. I love them! My favourite is Spider-man. He's Peter Parker, a young student who was bitten by a spider one day and miraculously acquired spider-like qualities, like crawling up walls and producing his own webs. I like it when Spider-man fights with a foe (synonym for enemy), some bearded criminal dressed in green, who also has some special power but wants to destroy the world with it. I like the way Spider-man and this guy have a conversation – 'take that, fluffy cheeks!' – while they're teetering on the edge of a skyscraper or swaying from a tower.

I like the way Batman and Robin are both birds' names but nobody else in Riverlea notices.

I like the way nobody around Clark Kent can see that he's Superman despite two whopping big clues – he looks exactly like Superman would look in a suit and specs and he's never around when Superman is.

Uncle Richard and I sit on opposite sides of the dining-room table. He gives me a *Spider-man*, I give him a *Superman*. He gives me a *Richie Rich*, I give him a *Little Lotta*.

The next day Allan comes over to our house. He sits next to me at our dining-room table and I read the comics out loud so that he can enjoy them too.

One day there's an unpleasant incident between me and Uncle Richard. I take my stack of comics and walk over to the Walburgh house. Uncle Richard and I sit down and start swapping. I give you two *Archies*, you give me a *Sad Sack* and a *Little Dot*. You give me a war comic for this *Pecos Bill*.

Then I show Uncle Richard a bumper *Superman*. These are rare: three or four complete stories in one super edition. Uncle Richard picks it up and flips through it. He seems very interested in the adventures of the caped crusader – the mild-mannered Clark Kent who hobbles haplessly into a telephone booth and emerges mere seconds later as the most powerful crime fighter on our troubled, crime-ridden planet. Plus the comic is in pristine condition; no dog-ears, no missing pages, no pages where a bored younger brother with a ballpoint pen has given all the women moustaches and sunglasses.

For this bumper comic I am mentally planning negotiations. I want no less than three comics and they would all have to be in mint condition too.

Uncle Richard grunts, stamps out his cigarette, holds up the *Superman* omnibus. He says, 'This is *my* comic. You stole it from me.'

I stare at him. I go weak at the knees, like my hero exposed to a big chunk of kryptonite. Uncle Richard's fingers are yellow and calloused from cigarettes and woodwork and too much cheddar cheese. He points one of them at me. 'Why did you steal this book from me?'

'I didn't, Uncle Richard. It's my book.'

'Where did you get it?'

It's hard to answer that one. Comics travel lightly and widely. It's possible that within a week one comic can be read by twenty different people. A comic bought in town by someone who lives in Riverlea could end up in Cape Town in three days' time or before you can say ZAP, could cross racial barriers from suburb to township before you can say BIFF BAM AAARGH.

As to where I got it? Well I just don't know. I do my swapping rounds almost every day. But, as sure as Peter Parker is Spider-man, I did not steal it from Richard Walburgh.

The comic-swapping session is over. I gather up my stack of comics – minus the big *Superman* – and stumble out of the Walburghs' house. I'm sobbing and hope there aren't any girls playing skipping or hopscotch in the street. I'm in a great hurry to get home.

Barely two minutes later I'm at home, still sobbing bitterly, with more volume now because I want my ma to come rushing out from wherever she is. I have serious problems and I need her NOW. And, sure enough, she comes rushing into the bedroom, where I have flung myself on the bed, face down.

'What's it now?'

'Unc-cle Rich-chard-says-I-stole ...'

Mothers have special powers and in no time she's worked out what I'm saying. In fact Ma reads my comics too, so she even knows which one I'm talking about.

'Come-come-come,' Ma says. 'Let's go sort this thing out once and for all.'

Minutes later, I'm back at the Walburghs with Ma leading the charge (well it's half a charge really with Ma looking ready for battle and me the walking wounded).

'But, Richard, if he stole it from you, would he bring it back here?' The look on Ma's face is sort of like a smile. But I know it's actually a look that says, 'You're an idiot'. You can ask Dad because until now it was a smile reserved for him exclusively.

Minutes later we're back home. Me, Superman and Superwoman.

Auntie Nita has long jet-black hair. She will let no one cut her hair but Ma. She says Ma's got a good hand and that her hair grows quickly when Ma cuts it. There's something I don't understand here: if she wants her hair to grow quickly then why cut it in the first place?

When her hair grows just a little too long for her liking, she sends Allan over and he says, 'Auntie Shirley, my mother asks if Auntie Shirley has time to please cut her hair?'

'Ask your mother if tomorrow night's OK.'

He runs home and three minutes later he's back with a yes, Auntie Shirley.

Auntie Nita comes over with her comb, her scissors – in case Ma's aren't sharp enough – and a thirty-pack of Van Rijn cigarettes, the same brand as Ma's.

We clear the lounge of people and they get to work. Ma snips away and Auntie Nita's black tresses float on to the linoleum floor.

'Oh God!' Ma says and stops cutting.

'What's the matter?' Auntie Nita says, alarmed.

'Grey hairs, Nita, grey hairs! Look.'

'Oh shit, Shirley. Do you have to show me?'

They explode with laughter.

'I tell you, it's that Richard. Turning my house into a bladdy factory with that carving of his. You won't believe where I find wood shavings, Shirl, in the kitchen, the toilet, between the bedsheets. Even in …'

I don't hear the end of the sentence because it's whispered. But for the next few hours I wonder what Auntie Nita could've said that made them laugh so much.

Later, her hair cut, Auntie Nita takes out of her purse five rands and hands it to Ma.

Ma refuses it point blank.

'Don't be bladdy foolish, Shirley.'

'You're the one that's being foolish.'

Eventually Auntie Nita says goodnight, accidentally leaving a full, closed packet of Van Rijn on the table.

The next day I ask Ma for twenty cents for the movies.

'I'm broke,' she says. She lights up a Van Rijn and opens her paperback novel.

So one day, in 1966, a man gets knifed and dies and it's so serious that we all get sent home from school early the day it happens. This is a real treat! We're caught so off-guard that we almost don't know what to do on this unexpected holiday.

When Dad gets home from work (normal time) I tell him we got home early.

'So what did yous do all day?'

'Played.' I shrug.

'What about the yard?'

'The yard, Da?' I don't know what he means.

'Why didn't you clean it?'

Because I was too busy playing. But I don't say this.

There's a head-and-shoulders photo of an unsmiling white man on the front page of *The Star.* Dad's sitting on the couch. He has turned to his paper and is staring at the face and reading the story.

'Is that the man who died?' I ask.

'Mmm-mm.'

'What's his name again?' They told us at school but I can't remember.

'Dr Verwoerd.'

A few years earlier, before my school-days began, Dad used to make me a toy called a bullroarer. Thread cotton through a big button, twirl about a dozen times and pull. It goes voorrrrvoooorrrvoer, which is why its Afrikaans name is woerwoer.

'Like a woerwoer,' I say.

Dad laughs and says,' Ja.' He goes back to his reading.

Dad is not really a big talker. If I had asked Ma these questions, I would've known the entire history by now: birth, school, university, and untimely death. But I struggle on.

'Who's he?'

'He was the prime minister.'

'What does the prime minister do?'

'He's the leader of the country.'

My dad isn't really annoyed to be answering these questions, so I go on.

'But if he's a doctor, why doesn't he work in a hospital?'

'He's not that kind of a doctor, he's a … he went to university for many years and he studied hard and he's clever. If you study hard and you're clever they call you a doctor.'

I stare at the portrait of Verwoerd. 'Is it a sad thing that he's dead?'

'Not for me.'

This answer surprises me. 'Why aren't you sad?'

'Because he was an arsehole, an idiot.'

'But you said he's clever and he went to university and that!'

He sighs, and there's a half-smile on his face.

Later, I go over to the Walburghs. Allan and I sit in the kitchen. The rest of the family are all somewhere else in the house. They have just had dinner and dishes are stacked on the table, in the sink.

Behind the glass sliding doors of their kitchen dresser are little cards the size of business cards, with wise little bits of advice on them by somebody called Patience Strong. The Walburghs get these cards buried deep in the Pitco Tips tea and every time I visit their home there's a new piece of wisdom waiting for me to read. The latest one says:

Life is never empty while there is someone needing you
Life is never futile while there is something you can do

The card smells like Pitco Tips. The rest of the Walburgh house smells of cat pee because they have two or three felines pissing all over the house from top to bottom. But despite the pee smell I like this house; it's clean and homely and Allan's my best friend – at least for the moment.

While we chat Allan keeps dipping a finger into the mayonnaise jar and then licking it. He laughs mischievously, inviting me to stick my finger in the jar too. I wouldn't like Uncle Richard or Auntie Nita to catch me with my dirty fingers in their mayo. Besides I don't like mayonnaise anyway, so I shake my head.

'It's nice, man. Good for your … uhm …'

'Your stomach.'

We both laugh.

Allan always has a piece of philosophy or an idea that he sort of flings at you without warning.

'Christopher,' he says. 'Who are the two handsomest men in the world?'

I don't know why we're on to this weird topic. I shake my head because with Allan you'll never get such things right.

'You wanna tell me you don't know?' he says. 'Jesus Christ and Elvis Presley.'

I'm not going to argue with that. The Walburghs are big Elvis fans and have all the LPs and seven-singles. As for Jesus, if I disputed that I would be accused of blasphemy. I say:

'You could be right.'

'Not could be, am.'

I nod. I really don't want to start a fight with Allan, so I switch to something we don't have to argue about.

'Hey, did you see this thing about the prime minister that they killed in parliament?'

'Ja, that's why they sent us home today. Isn't it sad?'

'My father says he was an idiot.'

'Ja, that man who killed the prime minister. They should hang him.'

'No ... the prime minister, my father says he's the idiot.'

'What!' Allan takes a cloth and wipes off his finger, like a clown taking off his face paint when he hears bad news.

'An idiot,' I repeat. Allan knows exactly what an idiot is; he's been called one dozens of times by sisters and teachers – although I don't think he's one himself.

'I can't believe your father said such a thing.'

'I'm telling you what he said.'

'Do you know how much that man has done for Coloured people?'

This is like Jesus dying for me, for my sins, long before I'm even born. People are handing out gifts to me and mine all over the place and I'm not even aware of it.

'What did he do for us?' I'm not being sarcastic; I just really would like to know.

'Houses. He gave us all houses.'

'But my father says he gives white people better houses.'

'That's not the point. He gives black people worse houses so at least we're better off than them.'

In this very same kitchen, weeks later, I see something that disturbs me. When I come looking for Allan, the maid opens the door, we greet each other and she lets me in. She is an African woman with an English name, Janet. Our maid is Agnes.

Janet calls Allan and tells me to sit down. She is making lunch for herself and from underneath the sink she takes out an enamel dish, an enamel mug, a big spoon, a teaspoon and a fork.

Allan appears and we go into the street to find our other friends. When we're outside I turn to him and ask: 'Does your maid have her own plate and mug and stuff?'

He stares at me as if I've again said Verwoerd is an idiot.

'Don't tell me your maid drinks out of the same cups you drink out of?'

He waits for an answer and my silence is clear enough.

'Jesus, Christopher. You know, I've also noticed that yous, you and Derek, call your maid Auntie. She's not married to your father's brother!'

I find this disturbing. Because when Allan talks to me, I know when it's Allan. But there are times when he talks to me when I can hear his mother and father speaking with his tongue. I can sense without a doubt that the Van Wyks are sometimes the topic of conversation in the Walburgh household.

When I go home, Ma is reading a paperback novel. I tell her about my day with Allan. She keeps her folded-over book ready, to return to it at any minute. But when she hears, 'she's not your auntie', the book gets cast aside. She says:

'Auntie Nita isn't married to your father's brother either but they don't mind you calling her auntie do they?'

Damn it. Why didn't I think of that?

'Look,' Ma explains further, 'Agnes is my age so you and Derek and Shaun can't go about calling her by her first name. If the people around here do that, well that goes for them. But I won't allow my children to call a woman by her first name just because she's black.'

'Did Verwoerd give us this house?'

'Who told you that?'

'Allan.' I explain what happened.

'Look here. Those white hoboes that you see in the streets, they can vote but we can't. So fuck the Walburghs and fuck Verwoerd.'

'Dad told me you can get arrested for saying that.'

'For saying fuck the Walburghs?'

We both laugh at Ma's joke.

'No, Verwoerd.' I say.

'That'll be the fucking day.'

A few weeks after the death of the prime minister, I hear an Elvis song being sung in the streets. It's an Elvis tune but the words are about the assassinated Verwoerd. It goes:

It's now or never
Verwoerd gaan sterwe
Wie gaan hom begrawe
Sy eie soldate

Everybody's singing it, children and adults, and me too. But not the Walburghs.

Numbers

ONE SUMMER EVENING there's a knock on the door. I open it and it's Lionel 'Liney' Vergie from next door. He's my friend but he hasn't come to hang out. The Vergies don't hang out late. By eight at night it's lights out at their home. No playing hide-and-seek under the lampposts on summer evenings like we all do. Or listening to the radio like the Van Wyks, or reading. Everybody's asleep by eight.

I'm in primary school and doing my homework. Lionel tells me his dad would like to borrow my English dictionary. I take it off the little shelf in the passage where I keep it. It's called the Concise Oxford. My father bought it for me, together with a set of encyclopaedias. I use it all the time and I don't like being without it for too long. Lionel promises to bring it back the next day.

After he leaves, my father comes out of his bedroom where he had been listening to the conversation between Liney and me.

'His father borrowed your dictionary?'

'Yes, Dad.'

My dad stares at me, a little surprised.

'What's the matter?' I want to know.

'He's a *teacher* and he hasn't got a *dictionary*!'

Throughout his life, my dad has some overrated opinions of teachers. He believes they are super-intelligent, wise creatures who should be revered and respected by the rest of the community, the blue-collar workers like himself and Ma.

The Vergies are our left-hand next-door neighbours. They come from Kimberley and they speak Afrikaans.

Liney is two years older than I am. He's the centre forward for the Young Lions, where he causes all kinds of trouble for their league rivals, Arsenal, Gladiators, Rosebuds, Chelsea.

Mr van Rijn down in Ganges Street owns the team and on Thursday evenings they have club meetings at his home. If you don't go to the meeting, you can't get picked for the game on Saturday. That's the rule.

Liney is the club's secretary so he has to write a three- or four-line match report, which he has to read out every Thursday evening. Even though Liney and fifty per cent of the club are Afrikaans speaking, the match report is always in English. And always includes this sentence: 'We played with alacrity' together with the score. A full match report would go like this: 'We won because we played with alacrity. The score was: Young Lions 5, Chelsea 4.' Or: 'We played with alacrity but we lost ...'

Maybe it's in my dictionary that they stumble upon this word 'alacrity'.

One Sunday morning I pop over to the Vergies to hang out with Liney and Toolbag. The Sunday newspaper is on their dining-room table but it's not the *Sunday Times* that we buy, it's the Afrikaans newspaper *Rapport*. I'm curious so I page through the paper reading the headlines. There's a special section for Coloureds, mostly Coloureds in the Cape where ninety per cent of us live. This news amuses me because it's not actual news; it's about fetes and weddings and stuff like that. There are a lot of fezzes and kufias in the photos.

There's even a comic section and it's called *Strokies Rapport*. And guess who I see there? Old friends from the *Sunday Times*, Dagwood and Blondie and 'Bringing up Father', all in Afrikaans. 'Bringing up Father' is called *Pantoffelregering*. Whatever's that? A *pantoffel* is a slipper and a *regering* is a government. Oh! I see it now. It's like the English Petticoat government.

I'm quite proud of myself for having made such a discovery all on my own. But I don't share it with Liney or Toolbag or any of my friends. Nobody in this township seems too interested in words. Ag, what, I just keep it filed away somewhere in my brain to impress my Afrikaans teacher the next time I write an *opstel*.

The Vergies are numbers people. When I chat to Liney and Toolbag in the street about families, they claim they are from Indian stock. I'm surprised that they tell me this so easily. In this township nobody wants to admit to their origins unless those origins are white.

Looking at Mr Vergie (which I do almost every day of my life)

I think I can see something Indian, long strands of black hair that he combs from the left side of his head, across a big bald section, to the right side. In summer a waterfall of sweat comes cascading down from there and then he takes off his glasses every five minutes and wipes it away with his big hanky.

Mr Vergie has the strangest nickname, Baby. In the meantime his youngest son Wayne is called Man. Once again nobody else but me finds this a little odd.

Mr Vergie is a schoolteacher at Riverlea First Primary where he teaches Standard 5s. And in the afternoons he is home early enough to work at his other occupation, that of fahfee runner. This fahfee thing is worth explaining.

It is an illegal gambling operation, run in many Coloured townships, usually by a Chinese man or woman. In our case, she is Julie.

There is a set list of 36 numbers you can bet money on. These numbers also have names, using various different languages:

1 – king
2 – apie (monkey)
3 – seawater
4 – dead man
5 – tiger
6 – os (ox)
7 – skelm (sly one)
8 – vark (pig)
9 – moon
10 – eggs
11 – carriage
12 – dead woman
13 – big fish
14 – ou vrou (old woman)
15 – slegte vrou (bad woman)
16 – pigeons
17 – diamond lady
18 – small change
19 – little girl
20 – cat

21 – elephant
22 – ship
23 – horse
24 – chatta (mouth)
25 – big house
26 – bees
27 – hond (dog)
28 – herrings
29 – kleinwater (small water)
30 – hoender (fowl)
31 – fire
32 – gold money
33 – little boy
34 – stront (shit)
35 – katpan (vagina)
36 – nunkwayi (penis)

There are two draws, one at around 3.00 p.m. and another around 7.30 p.m. Mr Vergie is one of about ten runners all over Riverlea who go around, knocking on doors, asking neighbours to bet, and they get paid a commission.

If you bet a sixpence and win, you get twelve bob.

Some evenings, if I've got nothing better to do, I go around with Liney to the various punters.

At about seven in the evening Julie arrives in her Volksie with the winning number. It's written on half a sheet of paper and folded up – a big secret, which will remain a secret for another half hour or so. Julie places the number ceremoniously in the centre of the table underneath a vase or saucer. All the runners hand in their 'bags'. Julie counts all the money. One runner is chosen to unfold the winning number and call it out – followed by a chorus of curses and cheers.

'Shit! I looked at the 8. Thought of playing it, played 9 instead.'

'I played the 8 yesterday!'

'I've got a shilling on it at least.'

When Mr Thomas wins big, Liney takes him his winnings and I go with my friend.

'Twenty-eight, Mr T,' Liney says. The punter's face cracks into a grin and all his children come to the lounge to be part of the excitement. Mr Thomas says, 'I knew it! It had to be herrings!' as if there's a system. He calls over his shoulder, 'Mary!' His wife comes to the dining-room.

'Just tell these boys what I told you last night?'

She looks puzzled and I don't blame her; he must've told her a hundred different things last night.

'When you were making coffee?'

'About what you heard at the bus stop?'

'No, man! The pilchards! My dream about the pilchards!'

'Oh that!' she says and tells us how he came from work yesterday and said to her, 'Mary, why were there no pilchards on my lunch today?' 'Because I put polony on your lunch,' she said. 'But I distinctly saw you put pilchards on my lunch.' You must've been dreaming,' she said. 'I don't know when last we had pilchards in this house.' Then it dawned on him and he smiled and said, 'You know something, it was a dream.' And he said:

'The Chinaman's going to pull herrings,' they finish the story together.

Mr Thomas gives Liney a shilling and we go and buy sweets at Mrs Lang's, the house shop.

Because fahfee is illegal, everybody has to be careful; we have to be on the lookout for the cops all the time. And this often results in some strange sign language in the township. Let's say the Chinaman has pulled number 36, which is you-know-what. Liney is on his way home from the house where the draw was made and the whole of Riverlea is on tenterhooks, wondering if they've won or lost. Liney chances upon a punter a hundred metres away down the street. Instead of calling out the winning number, Liney holds his fist in the air – the fahfee sign of the penis. A few years later, a very similar sign would become the famous black power salute.

Sometimes there's drama on a Saturday afternoon. The police spot Julie coming into the township in her blue Volksie and they give chase in their white Opel Record. Julie doesn't wait for small change, as they say. She flies down Flinders, up

Galana, swerves into Colorado Drive, all the way past the shops into Zone 2 … and the poor cops are driving in her dust and we're cheering because Julie's getting away!

And then one day, on her way home from work, Ma passes a rubbish dump. It's piled high with nothing but old, discarded shoes. This means only one thing, Ma decides, Julie's pulling 22 today. Ma takes not five bob, not ten bob, not three rand, but a whole five rand! And puts it on 22. My God, she thinks, what have I done? That's half the rent money, bread for a month … she can't concentrate, forgets to put salt in the pot, can't laugh at George and Rita on the radio, smokes three cigarettes in one hour, glances at the front door a hundred times waiting for Liney to come and tell her … Half past eight the knock comes. It's Liney come to give good news or bad news.

'Twenty-two, Auntie Shirley. You broke the bank.'

Our house tinkles with the sound of money.

Crumbs in the cooldrink

SOMETIMES WE'VE ALL GOT MONEY, all the guys. Then we feel good and important and we call each other 'gents'.

'Hey, gents, lets *koezat* and *slaan* a biff.'

That means: Hey, gents, let's pool our money and buy some chips and bread and cooldrink.

Allan is the oldest so he gets to keep all our money in his pocket. He's in charge of the finances. We hit the road to the shops, half of us are barefoot, the others have on their old shoes, which are falling apart, T-shirts with holes in them the size of tennis balls.

We walk down Flinders Street making a helluva racket. But it's OK because it's school holidays and there's lots of noise around us. Somebody's door is open; the radio is on and the Beatles are singing 'Ob-la di, ob-la-da'. I sing along with them and Toolbag says, 'Jislaaik! That song only came out last week and ou Kuller knows all the words already.'

Ahead of us Delfine and Stephanie Press and Anita Lawrence are playing skipping rope and we hear them go:

Daar onder by die dam
Daar woon 'n slamse man
Gadija kook die kerrie kos
Die kinners se bekke brand
Volstruis
Jou lank bek
Jou pap bek
Met wie gaan jy trou? …

When they see us coming they go stiff and the rope goes slack and they stop their song about the Muslim woman who gives her children such hot curry that their mouths are set on fire. Because here come the boys to bomb up their game and pull their hair …

But we do no such thing – this time – because we're on a mission.

Hippie Johnson wants to tell us all something, a scene from a John Wayne movie, so what he does is he walks ahead of us but backwards so that he can face us.

It's nice and hot and we're already too far away from our homes for anybody's ma to call him to come and do some stupid chore. Mothers don't realise what damage they cause. A group of boys are out having a good time. A mother calls one of them. After that the spell is broken and it's not so nice any more.

There are six of us.

We buy two packets of polony and chips, two loaves of bread, each sliced into three equal portions, atchar, a litre bottle of Fanta. There's ten cents change and Allan buys Chappies bubble gum. He shares it among us and says, 'Don't chew now, this is dessert.'

We hit the veld behind the Evangelical Bible Church. This is one of our spots. We've got lots of spots. Around here there are lots of mineshafts. Each one is fenced in but the fences are all lying flat from our jumping right on them and over them. We go as close as we can to the mine shaft. We take stones and chuck them down the hole. We all keep quiet until we hear a splash and then we all say, 'Jesus! It's fucken deep.'

Standing so close to the edge of the hole is scary because what if your friend pushes you in? Guys like to pretend they're going to push you in just to give you a *skrik.* But what if they shove too hard?

About five hundred metres away we can see the red roof of Widas the Jewish shop, sticking up above the long grass and the trees. The shop was there even before Riverlea was built in 1961 and sold stuff to the miners that went down these mine holes.

Widas still operates even though the miners have long gone. He has those glass counters and you can see the stuff he sells underneath the glass. He sells cups and saucers and knives and forks and wallets for men and purses for women and Bicycle playing cards, red and blue, but used. You can see the seal has been cut open. Ma says professional gamblers use a new pack for every game.

'For every game, Ma!'

'I'm telling you,' Ma says.

'But what if they play a hundred games a night?'

'Then they use a hundred packs.'

'But why?'

'So that nobody will cheat. If they play with the same pack over and over again, some gamblers mark the cards by making pinholes in the Ace of Spades or the King of Diamonds or something like that.'

I shake my head. 'And what do they do with all the used packs?'

'You can buy them in the shops, by Widas. You get a discount.'

Widas also sells pocket radios, bicycles, patch and solution for bicycle punctures, fish and chips, paraffin, meat, sweets, lamps, primus stoves, linoleum, chimney pipes.

Hippie Johnson once bought a gold chain with a heart dangling from it from Widas. If you clip open the heart there are pictures of Hollywood movie stars that we never heard of, Jean Harlow and Montgomery Clift. But that's just to show you what you can do – put in a picture of yourself and your girlfriend. Poor Hippie. He bought it for Denise Barlow, a girl in his class whom he fancied. But he didn't have the guts to give it to her and the gold came off the heart.

Mr Widas always watches us very closely because he thinks we're there to steal his stuff. For instance, if we split up and half of us stand by one counter and half by the other, his eyes start darting around from one bunch to the other, watching.

I heard once that a boy did try to break into Widas. But a horrible thing happened. He went late at night and climbed on to the roof and sailed down the chimney. But he got stuck.

The next day Widas and his wife and two sons came into the shop. The boy shouted for help but no one heard him. They made a fire in their stove. The shop filled up with black smoke and they tried to clean the chimney and there was the boy, burnt and dead.

This veld is also the spot where we pick *morogo*. One day Ma was broke. All there was for lunch was a packet of mealie meal. She gives me and Derek a big plastic packet each and she says, 'Go pick *morogo*, as much as you can get.'

My brother and I fill our packets and go home telling each other, 'Ma's gonna be pleased.'

Ma is indeed pleased. But she empties the packets into a dish and says, 'Go pick some more.'

'Aw, Ma!'

But we go and fill the packets again.

Ma cooks it up with pap and that afternoon we have a meal that's even better than the bread and jam we have every day.

We've got other spots.

There's the top of the mine dumps. We climb up right to the top and from there we can see the whole of Riverlea. Everybody's tiny and the cars are like Dinky toy models. If we look down the northern side we can see the 'Whites Only' drive-in cinema with its big blank screen and those parking-meter type poles.

'Those poles have got a microphone. You hang it in your car and you can hear what they're saying on the screen.'

'Plus if you wanna buy Simba chips, cooldrink, stuff like that, a guy comes and clips a tray on to your door and he puts the stuff there for you and your girlfriend to eat.'

'Shit, that's fancy.'

'And,' Norman Crowie says, 'while you watching the film you can play with your girlfriend's *tieties*.

We all laugh.

A few days ago Norman calls me aside and says he wants to tell me a secret, which he says, don't tell nobody. I promise not to tell. Actually they are two secrets. For the first one he takes me to their backyard and into a small wood and corrugated zinc shed where his father keeps all his tools and stuff. He opens a tool-box and takes out his father's dagga pipe. It's actually the neck of a beer bottle with some silver paper stuck inside the neck.

'That's to stop the dagga from going into your mouth.'

'Jislaaik!' I say.

Everyone in Flinders Street knows Norman's dad smokes dagga. Most nights we get the unmistakable whiff drifting on a breeze down the street. Many dagga smokers get caught and jailed, but not Norman's dad. Their yard has a high fence topped with barbed wire and no cop has ever attempted to jump over that.

The second secret is much nicer.

There's a girl called Beulah, who lives in the house behind theirs. Norman's in Standard 5 and she's in Standard 6. But in actual fact she's supposed to be in Standard 9 or something like that. She passes one year, fails the next, passes, fails …

She's got nice, big *tieties*.

After school, when her ma isn't at home, she calls him, 'Norman!' He leaves his bread and jam and his tea and he hops over the fence. He goes to stand by her bedroom window, where she's getting out of her gym and into her shorts and blouse.

She says, 'So how was school today?'

'Ag, not bad,' he says.

Did you get a lot of homework?'

'Ja.'

She waits to hear what homework but he doesn't answer.

'What homework?'

'Huh? Maths.'

'Just maths?'

'Ja … I mean no.'

The reason why he's not paying attention is because he's seeing her in her panties and her bra and it's becoming very hard for him to concentrate on schoolwork.

So one afternoon he comes right out with it and he says to her, 'Beulah, don't think I'm forward or anything, but don't you wanna show me your *koek* and your *tieties*?'

She stares at him, shocked. Obviously she has never been asked such a thing before.

'OK, just your *koekie* then.'

She's glaring at him, standing there in her bra and panties. This is the scariest moment for any boy because it's when a girl is busy deciding whether she's going to show you her stuff or going to tell her mother about you.

Also at this point there's only one phrase in the whole world that will make a girl laugh. And, of course, Nokker comes up with it, and says it:

'Please, Beulie, baby.'

That's it. She bursts out laughing and she ends up showing him both things – well, three things really, if you're counting. What's more, she shows it to him almost every afternoon.

I'm so envious of Nokker. He's a whole year younger than I am and already he's seen things I don't think I'll ever see. I ask him if he can't arrange for me to become a part of this secret.

'Ask Beulah if she can show me too, I won't tell anybody, 'strue's one living God.' I'm so desperate that I add, 'Tell her my eyesight's not good so I won't see much anyway.'

'I'll see,' he says. But the minute he says it, I know he'll do no such thing. If Beulah hears he's been bragging to his friends, she'll get scared and shut down the entertainment immediately, finish and *klaar* ... and this is one show Norman wants to stay open as long as possible.

Norman's got charm. Sometimes he comes looking for me or Derek. He knocks on the door and Ma opens. He says to her:

'Howzit, Shirley? How's Nick?'

'Oh, he's not too bad thank you,' Ma says, playing along.

He spots her cigarettes on the table, takes one out and pretends that he's puffing away.

'How's Christopher,' he says, 'still so lazy?'

By now it's become too funny for everyone and me and Derek and Norman and Ma, we're all laughing and Ma says, 'Get out of here, you little shit!'

Ma and all the other grown-ups say, 'That Norman, he's too polite!'

Our other favourite spot is the *vlei*. It's a brackish, weak stripe of a stream that runs through the southern part of Riverlea. This is the poorer section of the township where the people have outside toilets and no lights or inside running water. A local politician called it Zombietown because, he said, it's a place only fit for zombies.

When it's school holidays we go down to the *vlei* to swim. It's filled with broken bottles and rusty cans so if you don't drown in the water, you can cut yourself in a hundred places. One or other of these accidents has already happened to a lot of boys.

That's why, all over Riverlea during school holidays, before mothers leave for work in the mornings they say: 'If I hear you were by that *vlei* I'm going to beat the shit out of you.'

But we all go anyway.

When you come home from the *vlei* you're covered in a greyish tint. This is a funny thing because, you see, we're all called Coloureds but after a swim in the *vlei* all Coloureds turn grey. That's when your mother kills you because 'you could've drowned'.

To prevent the greyness, and the beating at home, you smear yourself in Vaseline. And then your Ma gives you a beating anyway because you've used up a week's supply of Vaseline in one day.

No matter which spot in Riverlea you go to, you take the evidence home with you. Go to the mine dumps and you come home with yellow sand in your pockets and shoes. Go to the *vlei*, you come home grey. Go to the veld, you go home with blackjacks stuck to your clothes.

Now we're in the veld with our biff. There are no adults in the veld so we can do as we like. We swear as loud as possible – especially if it's somewhere that gives you an echo because it sounds funny:

Jou ma se moer – *jou ma se moer … se moer … moer*
Fuck you – *fuck you … uck you … uck you*

We swear in English, Afrikaans, and even in Zulu and Tswana, which we pick up from the domestic workers and our fathers, who work in factories with men from Soweto.

Most of the words describe men and women's private parts, fifty per cent of which none of us – except of course Nokker – has ever seen.

Our biff. This is a kind of veld party. We remove the inside of the bread, fill the hole with chips, polony and atchar, and put the inside back. It looks like it won't fit but if you squeeze hard enough it does go back in place.

Ah! Just as we're about to bite into our biff, Gregory Johnson says:

'Wait!'

Aw! What's wrong now?

He asks us all to close our eyes. We do, and he prays:

'Dankie Here
Vir die kos en klere.'

It means, Thank you, Lord for the food and the clothing. But it's actually a funny prayer because it rhymes. We all laugh and ou Gregs is very proud of his joke.

We sit on logs and rocks and eat and talk – and it's 'gents this' and 'gents that'. Each gent has his own biff but the litre of Fanta gets passed around.

Somebody farts. It's Norman. He smiles, looks around and says, 'Shakespeare said: 'Let winds be free.'

He says this just as I'm about to take a gulp of Fanta and my laughter bursts into the mouth of the bottle and sends crumbs and stuff floating up into the cooldrink.

Norman has put everyone in the mood for a laugh. Allan says:

'Hey, you know that song Mr Alexander taught us: *Hoe ry die Boere, sit sit so, sit sit so …'*

'Ja, ja.'

'Ja.'

He sings his own version: *'Hoe ry die Boere, drie op 'n drol, vinger in die hol.'*

By now everybody's crumbs are floating around in the Fanta. But so what, we're gents.

When I go home Ma says, 'How much d'you have left from that twenty cents I gave you?'

'Nothing, Ma.'

'My God! What did you spend it on?'

I tell her.

'Are you serious?'

I don't know how to answer this one.

'That was a whole week's pocket money.'

I put my hand over my face and pretend to be sorry and ashamed. But what I'm really doing is smelling the delicious atchar and chips aroma that the afternoon veld party has left on my hands.

The queue

I CAN'T SEE THE BEGINNING and I can't see the end.

I'm about nine years old and I'm standing in the longest queue I've ever seen.

I've been in queues before. When Ma or Auntie Venecia takes me to St John's Eye Hospital we sit there the whole day. I even have to stay out of school and take my school lunch and a book with me. We sit on benches and slide along them, moving up one bum space every half hour.

At the rent office there's also a long queue every month when Ma sends me to pay the rent. It goes out of the rent office door, down the steps into the yard of the community hall and way past the library. It's a good thing half the people of Riverlea don't pay their rent or it would be twice as long.

But this is the queue of all queues. We are four abreast. I'm with my brother, Derek, Glen Philips and Gregory Johnson. The queue starts at the park in Colorado Drive opposite the football grounds. It winds like a giant and very noisy snake all the way up Colorado Drive, past the football grounds, past the shops, and well into Zone 2.

There is much excitement in this queue because at the end of it await the following goodies for each person: one packet of potato chips, juice in a plastic bottle (raspberry or orange, but word coming down the line is that you can't choose, you just have to take what you get), and a fistful of sweets and toffees in a plastic bag.

The people handing out these treats are white students from the University of the Witwatersrand. They are all volunteer workers from Witsco. Witsco is a charity organisation and, of all the black townships within a thirty-kilometre radius of their campus, they have chosen Riverlea as the township they would like to help. These students are so busy helping us, I don't know where they find the time to study.

The place where all the action takes place is the community hall. The students come every day of the week to teach, play with and entertain us. There are sewing classes, soccer, hockey, table tennis, puppet shows. Even guitar and piano lessons.

Some days they pack dozens of kids into Kombis and take them to the Coke factory in Cleveland to see how Coke is made – and of course to get a free Coke – a luxury that many of us only get on Sundays. Or to Chapelat, the sweet factory in Fordsburg.

It gets better. These Wits students built a crèche in Riverlea. So now working mothers can drop their toddlers off there in the mornings instead of having them wandering around the township streets with snotty noses and soiled nappies down to their knees.

They have a dentist on Thursday evenings. You can go and have your cavities filled and your rotten teeth extracted free of charge.

Years later, when I'm about eighteen, I make use of the Wits dentists. A molar is rotting away and causing me lots of pain, sleepless nights and a fortune in Disprins. A student dentist makes me say 'aah'. After about twenty seconds he says, 'You can close your mouth now, Chris.'

'But when are you gonna take it out?' I ask.

'I just did,' he says with a smile, showing me the offending tooth gripped between forceps.'

They have a legal advice office on a weekday evening. Your boss fires you without reason or you get short-changed on your holiday pay, you go see a bunch of Wits students and their lecturer, who sort these things out for you – no charge.

There's more.

At school, the teachers tell us that those of us who would like extra lessons in Maths or English or Geography or any of our other subjects can have a student come to our home once a week to help us. A personal helper – free of charge!

When the teacher wants to know who's interested, the hands fly up as if the ceiling's about to come crashing down.

I really don't need help with English. But I do have serious problems with Maths. Still, I don't put up my hand. I have my reasons and they go like this:

Every now and then we run out of Nestlé condensed milk for tea. Ma just doesn't have money and we have our tea black. If you have it a little weak then it's not too hard to swallow.

Our vase on the dining-room table has never known the fragrant presence of a rose or a lily. For all my 9 years, I've only known it as a storage facility for reels of cotton, Sellotape with one sticky circle left, a Christmas card from *19-voetsek*, a screwdriver, a spinning top without a peg and sometimes even used bubble gum.

Then there's the problem of toilet paper. Dad buys three or four rolls on Friday and by Wednesday we're back to square one, square one being sheets from yesterday's copy of *The Star* neatly cut into manageable squares and hung on a nail on the toilet door.

There's no way I'm going to let a pretty white lady from some larney suburb, used to a lifestyle of two-ply Kleenex, come and use our loo.

The home situation of my current best friend, Keith, is basically the same as mine. But these considerations are the furthest from his mind. His hand flies up and a week later a lady, blonde and pretty – in her own little Volksie *nogal.*

She comes on Thursday afternoons, and on Fridays Keith comes to school with all his multiplication and division sums in order and his verbs and nouns in the right places, all ready to get those famous red tick marks from Mr Rasdien's Bic pen. During breaks he tells me about Joanne and how they sat alone in the lounge.

'My mother made biscuits and I gave her some in a saucer, on a tray. And guess what she said?'

'What?'

'Come on, Keith, what's with the silly tray.' He makes sure to do the accent every time he says her words. 'Am I the queen or something?'

'Joanne says skin colour doesn't matter.'

'Really?'

'Joanne lives in Parktown North.'

'Where's that?'

'Not so far from here. Maybe half an hour's drive. She's studying Sociology.'

'What's that?'

'I don't know, I'll ask her. She belongs to New Suss.'

'What's that?'

'It stands for National United Students of South Africa Something.'

'Oh, it's an abbreviation, like SPCA. What do they do?'

'They ... like ... have meetings and they say apartheid is wrong.'

One day Joanne has a surprise for Keith and his younger sister Desiree.

'You know Saturday is Wits Rag Day?'

'Ja.' There are posters all over the place advertising it: RAG DAY 16 MAY. And because it rhymes it stays in my head. Plus, the day before, *The Star* always gives a map of Jo'burg showing the route the Rag parade will take.

A week before Rag Day the students sell their Rag magazine. It's called *Wits Wits*. Dad says it's a clever name because it means 'the witty people of Wits university'. Dad buys it every year. It's full of jokes and cartoons. One cartoon made the government cross. It showed the prime minister, John Vorster, sitting on a toilet. I didn't know what it was all about but I think the students were made to apologise to the prime minister himself.

'Joanne's coming to pick us up to see the Rag,' Keith tells me

I wish I wasn't so full of stupid things in my heart and my head. I'm scared of this, worried about that, embarrassed about most things, especially white people. Nobody actually tells me, but I'm beginning to understand that, according to the law, I am not as good as a white person. So when my granny talks to a white man in the bookshop, I check him out from top to bottom to see what it is that makes him better than me. I listen to them carefully on the radio, taking note of what makes them laugh or sing out loud. When Ma and Dad talk about their bosses, I listen to what makes them angry, what irritates them. Then there are those Afrikaner police who raid the shebeens or come screeching into the township every time there's blood in the streets. They glare at us and call us bushmen.

I'm too wary of these people, this wonderful race of humans. There are two things we never talk about in our home: sex and where babies come from, and why white people and Coloured people and African people and Indian people live in different places. But slowly I read little bits here and hear a snatch there of both these subjects. And the pictures in my head are turning into one strange tapestry.

So if I wasn't so confused and full of shit then I could also now have a pretty white tutor taking me out to see the Rag parade.

Ma and Dad never take us out. On New Year's Day the whole of Riverlea empties out. With bottles of homemade ginger beer and baskets of cheese and tomato sandwiches and a big fat watermelon, everybody goes to Mia's farm or Honeydew, a place by the river where they picnic and laugh and dance and get drunk.

Except, that is, for the Van Wyks.

Dad takes great pleasure in saying to us, and whoever comes by in the next three or four weeks, 'Why the fuck should I go and eat a sandwich with ants in it when I can have my bread and polony right here at home? Huh? Tell me that?'

It doesn't ever occur to him that we, his children, might actually enjoy eating cheese and tomato sandwiches by a river. That it might do our brains some good to get out of miserable, dusty Riverlea for just one day every year.

Don't even talk about movies. My father has never taken me, Derek, Shaun, Allison, Nicolette or Russel to a movie in his life or ours. Bonding. When the word first arrives in my vocabulary I believe it has something to do with glue.

On Rag Day mothers take their children by the hand, who in turn take their siblings by the hand – so that no one gets lost in the excitement and the bustle. They find a spot outside Ackermans or OK Bazaars where the people in front of them are not too tall. They eat curry balls and marvel at the passing floats and laugh at the eighteen-year-old bearded white boys studying to be doctors and dentists and civil engineers, who for now walk about with napkins wrapped around their bums and dummies in their mouths rattling tin cans, collecting money for Witsco.

The Van Wyks, in the meantime, wander about that yard in Flinders Street and stare out at the mine dump.

So, on Saturday morning Keith's black curls are given an extra dab of Brylcreem, his shoes are shining, his socks are folded around his calves, his shirt and pants cleaned with New Surf with Superblue and showing a symmetry of creases. He seats himself next to the lovely Joanne, Desiree sits at the back, and off they go in the Volksie; Rag parade here we come.

I wait in our dusty yard for Keith to return with his hamper of stories. And he doesn't disappoint.

There are floats piled high with brightly coloured artificial flowers, so laden that it's hard to believe it's just an old truck underneath. There's ice-cream and melted chocolate in the hot sun, there are jokes. And as if this is not enough, Joanne spots someone in the crowds, calls out, 'Jillian, hey, Jillian!'

'She says to me and Desiree: Would you like to meet Miss South Africa? So she took us up to this woman. Jislaaik! But she's smart looking.'

'Even prettier than Joanne?' Ask a silly question.

'Of course! Aw, she's Miss South Africa!'

I'm still in the queue with Gregory Johnson and Derek and them. The queue is much shorter now and I can see the white students bent over the big buckets of juice and the open boxes of crisps. They're so busy they don't look up, just hand it out, hand it out saying, 'There you go, there you go.'

In about six years' time, in my last year at high school, I'll begin to see all this in a different light. I'll have debates with older friends, mentors, which will go like this:

'These whities should fuck out of our township.'

'But they're here to help.'

'To hell with their help. They're making us dependent on them. Can't you see – the more they help you, the more they grow into supermen and women, the more useless you become.'

'They should be working to change the whole society, not putting a plaster on the sick one.'

'Where do they go when they graduate? To their wealthy parents' businesses, to Israel, to England. Far away from you and me and this mine dump where their parents dumped us in the first place!'

Wow!

The truth is that these students have been a part of our lives for many years. It has not only been their sweets and their table tennis and their puppet shows. It's also been their free dental care and optometrist and legal advice and crèche. But most importantly, the Witsco Clinic, I believe, once saved my sister's life. But I too want to be a revolutionary and maybe I'm too cowardly to say anything. So I keep quiet.

Mr Brown

STANDARD 1 IS A MISNOMER because it happens to be the third year of school. First you do Grade 1 and Grade 2 and then comes Standard 1. Does this make sense to you?

When I'm in Standard 1 our hand-me-down school becomes too small for all its pupils. While two new rows of prefab classrooms are being built, the temporary solution is to split us into two 'schools', a morning session and an afternoon session.

Riverlea has two zones, 1 and 2, and the arrangement is simple: one week we, Zone 1, go to school in the mornings and Zone 2 in the afternoons and the following week we reverse the procedure.

This arrangement lasts about two or three months.

I remember one thing about that time with amusement. Even though every other week school started at 1.00 p.m. instead of 8.00 a.m., we were still often late.

A street soccer match that began at 9.00 in the morning was usually still on at 12.30, when we should all have been dressed and ready to head off to school.

'Last goal, gents, it's 9-9. One team must win.'

And five minutes later …

'OK, let's see who gets 12 goals first.'

School is over at 5.00. But instead of flying off in all directions, we have to all gather at the big gates, arrange ourselves into a long row, four abreast, and be shepherded home by four or five teachers, one at the front, one at the back and one on either side. The reason: it's peak traffic time, the school is on Main Reef Road, the longest and one of the busiest roads in Africa, and teachers want to avoid us getting knocked down.

One day finds me and my friends at the very back of the long line. I have read a few things about sex and where babies come from and I'm happily imparting my knowledge to my buddies – except that I'm getting sequences and processes so badly wrong that I don't blame my friends for the looks of astonishment on their faces.

Eventually somebody has had enough of my forbidden little lecture.

'Hey, shut up!' I hear a voice behind me growl.

I look around me. Mr Brown! An Afrikaans teacher! How could I have forgotten that he was behind us?

'First thing Monday morning, you make sure that you come and see me,' he says.

'Yes, sir.'

Now, if ever there was a weekend spoiler it was this. Sentence had been passed; the guilty prisoner knew more or less what the punishment would be. I would be confined to my cell for the weekend, and on Monday I would make my way to school and into Mr Brown's classroom, there to bend and to get my bum whacked.

'If I were you, I wouldn't go,' my friend Kendrick advises. 'He'll never remember.'

'And what if he sees me later on in the week, then he'll remember, and then I'll only get it worse.'

'Ag, you just stay out of his way, man.'

I'm too weak with apprehension to argue. But I know that come Monday morning I'll be making my way to Mr Brown's classroom. Who knows, he might just be impressed by my honesty/obedience, whatever it was, and I'd get off with a warning. Or he might see how petty the whole thing was: all I was doing was telling my friends about sex, after all.

Friday nights are good times. Ma and Dad both get their wages and we get potato chips, sweets, pocket money. We listen to *Squad Cars* on the radio and to the Top Twenty. This Friday evening though finds me, for once, not a participant in the festivities but a sad bystander.

Greg Johnson, Glen Phillips, Norman Crowie, Allan Walburgh, all come around to see if I'm interested in taking a walk to the shop to buy chewing gum, or just to hang out in the street under the lamppost. I have an appetite for none of these things. I get into bed early and take a long time to fall asleep. What happens the next morning you are not going to believe, but it's true.

Saturday morning, Greg Johnson wakes me up at about six.

'Kuller, hey, Kuller,' he shakes me awake.

We speak in Afrikaans. I say, 'What's going on?'

'Mr Brown is dead!'

'What are you talking about? Which Mr Brown?' I sit up in bed.

He says it more emphatically this time. 'Mr Brown, our schoolteacher, he's dead. Come, I'll go and show you.'

I think he's playing some stupid prank on me. But I remember that I had not told him one word about my Friday afternoon encounter with Mr Brown.

Within three minutes I have on my shoes – without socks – and we're galloping out of our gate.

'Galana Street,' he says, proud that he had been the bearer of such terrible news.

The world has changed in unimaginable ways while I had been sleeping in my bed with its coir mattress and its ancient bubble gum stuck to the headboard. But Gregory has been awake and has heard the news, seen the people gathering and has thought about his chommie, me, who knows nothing about what's going on.

Galana is the street after Flinders. Between the corner house at the bottom of Galana and the football field, is a patch of open veld hardly more than a hundred square metres. It's filled with tufts of grass, stones and broken bottles. And, on this early Saturday morning in summer 1965, with the bloodied body of Mr Brown.

When I arrive with Gregory on the scene, the show (which has played itself out so often since then) has already begun: a big crowd is gasping and chattering around the corpse, men smoking cigarettes, women in curlers and slippers also smoking cigarettes, one or two boys pushing their bikes, kids on foot.

I find a vantage point as close to the corpse as I can be without being closer than anybody else. It is indeed Mr Brown. In fact, it looks like he has not had a change of clothing since he told me to shut up yesterday afternoon, less than twenty-four hours ago. Light brown pants, maroon jacket, and a brown tie. To this has been added generous splashes of red, courtesy of a township thug or two. His shirt-front is spattered with blood where the knife has torn material, skin and whatever's inside: lung, sinew and flesh.

White cops come screeching to a halt in a kwela-kwela, sending up some dry Riverlea dust. They hop out, in blue uniforms and peaked caps and come and glower at all of us as if we have all murdered Mr Brown together. Actually it's probably just that we have spoiled their weekend, violent, wild, barbaric bushmen that we are.

They are from the Brixton Murder and Robbery Squad. Once when my father and his friends were talking and drinking in our lounge, I heard one of Dad's friends talk about Brixton Murder and Robbery. He said:

'If those *boere* come knocking on your door and say to you, "Where's the gun?" And you don't have a gun and never owned one in your life, I tell you the best thing is you just go and borrow someone else's and say, "Here's the gun, baas."'

We wait until the mortuary van comes and takes Mr Brown away. Nobody wants to go home before then and risk missing out on a sudden dramatic turn of events.

We stand around for a while, discussing the whole thing. The names of the usual suspects come out. Spotty, Lekkerbek, Dirk, who are in and out of jail for crimes such as muggings, knife fights and rape. It appears that Mr Brown had spent Friday evening at one of Riverlea's shebeens drinking and gambling the night away. He staggered off home in the early hours of Saturday morning. With money in his pockets that the thugs knew he had. They lay in wait for him and the result of that now lies under a blanket waiting for the mortuary van.

Quite frankly, I don't know what to make of this teacher's death. But I cannot deny that I do feel good knowing that our Monday morning appointment is cancelled – for ever and ever.

A few years later, I would enter the class of one Melbourne Kelly for a full year. Now there's a teacher who I wish had been brutally knifed to death. But more about him when the time comes.

Sunday soccer

A MERE THIRTY METRES from where Mr Brown has been murdered is the football 'grounds', as we call it. It's a proper football field: white lines, goalposts, nets – except that there's no grass on it, not one miserable blade. I remember, years later, when I first see a picture of a football field and notice the white lines on green manicured grass, I'm puzzled. The picture is of course of a field where white people play football.

But, lack of grass notwithstanding, the football grounds provides many weekend hours of thrilling entertainment for the residents of Riverlea, where amenities such as movie houses, parks, putt-putt and bowling alleys are the preserve of 'Whites Only' in the suburbs.

In addition to the entertainment, the football field is also a place of pride for my brother Derek and me. You see, my father is the goalkeeper for Rosebuds, one of the most exciting football teams in Riverlea. At the time I accept this name without question. Later though, I would say to myself: but of all the plants and animals in the world, why a rosebud? I don't know. Nor do I know why there were Arsenals, Blackpool, City Blacks ... But I have a feeling that I was in a minority of one when it came to thinking about these things. Everybody is interested in the thrills and spills on the field rather than the reasons for the club names.

On Saturdays and Sundays, Riverlea comes out in force and its finery to cheer on their team, forming a colourful rectangle of hundreds of supporters around the grounds.

Derek and I always sit behind the goalposts where Dad does his goal-blocking acrobatics. Rosebuds' colours are red and white. He wears white shorts and a red jersey.

Often the fans don't know that Derek and I are his sons and it's fun to hear them cheering whenever he saves a goal. And very often a nubile young girl, her arms linked together in a row of three or four other girls, would call out to Dad: 'Hey, Mr Goalie, I live at number 17 Kentucky Street ... ' Then she would gasp and giggle at her own audaciousness and, egged on by her buddies, 'my parents won't be there tonight ...' followed by more whoops of laughter from her friends.

Dad, six feet tall and handsome, ignores them completely. Derek and I grin at each other with embarrassment, both having a general idea as to what's going on here.

At half-time the entire team squats somewhere in the centre of the field – there being no cloakroom at the time – to discuss their game plan while they all suck on oranges handed out by Mr Paulsen, the coach and owner of the club.

Tired of being the anonymous sons of one of Riverlea's most famous goalies, Derek and I make our way on to the field just to say howzit to Dad, give him a hug from behind as he sits flat on the sand, ask him some mundane question ... knowing that the whole of Riverlea is watching.

After the match, the entire team strolls up to Mr Paulsen's home in Zone 2, a leisurely twenty-minute walk away from the field. This stroll takes the twelve to fifteen players past the local library, the community hall and the shops. Workmates at factories during the week, today they're a team of popular, triumphant athletes, joking, laughing, teasing each other, talking football, being friends together.

All the time Derek and I tag along, tolerated, but knowing full well that we are, in fact, nuisances who should be somewhere else playing with our own friends, or doing homework or something.

Actually, a strange reality is dawning on me these days. It seems like the more children my dad gets, the less he's able to tolerate them. We're four kids at this time and there are two more to come. But with every addition to the family he swears and curses more and more, and ask him for ten cents and he goes, 'Oh fuck it!' whether he gives it or not. Sometimes he calls me by one of my brothers' names: 'Derek, come here ... I mean Shaun ... Shit! You! Christopher! fuck ... You! I'm calling you! Fucken come here.' This sometimes happens when he's having supper and the rice spills from his mouth and it looks gross.

Don't be around when he's looking for something – the scissors or a sock or the cap of a pen or the nail clipper. He says to me:

'Have you seen the fucking nail clipper?'

I say, 'No, Dad.'

'Don't just say no, think.'

I go, 'uhm, no, Dad.'

'You never know where anything fucking is.'

I would like to say, well, nor do you because you're forever asking me. My tongue burns with this retort but I have to swallow it.

He likes calling me a sonofabitch, until Ma says to him one day, 'So am I a bitch then?'

'What do you mean?'

'If he's a sonofabitch then I'm a bitch, isn't that so, Nick?'

At this point he gets that defeated look on his face.

He comes in from work, smelling of wood shavings and cigarettes and looking tired. We bombard him with:

'My teacher says we must each bring five cents for the seaside fund.'

'Agnes couldn't do the ironing today, the iron's broken.'

'I need money for brown paper to cover my History exercise book. Mr Rasdien says if it's not covered by tomorrow …'

Dad says, 'Oh fuck, fuck, fuck!' Or: 'Jesus Christ!'

Once or twice a year he comes home and finds us all sitting in the dark, cooking in the dark, crawling around on the floor in the dark.

'What the fuck's going on here?'

'They cut the lights, Daddy,' someone tells him.

'Fuck them,' he says. 'Who the fuck do they think they are?'

The Council rules are: Don't pay your water and lights and we put them off. Don't pay your rent and we throw you out. But Dad is not interested in the rules right now. He goes into our small, dark kitchen, opens the dresser drawer, and takes out our tin-opener. He stomps out of the front door, swearing all the way, and goes to the side of the house where the steel meter box is bolted up crudely against the wall. He opens it and fiddles inside with the tin-opener. Derek and I have followed him because this is an ex-citing event. Shaun and Allison have in the meantime switched on all the lights in anticipation of what Dad is about to do. Something in the meter box snaps and Dad switches on. Our house lights up and the inside siblings go 'Yeah!' and Allison even claps her little hands.

Sometimes Dad arrives home to find – disaster of disasters – Allison has lost her 'bobo' (bottle). Nothing on the seven-o'-clock Springbok Radio news could be quite as disastrous. This means that any minute now Allison will get hungry and will want her bobo. She will fling herself down on the floor and kick her little legs outwards and scream. There will be no peaceful supper for us, no happy radio listening, no placid conversation, nothing.

Allison is a toddler and she has toddler friends next door, two doors away, down the street. There are wire fences that divide up the neighbourhood yards. But that has never kept the Van Wyks or the Constances or the Vergies from going anywhere they wish, whether adult or toddler. So for all we know this bobo could be behind the bathroom door or underneath a dog's kennel two streets away.

'Why didn't you fucking bastards watch where she throws her bottle?' Dad fumes, turning as usual on me.

Does he really expect me to spend my afternoons, when all my friends are spinning tops or kicking a ball, walking after my baby sister?

His rage is so severe that he says to me, 'You're so fucking useless that you should've been a girl, a little bitch.'

The words stay with me all my life. And what does Ma do about it? Mostly nothing, except when he froths at the mouth and looks like he might go berserk. Then she says, 'Nick, Nick.'

Well, when his offspring are little 'bitches' they don't seem to make his life any easier, do they? Dad kneels before Allison, yes kneels, and begs her to tell him where she last left the bottle.

'Hey, baby. Tell Daddy.'

'Bobo gone,' she says tearfully, 'bobo gone.'

I look on, feeling pity for every one of us in a three-foot radius of Dad. And feeling embarrassed.

So we have to find this bobo now, quivering somewhere in a neighbour's yard under a broken car, a kennel or coal box, the dregs of Lactogen formula going sour, the teat a tourist attraction for flies.

Uncle Ron from next door has, in the meantime, heard the commotion and he comes over to join the search party. He tries to pa-cify Dad by saying things like, 'We'll find that bottle, ou Nicko,' 'Don't worry, ou Nicko.'

We all know the drill. We take sheets of *The Star* and twist them into thick rods. We light them and they become our torches. Primitive but effective, because before long someone will yell the two magic words, 'Found it!' Four magic words if that person happens to be Dad: 'Here's the fucking thing.'

Two or three days later the entire circus repeats itself.

One day I open the toilet door to go inside. But Dad is sitting right there doing neither a number one nor a number two. He's drinking a cup of tea and it seems this was the only spot in the house where he could do this, in relative peace.

Then one fateful day our status as minor nuisance on the football field changes drastically to *persona non grata*. And it's all our own fault.

It's a Sunday afternoon, the game is over and Rosebuds have won so the mood is good. The sun has begun to dip. The Rosebuds team are taking their customary stroll up to Mr Paulsen's home. But, being in no hurry, they stop for a while and sit on the perimeter wall of the community centre – a favourite spot for everyone wanting to relax and watch Riverlea passing by in their cars and on foot.

While the men chat and smoke, two gorgeous girls come strolling past in their tennis outfits, tennis racquets in hand. Conversation among the Rosebuds drops to a respectable silence and fifteen or so pairs of eyes take in every step. The first man to break the silence is none other than the goalkeeper. He says:

'Oh ... please let those racquets fall!'

This remark, for some reason, provokes a chorus of thigh-slapping laughter. Derek and I laugh too because it's fun to laugh at the grown-ups' jokes, even when we don't know what the hell it's all about. In fact we even go as far as to do some thigh slapping ourselves.

At this point we're still the unofficial mascots of Rosebuds. But unbeknown to us our tenure will come to a humiliating end before this day is over.

Later that evening we're back home, sitting in the kitchen and having supper.

Derek and I decide to try out Dad's joke on Ma.

'... so, just as the two pretty girls walk past, Daddy said, 'I wish those racquets could fall ...'

Ma has a very good sense of humour and we wait for her to collapse on to a chair with laughter. But she does no such thing. Nobody laughs and the funniest thing in that hot kitchen is the different look on the faces of everyone. Dad, grim, his mastications of food suspended, Derek looking eagerly from one face to the next, still hoping, it seems, that we would all burst into laughter any minute, that it's just a case of a missing crucial word or something before Ma gets it. Slowly it dawns on me that this is a joke not meant for Ma.

Ma breaks the silence with, 'So that is what you stand around doing on a Sunday evening. You and Rosebuds.'

'It's just a joke, Shirley.'

'Then why am I not laughing?'

As soon as he has a chance, Dad turns a very angry face to my brother and me and declares: 'No more tagging along with me all over the place, you hear me?'

What the hell, I had become tired of it anyway.

Months, maybe a year later, Ma gets her own back. Not that she's been waiting to take revenge; things returned to normal quite soon, except of course for the ban on the two mascots with the wagging tongues. The family goes to work and school, makes jokes in the evenings or listens to the radio, take turns in holding the new baby Nicolette, born a year after.

From time to time on a Saturday evening, Dad and his friends gather in a friend's lounge for a drink and a chat. There are no pubs in Riverlea, but shebeens scattered all over the township. Some of them are sit-down joints, others strictly take-aways.

When our house is the chosen venue, the men sit in the lounge and chat: about work, white bosses, white people generally, making money. Sometimes they talk politics – but very rarely. When they do, they lower their voices: the ANC is banned and, I'm told, that by merely mentioning their name you could be arrested by a passing cop and jailed for months, years even.

I marvel at how many trips to the nearest shebeen they make on these occasions. On one night four trips for two beers and a nip per trip rather than eight beers and a straight in one trip.

At the end of it, all the men stumble out of our house way past midnight, shooed away by Ma, who tells them they have had more than enough now, and, 'Your wives and family are waiting.' Ma then leads Dad to bed.

When the smoky coast is clear, Derek and I creep into the lounge and play the now sleeveless Frank Sinatra, Dean Martin and Sammy Davis Jr records scattered all over the place. Then we pretend that we are the grown men who had been there moments ago. We sip the dregs from their glasses and start a conversation, deliberately slurring our words and using their workmen's and township language.

A conversation goes like this:

'Aw, bra D, so how's the graft, ek sê?' (Hey, brother D, how's work?)

'Ah, bra C, *kak maar oraait*.' (Ah, brother C, shit but not too bad.)

'You reckon?' (You don't say?)

'Ja, man. That *larney sug* to pay man.' (Yes, man, my white boss is stingy and doesn't pay well.)

We wince at the taste of their beer and brandy, wondering how in the world grown-ups can actually enjoy these vile concoctions. Don't they know what a great drink Fanta Orange is, sweet, fizzy, orangey and giving the drinker enough sneezes and burps to turn any serious occasion into a festive one.

One Saturday the boys' get-together is not at our house. Somewhere in Riverlea, I'm not sure where, Dad and his friends have once again gathered and are making merry. On nights like these Ma stays up to wait for my father. Gangsters, muggers and drunks are out in force on Saturday nights and she won't be able to fall asleep until he's safely home. She listens to the radio, gives us supper, puts us to bed, and then she sits in the kitchen reading a paperback, drinking tea and smoking her Van Rijns.

After midnight she begins to worry and from time to time goes to stand by the lounge window, waiting, a jersey draped over her shoulders, smoking.

Eventually, the dogs down the street herald the coming of someone. Ma looks out of the window towards the pool of lamplight right outside our house, waiting for Dad to stumble into it like an actor who is playing a drunk man – except that he would not be acting.

And soon enough, he comes, stumbling along, with his friends who, despite being as drunk as he is, have insisted on bringing him home.

'Bra Nick, bra Nick, you OK? OK … O O O kayere?'

'For sure, for sure.' And then to the barking neighbourhood dogs, 'Shut up you bastards, fucken shits … go to hell.'

Ma, unseen, is smoking another Van Rijn, watching the stumbling, listening to the slurring.

'Hey, it's late man, ou Nick. You reckon ou Shirley will let you in?'

'Hey, gents,' Dad tries to get himself as straight up as the beer and brandy and cane spirit will allow, 'now who d'yous think is the bo-oss in this hou-house?'

Ma smiles silently behind the window.

'Hey, gents? Just answer me … that … tell me.'

The houses are so small – matchboxes we call them – that from the bedroom window you can see who is standing at your front door – indeed you can almost touch the person. Dad has managed to ascend the three tiny steps as if they are Kilimanjaro, and teeters there, knocking, while his drunken friends look on from the street. 'Shirley.'

Ma opens the window and says, 'Yes, boss.'

'Come open the door, Shirl.'

'When, boss? Now, boss?'

'Ag, Shirley, man.'

His friends start sniggering in the lamplight.

'Shirley, please, I'm not in the mood for your jokes OK, open up. D'you know how cold it is out here!'

'Really? Well inside here it's so hot, I've just made a fire in the stove and … whew, I tell you I'm sweating!'

'Please Shirley man!'

My mother's laughter

When I think of my mother's laughter
and how it ran through my childhood
I search for a way to bring it to you
and the nearest analogy of those
sounds that slaughtered the sadness
is this:

When I loosened the string
that choked my bag of marbles
and threw them on to the earth
they captured the sun in their prisms
even as they ran free
and transformed their little windows of light
into coins that I squandered on joy
with all my friends.

On Sundays my mother's laughter
swept the sombre crosses
off the shoulders of the churchgoers
flung us into the streets
with our white shirts pockmarked
with the talismans of tomato sauce
and the brooches of beetroot.

My mother's sheer laughter
filled the afternoon cheering football fields
flew through the nets of the goalposts
and the bags of the whistling orange vendors

Throughout her life my mother laughed
as she still does today
And even though there was much to cry about
as there is even now
so seldom does she weep
that I am forced to put her tears in parentheses

My mother's laughter grows out of our house
and people come to taste it.
Citrus mirth, deciduous pleasure. Evergreen.

My mother's laughter runs in the family.

One Friday night, my father goes out, I don't remember why, to play fahfee, have a quick beer with friends, see somebody about something.

'I won't be long, Shirley,' he says.

Dit woel op 'n Vrydag. (It teems on a Friday.) Friday night is the night of transactions. The dry cleaner's man comes with your cleaned suit on a hanger, wrapped in plastic, and he wants his money. Bill Jardine and his sons come selling fruit and veg, door to door, Ma sends you to the shop for fish and chips or mince, onions and tomatoes for a quick Friday night gravy, Dad sends you to a neighbour with a five-rand note. 'Give this to Uncle Eric.'

'But why? What for?'

'Don't worry, he'll know.'

'But what if he doesn't, then I'll look like a fool.'

'Don't try to be clever, just take it, he'll know.'

On Friday evenings in the township there is more money on the streets than on any other day: in the grubby hands of children coming from the shops, in the handbags of mothers getting off buses, in the pockets of fathers eager to get home or to pop into a shebeen for a quick one, in the vans of vendors.

And the thugs, the tsotsis, the clevers, they all know about this money. They smell it in the air, see it change hands, hear it in bags and wallets and pockets, imagine it in their own hands.

Riverlea is a Coloured township. That means it's not the safest place in the world. A boy could get his bubble gum and his ma's small change snatched away from him by a gang of teenagers. Or a man could get knifed in the dark at midnight staggering down a street.

Over the years some of the gangs and gangsters have become household names. There are the Yellow Vipers of Riverlea Extension or Zombietown. And there are the Kalomo Kids, named after the street where many of them live. The Kids started out as a well-intentioned boxing club. But something went wrong somewhere and they swapped the boxing glove for the Okapi knife, the square ring for the dark alley, TKO for GBH.

The gangsters keep the tongues wagging and the police cursing every day. There's Popeye Sauls. Before he turns fifty he will have spent a total of 27 years in prison – at various times.

There's also Dirk, who goes by the disarming nickname of Lekkerbek (Nicemouth). He goes about robbing, raping and probably killing, keeping Riverlea in a grip of terror and supplying the *Post* with many of its shocking headlines.

Lekkerbek's life comes to a violent end on a Saturday night at the Blue Danube nightclub in Fordsburg when one Dan September puts a bullet in his head.

But the most famous of them all is Spotty Hall. He's a fair-complexioned youth with a spatter of freckles on his face, which has given him his nickname.

Spotty and his company of clevers hang around at the shops all day shooting dice, drinking, smoking dagga and taunting the girls who are sent there. At night though, he gets down to business. Then the knives come out and the blood spills into Riverlea's streets.

One day, during a long spell in jail, Spotty writes an open letter to the people of Riverlea published in *Post*. In it he begs our forgiveness and promises that the Spotty who will be released from jail in a few years will be a new Spotty, a churchgoing Spotty, a working Spotty, a Spotty who will throw away the knife and stay out of trouble for ever.

Spotty's letter becomes the talking point all over Riverlea, at the shops, shebeens, on buses and at bus stops.

Spotty is released a few years later and, without so much as a second thought, returns to his life of crime. A leopard doesn't change its spotties.

But back to Friday evening. My brothers, Derek, Shaun and I are listening to Squad Cars on the radio, trying to make our Friday evening rations of sweets last as long as possible. There's a knock on the door.

Now who's going to answer, nobody wants to miss …

'Is anybody going to answer that door?' Ma calls from the room. But the callers have lost their patience and fling the door open. They are four men, young men, men I either know or at least have seen around Riverlea. They're carrying a man who's unconscious. Without saying a word, they heave the big man up from the dark stoep into the light of the dining-room. They put him on the couch while Ma, who has come to the lounge, looks on, gasping.

The unconscious man is my father. For five or six seconds I do not recognise him. I think it's because I have never seen him so full of dust and bits of grass and with half-dried blood on his temple, with his head flung far back and his Adam's apple aimed at the ceiling like an arrow, and a grim look of unbearable pain on his face and the indignity of it all.

'Where did this happen?' Ma asks the men.

'The patch of veld in Galana Street.'

It's the same place where Mr Brown was killed a few months ago.

I look at my father on the couch. He must be dead, I think, or dying. And how does it make me feel to have a dead father? I don't know. I'm in a gap in time. The clock has stopped, and sometime later it would start again, slowly, dragging out the days.

My father was accosted by thugs. They confronted him in the dark, away from passers-by or the glare of a lamppost. They beat him up and smashed a brick against his head and he fell to the ground. They went through his pockets and found money, not much. Like all Coloured and African factory workers he earned very little to begin with, and had spent most of it already, on groceries, accounts, handing some to Ma for the rent.

Chances are the thugs also had knives but didn't use them. Maybe they didn't think it necessary; maybe they thought they'd killed him already. It could be that a shout from a nearby window or the footstep of a passing child disturbed them. Anyway, they left him for dead.

Ma made no case. What would the police do? Write out a docket in ungrammatical English and file it, under V for Van Wyk, or A for attempted murder, or C for Coloureds or W for whatever. I don't know.

All I know is that my father was out of work for about three months and that he couldn't remember what had happened and that we thought he would never be the same again.

The next morning Ma takes him to Coronation Hospital where he is admitted and kept for a week. In the middle of the night, when all is quiet, he calls the night duty nurse and asks her if she can get the people in the ward to shut up so that he can get some sleep.

A week later, after he's discharged, he comes home and sees my sister Allison on Ma's lap. She's happy to see her Daddy, but he turns to Ma and says,

'Who is this child?'

One afternoon, a week or so later, I come home from the football field and find Ma home from work and standing at the sink peeling potatoes.

I greet her. She greets me, but instead of her usual smile she has a puzzled look on her face and is looking at my hands.

'Where's the mince?' she asks me. 'I've been waiting here …' She points to onions braising in a pot on the stove.

'What mince, Ma?'

'Your father says he sent you to the shop for mince.'

'Not me, Ma. Maybe Derek.'

'Oh shit,' she says. 'Oh shit.'

It was that knock on the head that was causing all this trouble.

One day my father gets up late in the morning, gets dressed and gets on to a bus to town. He makes his way to the OK Bazaars in Eloff Street. He takes a trolley and begins filling it with the usual fare. Cheese, butter, apricot jam, tinned baked beans, spaghetti, sweetcorn, condensed milk and, of course, a packet of mixed sweets for his children, those of us he recognises and those he doesn't. He pushes his trolley to the till and unpacks his purchases. The cashier adds it all up and gives him the total while a packer, in the meantime, packs it all into packets.

Dad sticks his hand deep into his trousers pocket, takes out a stack of brown paper and presents it to the cashier.

'What's this, sir?' the confused cashier wants to know. But then she looks into Dad's eyes and realises something's wrong somewhere. She alerts the manager who leads my father out of the store saying, 'Don't worry, sir. We'll deliver.'

Ma and I see the funny side and we both laugh and, of course, Ma entertains relatives and friends with the story long after Dad has recovered.

During the time of my father's illness and his long months of recovery, life becomes a little tougher than usual. There are lots of things we have to do without. No milk in our tea, or sometimes no tea at all. No toothpaste: you lay the old tube down on the bathroom floor and stamp on it 'to get out the lasties'. Otherwise, you put some salt on a damp finger and scrub away at the ivories. I also hear that ash is a good substitute for toothpaste but I choose to give that one a miss.

Soap is in short supply, the portions of meat on our plates are getting smaller and smaller. Don't even talk about sweets. They're a luxury that's out of bounds. Ma is the only one working and once or twice she doesn't even have bus fare to get to the factory in Doornfontein.

I watch Ma going through Dad's jackets' pockets in his wardrobe in her search for a few coins. Fifteen cents could buy a tin of baked beans or condensed milk. Thirty cents could get us a decent parcel of mince. A one-rand note, folded and forgotten in a corner in a time of plenty, could now buy a week's supply of bread, butter and jam.

The pockets yield nothing but the odd bus ticket, a crumpled hanky and a Gold Dollar packet which once held ten but now is home to a solitary half- nipped *stompie.*

'Go and ask Auntie Louie if she hasn't got thirty cents to lend me. Tell her it's just till Friday.'

Auntie Louie, Ma's cousin, says, 'Ag, shame, Christopher tell your mother I'm just as broke. I was gonna send Mary up to her for a cigarette.'

One Friday Ma comes home from work. As always, she asks one of us for half a blank page and a pen, to make a shopping list. The way Ma looks writing out that list, it's exactly like a pupil writing an exam for which she hasn't studied. There's a lot of thinking and wanting to write down something but she keeps changing her mind or writing something then scratching it out again. Every time I hear her saying, 'Oh shit.'

In the end I set off for the shops with a list made up of a quarter of the stuff I usually buy. On the list are mostly things that go a long way, like pilchards and condensed milk and mealie meal for pap. There's no meat on that list. And definitely no sweets

On my way back from the shop, as I walk past the community hall, I look down and there staring up at me from the pavement is the smiling face of Jan van Riebeeck, adorning a twenty-rand note. My heart rattles against my chest and I do a quick check to see who's watching – you look behind you, in front of you and on either side of you to see who's coming on – and then I stoop and scoop up the treasure into my little fist and casually walk on. It's a Friday, late afternoon, and the place is busy with people going up and down. And yet nobody has seen me pick up the money.

At home I plonk the groceries down on the kitchen table. Then I turn to Ma and, opening my hand, I say: 'Ma, look.'

Ma's eyes almost pop out of her head. This is twenty rands! Six rands more than her weekly wages. 'Where did you get this?' she says, already holding it in her hands.

'I picked it up.'

'Where?'

'By the hall.'

This is too much for Ma and she has to sit down on a kitchen chair.

'God has answered my prayers,' she says. 'You won't believe me, my son, God has answered my prayers.' For the second time that evening she calls for pen and paper. This time the list includes mince, chops, jam, a packet of Bakers Assorted biscuits, even sweets.

I go back to the shop, pleased that I had brought some light into my mother's eyes. On my way back, a heavier bag in hand this time, I pass the hall where I found the money. There are these three Jacobs brothers from Colorado Drive, their heads bent down low, searching the pavement. The younger two keep asking their eldest brother: 'But are you sure you lost it here?' The eldest is too upset to give a clear answer. He's sobbing for all of Riverlea to hear and nodding.

I stand still for a while and watch them. I know exactly what they're looking for. But Ma had said that it was God's doing … And that was authority enough for me: God and Ma.

I decide not to tell Ma about the three desperate brothers. And after supper, as I chew my Ski Hi bubble gum, I wonder exactly how right Ma and God had been.

Errands

THE RIVERLEA COMMUNITY HAS MANY UNWRITTEN LAWS. One of them is that if a neighbour sends you to the shops, you have to go. If it's an old granny with arthritic legs, I go, to buy her a Grandpa headache powder and half a loaf of bread. No problem. Or if a son is recovering from mumps or an appendix operation or something like that and can't go to the shops for his ma.

But sometimes I dare to break this unwritten law. Auntie Rose Lawrence stands in her back doorway and calls me from the street. I vacate my left wing position and, even though we're two goals down, I run to see why she's calling me, suspecting that she wants to send me to the shops. I say 'shit' under my breath. Auntie Rose and her husband, Uncle Pat, and my parents go back a long way. They've known each other since before we were born, they were our neighbours in the Newclare days. Auntie Rose, a schoolteacher, comes and visits Ma often, and Uncle Pat and Dad swap the *Reader's Digest* from time to time.

I stand in the kitchen door and Auntie Rose says, 'Kuller, won't you go to the shops for Auntie Rose please, my angel?'

I'm about to say yes, when I spy her son Jeffrey reading a comic.

Now another unwritten law comes into play: I cannot go about questioning authority because to do so is regarded as rude. But I'm a little irritated that I have to go to the shop while old Jeff, who is a year older than I am and just as healthy and able-bodied, lounges around indulging in the moneyed adventures of *Richie Rich* and the inane antics of *Archie and Jughead*. This is no surprise. Everybody knows what kind of a guy Jeff is.

One day I visited the Lawrences and found myself the focus of a low-intensity argument between mother and son. 'Look at Kuller,' said the mother, 'no shoes.' We all three looked down at my poor dusty pigeon toes. Auntie Rose told her son, 'Kuller and Derek play barefoot all the time, so why can't you?' I could work out what was happening: Mother wanted to save her boy's footwear for school or for Sundays, but he wanted to be posh and go about in shoes and socks all the livelong day, like some white boy.

Right now I'm about to break a community bylaw.

'Uhm – ' (it's good to begin with 'uhm' because it takes away some of the effrontery) 'Why can't Jeff go, Auntie Rose?'

'Ag, don't worry about him, he's just a lazy thing. Just a loaf of bread and 20 Cavalha.' She tries to hand me the money but I don't take it. I would like to tell Auntie Rose a few things but of course the unwritten laws prevent me. For instance, I would like to say that Jeff should be made to go to the shops, no question. And if she can't do that, with tongue or belt, then she should go herself. Now there's another strange rule: moms and dads never go to the shops themselves. It's a child thing.

'I can't go, Auntie Rose,' I say.

'Why not?'

Because Jeff should go, surely it's obvious. But I say instead, 'I've got homework.' I turn on my heel and want to go back to being left wing in the street game, but I have something to attend to first. I go home and tell my mother what has just happened. This is a pre-emptive measure. You see, Auntie Rose will surely come over and tell Ma what a disobedient child she has, and I think I've got a good case for why I didn't go to the shops.

Ma listens carefully and in the end she says, 'So Jeffrey was just sitting there reading comics?'

'Yes, Ma.'

'Hm. So his mother thinks her son is Prince Charles and that my children must run around like servants?'

I would like to fold my arms and say, 'Ja, how do you like that, the nerve of it,' but yet another unwritten law stands in my way.

'I'm glad you didn't go,' Ma declares.

I go back to my game happy.

We, the boys of Flinders Street, have our favourite people to run errands for. Most people give you a cent or two, but the favourites give you five, six, even seven cents. This is the equivalent of a week's pocket money and could keep you in sweets for two days solid – as long as you don't buy those stupid marshmallows that last about ten seconds.

Mr and Mrs Clarke, now there's a strange couple to run errands for. They look like white people, very fair with light hair, and speak an Afrikaans that we've never heard spoken, even by our Afrikaans teachers – a kind of Afrikaans that has never been removed from the box it came in. They're in their fifties, soft spoken, well-dressed and quiet as two white mice. No loud talking, no boisterous laughing, breaking of bottles and glasses on a Saturday night, no maudlin, drunken singing. Even their little fox terrier hardly ever barks, just stands around in the garden and gazes at you through the fence. Their Cortina is a white mouse on wheels. They live on the corner of Flinders Street so that every boy or girl in the street has to pass their house on their way to the shop – or else take an unnecessarily long detour down the other end of Flinders, into Galana and up Colorado Drive or down Galana across the soccer field and around the back of the community hall.

'Son,' the very pale woman whispers to me in Afrikaans from her tiny little garden. The way she calls out to me it looks like she's a prisoner in the grounds of an old castle and she has to pass on a secret message to me before a guard spots her.

'Yes, Mrs Clarke,' I whisper back.

'Are you on your way to the shop?'

I have an empty oil bottle in my hand. There's no other place you could take an empty oil bottle. I could've said: 'No, I just felt like strolling about the place with an empty oil bottle,' but sarcasm is an adult thing and besides who wants to be rude to Mrs Clarke.

'Oh, please, son, won't you go and buy Mrs Clarke a loaf of bread?'

I take the twenty cents from her and off I go. Twenty minutes later I'm back with her bread – and her five cents change. She has been waiting for me at her gate.

'Oh thank you, my boy, thank you. Please come inside for a minute, I have something for you.'

What I want is right there in the palm of her hand – the five cents change, which I had made sure was in loose coins of two–

and one-cent pieces. But I let her lead me into her spick-and-span kitchen – a gleaming checkerboard floor, the sun glinting off brasso-ed taps, a kettle dancing cheerfully on the stove, all proof that a child had not set foot in here in over a century.

'You sit down, my child,' says the old woman. She cuts a slice of bread from the loaf I had brought for her, butters it and smears it with smooth apricot jam. She cuts it into triangles and hands it to me.

'There you are,' she says.

'Thank you, Mrs Clarke.' I realise that this is my gift for going to the shops for her. So there being no other matters at the Clarke residence, I slide off my chair, say goodbye to the beaming Mrs Clarke and traipse up the road towards home – where my lunch of four slices of bread and apricot jam await.

One important unwritten by-law regarding errands was: Go anywhere you are sent except to a shebeen. These are illegal drinking joints and regarded as definitely not a healthy place for children. People get drunk there. Women with their skirts up to here slide on to the laps of men whose poor wives are dreading their drunken return home late tonight. Foul language is used as a matter of course; in fact after a while every sentence is started or ended with a four-letter word. A fight inevitably breaks out over a spilled drink or a flirtatious girl. And if the shebeen queen is not paying her dues to the cops, then there is a great chance that she could be raided at the very moment that the innocent young Christopher purchases his nip of cane for the neighbour. You could be flung into the *kwela-kwela* with all the other drunks, ending up in a holding cell at Langlaagte police station while your mother thinks you're playing football in the street.

But a shebeen is the place to be sent if you want to make quick money. The shebeen is closer than any shop. And those who send you are already so drunk …

'Kuller!'

It's Mrs Erentzen calling me as I pass her house on my way to visit Keith. She's a widow and her husband died such a long time ago that I don't even know what he looked like.

As I walk through her gate into her yard, I already have a very good idea why I'm being called. The turntable is working overtime with: 'Are you lonesome tonight?' and 'I fall to pieces each time I hear your name.' There's also a storm of laughter blowing from the lounge, the kind that comes from rude jokes and brandy. And there's cigarette smoke coming out of the lounge as if Lexington has declared war on Rothmans in there.

Mrs Erentzen says, 'Don't you wanna go to the shebeen for your auntie please, boykie.'

I pause, pretending that this request has come as a complete shock. After all, everybody, even she, knows the rules about children going to the shebeen.

'I know your mother doesn't want you going to the shebeen, but I'll give you twenty cents.'

Twenty cents! The equivalent of payment for ten trips to the shops. But the people who are boozing and jiving the weekend away are generous souls. Invariably they'll wake up from a troubled sleep on Monday morning with one helluva *babalaas* and wondering what happened to all the wages they brought home on Friday, the twenty-rand note in the purse, the stack of coins on the kitchen dresser. I pause for a while, thinking what a lucky fellow I am to have walked past here before any of the other boys.

'OK, Auntie Jane, I'll go,' I say with a heavy sigh, pretending that my decision has nothing to do with her generous offer of cash.

I trot up the road and around the corner and buy two beers and half a jack brandy at Auntie Mamie's. I'm back in ten minutes flat and twenty cents richer. With this fortune I can buy a packet of fish and chips and some atchar to make it go down really lekker.

One day Auntie Noreen Crowie calls me from her gate. Her son Norman's gone with his dad to fetch a re-charged car battery, her daughter Beverly's gone to choir practice at the church. She's got nobody to send and she's desperate. Would I go and buy a packet of sago for her.

'Please, boykie. It costs 15 cents a packet. Here's twenty cents. You can keep the five cents change.' She has a ladle in her hand

and I assume that on her kitchen table, even as we speak, is everything she needs for the sago pudding – eggs, milk, salt, castor sugar, baking powder – except the sago itself.

I jog down Flinders Street, drawing up a mental five-cents shopping list in my head. Two cents worth of Chappies bubble gum; at a cent for two, that's four. Three cents Sharps' toffees. The really dark, coffee-flavoured toffee is the best, then there's the one that has bits of peanut in it. The Le Rouxs put them all in the same compartment of their sweet counter and if you buy you can't say: 'Gimme two dark ones, two minty ones and a couple of nutty ones.' You just have to take what is thrown on the counter. But it doesn't matter because they're all good. I begin to salivate.

There are a few boys kicking a ball on the football grounds.

'Kuller!' they call out a friendly greeting.

'Gents!'

'Kuller's on our side,' somebody shouts.

'Sorry, gents, can't play now.'

'Where's the move?'

'Shops.'

On my return I would have to use a route that would not bring me back this way. These boys are a sweet-munching horde and there are far too many of them to *diezie*.

I go to Raymond, the corner café.

'We don't sell sago. Next!'

The middle shop is the Le Rouxs. They're a general dealer and have lots and lots of things in packets – three varieties of lentils, four different kinds of beans, sugar, castor sugar, desiccated coconut, even stuff I've never in my life tasted before. But no sago.

'Somebody bought the last packet an hour ago.'

Henry is the corner shop. That shop is so small that he probably stocks no more than five or six of everything he sells. I don't think he will have sago, but I try anyway. I'm right.

'No sago, sonny.' He shakes his head.

I'm devastated. I have a twenty-cent coin in my hand: fifteen cents is for sago, five cents is for me. What do I do now? None of the three shops has sago, but that's not my fault. I've done my bit. I go back to the Le Rouxs and buy my chewing gum and Sharps toffees.

Auntie Noreen is waiting at her front door, apron in front, bow at the back and powdery hands all fluttering impatiently in the air. She sees no sago in my hands and her bosoms sag in disappointment.

'You tried all three shops?'

'All three, Auntie Noreen.'

'Ag, thank you, Christopher,' she says with a sigh. She opens up her hand for her money and I give her the fifteen cents.

'What's this? I gave you twenty cents.'

'You said I could have five cents.'

She is speechless. 'Yes, but you didn't get the sago.'

'But I went to the shops for you, Auntie Noreen.'

'But you didn't get the sago!'

I shrug and suck on my second toffee. This could go on all afternoon.

She laughs at me, but more in disgust than anything else. She turns on her heel, goes inside and slams the door.

I'm right, I keep telling myself as I make my way home. But why am I feeling so lousy?

The sweets don't taste as nice as usual.

The Terrific Three – minus one

I'M EMBARRASSED TO TELL YOU THIS STORY. But, what the hell, here goes.

I'm in Mrs Manuel's class. She's teaching us history, but it's a hot summer afternoon and we're all wilting under the heat and the dates and all the stuff that happened even before my granny was born and when the Dutch came to the Cape of Good Hope and …

Clunk! Something falls on my desk. I sit up straight. I can see it's a note, folded a hundred thousand times to make it heavy enough to end up on the receiver's desk. I pick it up and am about to unfold it and read it under the desk when I hear Mrs Manuel say:

'Christopher, bring that here.'

'Ma'am?'

'You heard me. I said bring that note here.'

I slide out of my desk, walk up to her, surrender the note and go back to my seat. The entire class watches closely, not so droopy anymore, while she reads the note silently. She looks to me like an owl with her thick glasses and her bun hairstyle and her plump granny body.

For the class this is far more exciting than knowing what the Khoikhoi would do when they come upon Van Riebeeck staggering on to the beach way back in 1652. They all wait patiently hoping for a titbit from Mrs Manuel. And she doesn't disappoint.

'Who are the Terrific Three?' she asks me.

My jaw drops. It's a secret. I can't talk about it to anyone. But I can't say that to Mrs Manuel. Nowhere in history has a pupil ever told a teacher, I'm sorry that's classified information, I can't tell you.

Somewhere behind me a hand flies up, and I hear, 'Ma'am, Ma'am!' It's Neil Edwards and he shouts out for the world and his cousin to hear: 'It's Chris van Wyk, Keith Ferris and Gregory Ilett … they're a secret gang, Ma'am.'

'A secret gang?' Ma'am says, and her glasses do a little bounce on the bridge of her nose. 'What does a secret gang do?'

'They have meetings, ma'am, and they discuss things. They think we don't know about them.'

The class is out-tittering the birds in the trees outside.

Mario Butler's hand flies up and he shouts, 'Ma'am, ma'am. They've got a secret sign.'

'A secret sign?' She tells Mario to come up and write it on the board. He leaps out of his seat and in white chalk scrawls it out for the world and his cousin to see:

T
T
T

The Terrific Three. A secret organisation, which, it turns out, has not been as secret as we had thought, and is now public knowledge. Thanks to one of our members, Keith Ferris, sending me a letter from three rows away. If he had waited until break then none of this would have happened.

Our classmates think that somehow we will be punished for being The Terrific Three, but the owl-like Mrs Manuel delivers her wise verdict: 'I don't see anything wrong with the Terrific Three. I just wish you all had some imagination like Chris and Keith and Gregory.'

So there!

We're Terrific because we're three. If there had been four of us we would've been the Fearsome or Fabulous or Ferocious (but not Famous because Enid Blyton had already used that one) Four.

We meet at my home on Thursday afternoons. We eat sherbet, which comes in tiny packets with its own little plastic spoon – small enough to fit into the mouth of a mouse. On the agenda, every week, we discuss how to write invisible letters using milk or onion juice as ink – which seems a waste of time when your teacher intercepts your letters and they're in standard, Department of Coloured Affairs ink.

Also on the agenda, I raise the issue of a lack of adventures. This is serious and is worrying me quite a lot. Since the inception of the Three there have been no abductions of children or wheelchair-bound adults, there's no bank in Riverlea that could be robbed, providing us with an opportunity to put our skills to the test and arrest the robbers. There are no museums or centuries-old buildings where treasure maps could be found underneath loose floorboards or in the orifices of ancient statues. The nearest ocean, where old galleons might be shivering with gold and diamonds on the seabed, is six hundred kilometres away in Durban. And even if we ever chanced to get there, none of us can really swim. From the mine dump to the *vlei* is nothing but rusted tin cans and bits of old cars. Riverlea, I tell you, is not the ideal place for three intrepid investigators.

One day the Terrific Three almost breaks up. Gregory fails to turn up for our weekly meeting two Thursdays in a row. As boss of the Three, I decide that I would be failing in my duty if I did not enquire into the dereliction of his. I write him a letter:

> Dear Gregory
>
> I notice that you have not attended our meetings of late (two Thursdays in a row). Could you please inform me, by return of post, whether you still want to be a member. I also see that you are in arrears with your subs. Please pay up.
>
> Yours sincerely
> Chris
> (member of the TTT)

Before I put the letter in an envelope, I ask Ma, 'What does 'return of post' mean?'

She tells me. And I knew I was right. I also want to know about 'arrears' but I don't ask her that one. I once peeped into one of her letters from Levisons and saw that she was in arrears. I checked it up in the dictionary. I was right there too.

The following Thursday Gregs has still not pitched. I decide to speak to him about it. The next morning Keith and I find him playing football on the playground with ordinary boys who have no ambitions to investigate mysteries and bring criminals to justice.

'My mother found the letter you wrote to me,' he says. 'She told me not to go near boys who demand money from me.'

(Shit! Again I'd forgotten to use the invisible ink.)

'Don't worry,' I say to Keith. 'We'll be the Terrific Two. Lucky for us 'Two' also starts with a T so we don't have to make any big changes.'

In a way, the Terrific Two lasts far longer than we both realise. For years, in fact. We go everywhere together so that, whenever I'm alone, people say, 'Where's Keith?' And of course, that's exactly what he's being asked wherever he is too.

We first meet the year before we go to Mrs Manuel's class. Our teacher's gone out and of course the class is in a state of happy chaos. I walk down an aisle to get to a friend and there's this short guy, a new boy, standing in the way, and he won't let me pass.

'Excuse me,' I tell him.

'What d'you want?'

'I wanna pass, sonny.'

'Who's your sonny?'

'You are. Now lemme pass.'

He refuses. The only thing left to do is to push him out of the way. I put my hand on his chest and give him a shove. But he doesn't move. He's like a big rock there between two desks. I could go all the way around or climb over one or two desks and the problem will be solved. But I can't do that because then he will have won. He knows what I'm thinking and he smiles. Then I'm saved by the bell.

School's out and I'm walking home. Someone comes and puts his arm around me. It's him. He says, 'Come home with me I've got something to show you.'

'What?'

'I can't tell you, but it's very interesting.

They've just moved into 71 Colorado Drive. That's less than ten minutes from home, so I go home with him. When we get to their door he tells me to be very quiet, not to make a sound.

'Just follow me, OK?'

I nod.

He opens the door and tiptoes through the lounge to the kitchen, and I'm right behind him.

There, bent over the kitchen table is a man in black pants and white shirt, long sleeves rolled up to his elbows. He's very grey and wrinkled. On the table in front of him is what looks like a tattered photo album or some kind of a book with pictures in it. He has a reel of Sellotape in his hands and he's trying to find that strip of Braille that indicates the beginning.

Keith goes 'BOOM' stamping his foot and clapping to give the sound extra volume.

In an instant the old man leaps up from his chair, dives under the table and shouts, 'The fucking Germans are coming!' Then he spots Keith and says, 'You bastard! Come here, let me kill you!' But Keith runs outside and I follow him.

'That was cruel,' I tell him.

'I know. But I just wanted you to see. He's my oupa, he was in the army. He suffers from shell-shock.'

'What's that?'

'He heard so many bombs going off in the war and now he jumps every time he hears a noise and thinks the Germans are coming.'

I am very impressed. I tell him about my oupa who also fought in the war and fell into shit. Now he's impressed too and we're buddies. Keith is one clever guy, I'll tell you that. He knows everything. If you don't have patch and solution to fix a puncture, he'll find a substitute. If somebody has ten pellets stuck in the barrel of his pellet gun, Keith removes them no problem. A neighbour has a fish-tank that leaks all the time and he wants to throw it away. Keith says, no, don't throw it away, give it to me. The next thing the tank is fixed up and the fish are swimming away happily and for the next couple of months all I hear about are filters and thermostats. That's Keith for you.

He also knows the whole of Joburg, including the white areas where very few of us have ever been. If a white guy drives into Riverlea and wants directions to Kempton Park or Houghton, we call Keith.

Keith admires me for my vocabulary and general knowledge: for filling in crossword puzzles and for beating the white contestants on all the Springbok Radio quiz shows. But sometimes I wish I could be like him, just knowing how to get around.

During the summer school holidays we plan an outing to the zoo and Zoo Lake. For this trip we had planned for at least a week, saving our pocket money and making a list of things to take along. Cheese and tomato sandwiches, a flask of tea, Sharps toffees and a packet of Eet Sum Mor biscuits. We dress up in identical safari suits and carry our goodies in small haversacks, which we sling over our shoulders. We take a bus into town. From there we have to go to another part of town where there are European buses, smart double-deckers, which the City Council gives to the Coloureds and Africans when they get old and rickety (the buses, that is, not the Coloureds and Africans!). Keith knows which bus goes to Zoo Lake and he also knows we have to sit upstairs on the backseat because we're Coloureds. He sits by the window because he needs to see where we have to get off.

At the zoo the whole place smells like shit.

Keith has a camera that looks like he got it out of a five cent lucky packet, but it takes real photos. We take pictures of each other, with various animals in the background – an ostrich, an elephant, a giraffe. And then we want a picture of the two of us together but we don't know who to ask. A white woman strolls up behind us with her toddler, gazing into the cages at the animals.

'Let's ask her,' Keith says.

'You must be mad.'

'Why?'

'She's white.'

All this is said in whispers because the woman is very close to us.

'So what?' Keith says. He goes up to her and asks her, just like that. And just like that she says:

'Of course! Smile, guys. That's it.'

The eating-places are for Europeans Only, but it's no problem. We've come prepared.

We save our pocket money together and when we have enough we buy second-hand hunting caps from ME Stores in town, where they sell tents, sleeping bags, torches that can light up a whole veld and Swiss army knives that can do a hundred different things.

We save up some more money and go to Roy's for Toys in Simmonds Street. We buy itching powder, stink bombs, a spyscope (a special telescope for sleuths), and a little flat thing the size of the host Father McCullagh puts in your mouth on Sunday mornings. This is the thing ventriloquists all over the world use to throw their voices.

(When I see the word 'ventriloquist' I decide to use it in my next essay, no matter what the topic.)

Me and Keith (we haven't learned about 'Keith and I' at school yet) have great plans with our Roy's for Toys stuff. But sadly, we discover that in Riverlea even if you invent your own adventures you still get short-changed.

Take the spyscope for instance. The idea is to use it to spy on the locals and catch them in the act of committing what would look like a crime, which we would then solve. What we want is to spot two men in hats and trench coats with the collars turned up swapping suspicious-looking documents or somebody stopping a car on a lonely road and heaving a suspicious-looking heavy sack into a donga.

But all we get for our money and our long hours of patient espionage are boys going about their mundane little jobs, such as chopping wood for the stove, girls playing skipping rope or hopscotch, mothers with clothes pegs running down the front of their overalls and dusters in their hands chatting across rickety fences, men in greasy overalls half-swallowed up by their rusty cars' bonnets. And all of this given a yellow tint by the dust that perpetually blows off the mine dump.

After a while we give up trying to solve non-existent mysteries and just do things together.

We go to the veld together, cooking food under a tree and telling each other secrets, like which girls we are hopelessly in love with.

When Keith's ma sends him to the shops, he pops in at my home and we go together. The three Le Roux sisters who serve behind the counter all think Keith is the cutest boy they have ever seen. They are all four or five years older than he is. The one serving behind the counter calls the others at the back and say, 'Hey yous, Keith's here!' Then they lean across and flick the thick wavy fringe that hangs down his forehead and say, 'But why don't you have older brothers, hey, hey?' They give him ten times the number of Sharps toffees he pays for. We always share them fair and square, even down to the odd one, which one of us bites in half.

There's a soup kitchen in the community hall where the Witsco charity run by Wits University, sells soup and bread to the poor of Riverlea (which includes almost everyone) at the ridiculously low price of about two cents a cup. Every winter Keith and I make our way up to the soup kitchen almost every day and buy our cupfuls and our customary 'two slices'.

Sometimes Keith pays for this treat, sometimes I do.

The Terrific Two shares everything.

The soup itself, well I've tasted better. It's thick, mud-brown and nothing in it has a familiar taste, such as onion or carrot or potato. But just standing close together and sniffing snot and slurping this Witsco concoction and talking about one day when we would be men and married (he to Arlene and me to Belinda), well, we feel Terrific.

My father has money problems – which means he doesn't have enough cash from one week to the next for food, rent, bus fare and for when a teacher says he wants each of us to bring fifty cents for some project or other and 'no excuses'.

Dad borrows money from a white moneylender. This borrowing of money is an adult thing between my parents and this white man who has an office in town. But every week for about six months I have to take a ten-rand note, get on the bus, make my way to some building, some chambers, get into a non-European lift, go up to the fourteenth floor, hand over the ten rand and wait for a receipt.

My mother and father say to me, 'Don't tell anybody about this.'

I nod. But I tell Keith. I have to. He's fifty per cent of the Terrific Two. We do things together. He has to go to town with me. Ma and Dad don't really mind me telling Keith; when they say, tell nobody, they mean nobody besides Keith.

So off we go together, every week, the Terrific Two. And the one fifty per cent of the Terrific Two never asks the other fifty per cent uncomfortable questions like: Why did your father borrow money? How much? It's like our invisible ink.

One day Keith does a terrific thing. My mother, he and I are sitting in the kitchen chatting. Ma mentions that, a few years ago, a doctor once suggested that I wear an eye patch to correct my squint. I did try wearing one, with disastrous results. But Ma says that I should try again.

Even though I want more than anything in the world to have eyes like everybody else, I refuse.

'Why not?' Ma asks me. 'The doctors can't help you if you don't play your part too.'

I'm too embarrassed to tell her, but I'm sure she can guess why. Everywhere I go I get spotted a mile away, Here comes Mr Cockeye. Half the boys in Riverlea have almost grown too tired to keep up the constant taunting. Either this or they don't notice it any more. To these tormentors an eye patch would be a great gift, a wonderful opportunity to go after Cockeye with renewed vigour.

Keith knows why I won't wear this pirate's accessory and he turns to me and says, 'Hey, I'll wear one too.'

I still refuse. But it's an offer I will never forget. Keith was prepared to share the teasing.

One day I go over to Keith's house. His father is in their tiny driveway, doing something to his second-hand white Valiant station wagon with spanners and pliers and things.

'Hullo, Mr Ferris,' I greet him.

'Hullo, Kuller. Still not wearing socks?' he says with a smile.

This is an old harmless little jibe of his. I go about wearing shoes without socks. Nobody ever gives me so much as a second glance for this habit, except for Mr Ferris who believes I am causing some damage to my feet. But his comments are jocular and good-natured. Not so jocular is what he says to me next.

'Does your father still drink?'

My chest heaves from the shock. But I answer, with a little nervous giggle, 'Yes, Mr Ferris.'

'He should stop,' says Mr Ferris.

This is not the kind of conversation a neighbourhood boy has with his friend's dad. I search for a polite way to let him know that I'm very uncomfortable. But the only way would be impolite, and then I would get into trouble. I say:

'Uhm, he doesn't cause any problems when he's drunk, Mr Ferris.'

'What does he do when he's drunk?'

'He just goes to bed.'

'Well, even that's unnatural. He goes to bed because he's drunk, not because he's tired.'

I truly do not know how to proceed from here. I shrug my shoulders. Mr Ferris says, 'Your friend's inside' and he goes back to his Valiant.

Mr David Ferris gave up drinking years ago. He has accepted the Lord Jesus Christ 'as my own personal saviour'. He and his wife, Sarah, and his six children have all left the Anglican Church. They now worship at churches that do not have an actual building with a steeple and a priest in a cassock and bells on Sunday mornings. They got re-baptised because the Bible says you have to be old enough to know what you're doing when you get baptised, not a babe in arms. And not this little drop of holy water on the forehead from a font – they all went to a river and stood in it, socks and clothes and all, and their pastor dunked the whole lot of them, one by one.

Mr Ferris, Keith tells me, has read the Bible from cover to cover and is now halfway through his second reading.

This impresses me greatly. In fact, I sort of find it hard to believe at first and I tell Keith that I don't mean to be rude but I don't think it's possible.

'But why not?'

I shrug, not because I don't have a reason, I do have one but I'm embarrassed to tell him. What I believe is that the Bible is such an awesome holy book that as soon as you've read all of it you drop dead because now you know everything there is to know about God. It's just like when Allan Walburgh says to me: 'If you look into the face of God, you're a dead man'.

Mr Ferris also has a very strange photo in his wardrobe. It's a black and white picture, about postcard size, of patches of pure white snow, in grass burnt black. Now, this picture was taken by a woman – somewhere in America I think, although I'm not sure. And, according to her, she was walking through the snow, with her camera and suddenly a voice inside her head said, 'Stop, dear lady. Look down. Take a picture of the snow and the black grass.' When she had the picture developed, she looked at it and, miracle of miracles, there was the face of the Lord and Saviour Jesus Christ.

So Keith brings the picture to school and during break we look and we look and we look. And Cliffie Weideman, Robert Rhoda and Roger Durrell all say, ja, they can see Jesus. Bones Garcia and Ian Aronson say so as well. I can't, but I'm beginning to feel left out so after a while I also say, Ja, I see it now.

The Ferris family worship mostly in a classroom of the local primary school. The men and women call each other 'brother' and 'sister'. Most of the men are former alcoholics who used to go about beating their wives and spending lots of time with other women and losing their jobs. I know all this because sometimes I go to church with the Ferrises and there is a section in the service where they 'give testimony' and beg God's forgiveness. A lot of white people also attend the services, nice people, clean cut and well mannered, who shake my hand and smile and say to me, 'Hi, brother Chris. Nice to see you with us praising the Lord today.' As with most things in the country, they seem to be in charge of the church.

'Yes … brother,' I grin self-consciously.

In this church they often talk about the rapture. This is fascinating stuff and goes like this: When God descends down to earth on the final day of judgement, he will take back with him all those who have accepted the Lord Jesus Christ as their own personal saviour and off they will all go to heaven.

'Will you actually be able to see this happening, physically happening, all these people going up, up, up, into space and getting smaller and smaller until they disappeared beyond the clouds?'

'Yes,' say the Ferrises, mother, father, and baby Ferrises all – including Keith.

That's the rapture.

But David Ferris has begun to experience a rapture of a very different kind. He begins having an affair with another woman. Affairs in Riverlea happen all the time, but this one takes the cake, as they say, this one is terrific.

Sarah – Mrs Ferris to you – has a young married sister called Zelda. Zelda gets divorced from the guy because he beats her up all the time and the next thing she's given shelter at the Ferrises, her sister's and brother-in-law's home. And the next thing David is doing more than just wiping away a tear and offering her some tea. Don't forget, this is the same David who told me that my father should stop drinking.

I'm only about twelve years old but I see what's happening – long sighs, fleeting moments alone in the kitchen, in the yard after sunset, then arguments in the bedroom. It's hard to keep secrets in a Riverlea sub-economic matchbox – two tiny bedrooms, a tiny kitchen, a cramped lounge, and a bathroom/toilet all piled into one. No long passages, hidden recesses, unused rooms gathering dust, shed at the bottom of the garden. So David and Zelda have a romance and Sarah goes to pieces. And I see and hear it all. But I say nothing to nobody. This is happening to my friend's parents and we're the Terrific Two.

Then it hits the township headlines, through a pregnancy that can no longer be hidden. The news is on the buses, in the shebeens, in the little matchbox houses.

David moves out, and of course so does Zelda.

Fast-forward to a year or so later. Keith asks me at school if I would go with him to town. I say yes. He says, 'Every month.'

'What for?'

'I have to go and collect the maintenance from the magistrate's court.'

'I'll go with you,' I say, 'no problem.'

'Don't tell anyone.'

'You know I won't.'

So once a month we board a Putco bus. We find a seat at the back and tell our little secrets, about him marrying Arlene one day and me marrying Belinda. We also chat about how many cuts we got at school, about the Beatles and the price of bikes.

I never once tell him about what his father had told me one day when he was working on his Valiant. About how his dad tried to be one of us and make it the Terrific Three again.

The mouse

I AM A TEENAGER WHEN I FIRST SEE THE MOUSE.

The people of Riverlea borrow and lend everything and anything from each other. Top of the list, I suppose, is money – five cents, ten, sometimes even a rand 'till next Friday' or 'the end of the month'. Then there are things like cigarettes, matches, a hammer, something to read, like a Mills and Boon novel, a dictionary, curry powder, the Aretha Franklin seven-single where she sings 'Don't play that song,' chillies, an onion, a piece of Sunlight soap, a dress and a necklace to go with it, sugar, a tea bag. A handbag. A shoelace. It's all a case of if it exists it could be borrowed.

Our neighbour, Auntie Eleanor, once sent her daughter Yvonne over with two slices of dry bread.

'Auntie Shirley, my mother says can Auntie Shirley please dip this in that nice curry that she's smelling.'

Ma dips it deep into her pot, no problem.

As far as I know, there's only one thing that you can't lend to anybody no matter what. It's just simply considered bad luck to take your salt out of your house. Auntie Eleanor either forgets or ignores the custom one day.

'Auntie Shirley, my mother asks if Auntie Shirley won't just give her a teaspoon of salt.'

Ma gives Yvonne a five-cent coin. 'Here, Vonnie. You go buy a packet of salt for your mother.'

Auntie Eleanor sends her daughter around to borrow Ma's heavy brass pestle (which we've nicknamed the stamper), and pot. Such a thing can be borrowed for half an hour or so before it's returned. You stamp your garlic and ginger, you wash it out nicely, you bring it back. Auntie Eleanor stamps, she washes it out, but she doesn't bring it back.

One Saturday afternoon Ma decides to make a pot of mince curry. She needs the pot and stamper but it's not there. She sends Derek over to Auntie Eleanor to fetch it quickly.

Derek is about nine years old. He has a vile temper, freckles that sparkle around his nose when he gets angry and a ginger crop of hair that says, don't mess with me. He is assertive and ready to do battle – physical or wits – at very short notice, no problem.

As it turns out he's perfect for the job at hand.

He knocks on the door and Auntie Eleanor says, 'Come in.'

Derek finds himself in the lounge with our neighbour and about three couples sitting at the table. These are not local friends but guests. They have been laughing and chatting and drinking tea and smoking. They may become *chommies* later on, but for now they're important guests.

In a year or two Derek would have sensed this. For now though he's here to do a job.

'Auntie Eleanor, my mother says can she please have the pot and stamper.'

Auntie Eleanor is a little embarrassed to be asked this in front of these people. She throws her head back laughing.

'Oh, your mother wants to borrow my stamper?' she says, and tries to shoo him into the kitchen away from the VIPs. But he stays put and says, very pointedly:

'No, Auntie Eleanor. My mother doesn't want to borrow *your* stamper, my mother wants you to give back *her* pot and stamper.'

One of the stranger requests between neighbours concerns me.

Auntie Eleanor comes over from next door. It's a quiet weekday afternoon a week or so before Christmas when everyone is at home. I'm lying on the bed reading about the adventures of some English kids who go on an innocent picnic somewhere and stumble on something suspicious.

'Shirley, where's Christopher?'

Ma calls me and I go into the kitchen where our neighbour is standing and waiting for me.

'Don't you wanna do your auntie a favour?'

'OK,' I nod. I think she must need something from the shops. But this time I'm wrong. She's alone at home cooking. Pots are sizzling and steaming away on the stove and she's sitting on a kitchen chair reading some or other romance novel. But a mouse has ventured into her kitchen and is putting the fear of God into her with its short little darts from one safe place to another.

From behind the stove to behind the sink:

'Aaaahh!'

From sink to combustion stove:

'Waaghhhhhhh!'

From combustion stove to kitchen dresser:

'Eeeheek!'

'I want you to come over and sit by me,' she says. 'You can bring your book.'

But what d'you want me to do if the mouse comes, Auntie Ell?'

'Nothing.'

'But then why does Auntie Ell want me there if Auntie Ell doesn't want me to catch the mouse?'

She turns to Ma with a deep sigh and says, 'You know, Shirl, I don't think this child of yours knows what it feels like to be alone in the house with a mouse running around all over the place.' To me she says, 'Come, Christopher. Bring your book and stop interrogating me.'

She and Ma have a hearty laugh. I fetch my book and follow her next door. She pulls out a chair facing hers and tells me to sit down. This whole excursion feels silly but I sit down and go back to my adventure in England, where bobbies are on the beat and the rain is pouring down. Outside it is Africa in a hot month. The sun streams through the window, I can hear my friends somewhere in the street calling to each other. A neighbour's yard tap is turned wide open and water spurts into a bucket. Auntie Ell reads her book and I read mine.

But my mind begins to wander.

Auntie Ell is about 32 years old. She's wearing a short, dark blue dress. She sits with her legs up on the seat of the chair, out of the way of the mouse, who might be attracted to her blood-red toenails and just decide to bite off a toe.

Auntie Ell likes wearing short dresses. Looking over the top of my book I spy a lot of her legs, more than I've ever seen before.

It's hot in the kitchen, despite the kitchen door being wide open. An Alice De Luxe coal stove really makes you sweat when it gets going. I try to concentrate on England where it's cold and damp, but it's not easy.

Auntie Ell often comes over to have a chat with Ma. Whenever adults come to visit, we children are told to 'make yourselves scarce' when we hang around in the lounge. Or Ma says to us, 'are you counting teeth again?'

I go to the kitchen from where I can't see the speakers, but I can hear them, as clear as if they were speaking directly to me. There are certain little tricks you have to observe to prevent yourself from being caught eavesdropping. Here's a quick list:

1. Don't sit quiet as a mouse. If you can hear them out there in the lounge, they can hear you here in the kitchen. And if you're quiet they know you're listening. Make busy noises like drinking a glass of water, singing bits from pop songs, calling to the dog outside. But don't overdo it.
2. Do something while you're listening. Read a book or do some homework. If they come into the kitchen to switch on the kettle or something, they see a boy struggling with maths and not just staring at a wall.
3. Be wary of jokes coming from the lounge. If someone in the lounge tells a joke, try not to laugh. They'll know you've been listening all along.
4. If Ma calls you, don't answer immediately. If you do it's a dead giveaway and means that you've had your ears tuned on them all the time.

You will not believe the kind of information you can pick up just by keeping your ears open. Here are some choice ones:

Denise Smith, a sixteen-year-old from Ganges Street, was the very first person in Riverlea to fall pregnant out of wedlock. After her there must by now have been about a hundred thousand.

Uncle Eddie Jardine lives across the road from us and you can see him most days of the week sitting on his stoep in his T-shirt, light cotton trousers and comfy sandals reading J. T. Edson or Louis L'amour cowboy paperbacks. If you look closely, you will also notice that from time to time Uncle Eddie has one or the other hand in a thick white bandage. Well, according to information from the lounge, Uncle Eddie works in a factory in City and Suburban. He works with lots of dangerous woodcutting machines. If by accident you cut off part of one of your fingers, your foreman rushes you to hospital. There you get bandaged up and a doctor gives you pills for the pain. He also gives you a form to fill in. The next day, if you feel up to it, you have to take the form to the offices of the Coloured section of the Department of Labour. You sign another form – if your hand isn't too damaged. Then after a couple of weeks you get sent a cheque for a hundred and fifty rands or so, the equivalent of about five or six weeks' wages. Plus you get to stay at home for a few months and read Westerns on your stoep.

When Auntie Ell comes over, she and Ma mostly talk about boring things such as who did what at work, cute things that babies said, things like that. Auntie Ell is not shy to say her say on any matter so it's easy to listen to her. She shouts and laughs out loud. She has big feet and she takes off her shoes to show them to Ma.

'Bigger than Nick's,' she says. And then she calls into the room, 'Do I qualify for Rosebuds, Nick?' and then she and Ma both laugh.

Auntie Ell tells Ma that when she was sixteen her mother gave her money to go and do a course in Pitman's shorthand. But instead of doing the course she went to Dan the Yankee in Sophiatown for dance lessons.

'Am I a stupid bitch or what, Shirley?' she says. 'Now I can do the foxtrot and the waltz but I don't have a proper job!' They laugh out loud and smoke Rothmans and drink tea.

Sometimes they discuss things that I didn't even know humans did!

Auntie Ell, for instance, says that she's slept with Mr Matthews – who is married and lives up there in Barrow Road. And slowly I begin to work out that when adults talk about a man and a woman sleeping together, sleeping is the last thing they actually do – in fact, sometimes this sleeping together doesn't even happen in a bed.

Suddenly there is a tiny bit of a noise behind the sink and I see a grey streak with a tail flying across the floor to the narrow space behind the cupboard. Auntie Ell has heard or seen something too and she screams and her legs go flying in the air in opposite directions. Whew! What do I see! Suddenly I'm not so unhappy about being here anymore. My body feels sort of achy and it's as if the mouse has leapt right into my pants and is huddled there in a quivering hump.

'Oh God, oh God!' Auntie Ell goes, losing her page. A while later she calms down and laughs and pulls her dress knee-wards and laughs some more and lights a Rothmans.

I laugh with her. I pretend to read but my eyes stray over damp England into brightest Africa. There's nothing much to see now. But I know that when that mouse makes another run for it, I will get another glimpse. It's quiet. The mouse is quiet. I'm quiet. Auntie Ell is breathing quietly and I can see her breasts heave, up and down, up and down, quietly. And she turns a page quietly.

A mouse, I remember now, can sit behind a place for a long, long time, just doing nothing. Not even sleeping or lounging around or counting its own little whiskers. A mouse can just sit and stare into the dark for a whole day. I'm not prepared to wait a whole day to see what I want to see. So …

'There's the mouse!' I jump out of my seat and point. 'There!'

Auntie Ell pops out of her chair and this time her dress flies up, up, up, and I see whole worlds I never even knew existed.

I begin to understand Dad's quip about the tennis racquet made a few Sundays ago to his Rosebuds team mates.

Ten years' experience

THE RITUAL AT THE SUPPER TABLE is always the same. Dad opens with the solemn, monotonous:

'Be present at our table, Lord
Be here and everywhere adored
These mercies bless and grant
That we may feast in paradise with thee.
Amen.'

'Amen.'
'Amen.'
'Amen.'

After my father speaks to God, my mother speaks to my father. All through supper, pausing only to chew and swallow. She has even mastered a method whereby she can operate swallowing and her vocal chords at the same time. And, whenever Ma speaks, I swear that she has forgotten all about the presence of the Lord at the table. It's not as if she swears or blasphemes or anything like that. It's just that the way she speaks is not the way you would if you knew God was listening to your every word.

My younger brother, Derek, and I sit between Ma and Dad, facing each other. His left ear gets the full blast of what Ma says while my right ear gets the blast from Dad. It's not too pleasant since we're not allowed to talk at the table. Eating is our business there. Sometimes we swap places for the sake of a little variety.

And Ma thinks no other topic better than N and B Clothing Manufacturers, where she works, so that I know that factory like my favourite fork; every prong and cranny of it. Although Derek doesn't have a favourite fork, he feels the same way about N and B.

'I don't know where she comes from,' Ma introduces a new machine hand to us. 'Mr Nissenbaum put her with us. Apparently she's very good on the jumper-basting machine so she does actually belong in our section. But as far as I'm concerned she doesn't really. She's just too bitchy that one!'

See what I mean about forgetting the presence of the Lord?

'Now we sit like this at our tables …' With her fork Ma traces a U-shape which includes Derek and me and which never fails to give us a pleasant sense of involvement.

'OK,' Ma has to admit, 'she is good on the machine, bladdy good. And that is the proper place for her to be seeing that she has to pass the jackets to Doreen for lining. I think she used to work at Dugson's down there in Fordsburg.'

'I got Elaine on the bus this morning. Elaine works at Dugson's and she tells me that this thing used to work there. Elaine says she works damn good but she was such a troublemaker with the girls there and that she got fired because of her shit!'

'Now she sits there (at the base of the U) 'and whenever she sees one of us talking – you know we can't talk too loud because of rules and that – she thinks we're talking about her. Just this morning, Lettie was telling me she wants to rush down to the furniture shop lunchtime to pay her account. And won't this stupid woman jump up and say, "Ja, talking about me again, nê. *Skindering* again."'

'So Lettie tells her – you see I told Lettie what Elaine had told me on the bus – Lettie tells her she's not at Dugson's any more because of her bitchiness and she'll be out of N and B too because of that same bitchiness.'

'Jesus, you should've seen her face. You see, she didn't know we knew where she worked before. And when Lettie told her that, I said to myself, well you asked for that, you cow.

'And what could she say? What could she say? You should've seen that look she gave Lettie.'

I give Derek a look and he gives me one back. This is dangerous because the next time we look at each other we're going to get the giggles.

'Well,' Ma goes on 'she did afterwards mumble something. She said that with her experience on the jumper-basting machine she could go anywhere for a job.'

'I think the woman's got a serious complex,' says Dad.

'Well, if you ask me, I think she should leave that complex of hers at home.'

A frown darkens my brother's face. I suspect the adults had lost him somewhere. It seems he's trying to work out whether a complex is a sickness that only women get or whether it could be packed into a bag together with lipstick and a bus coupon.

'And you, Mister, you better eat that cabbage.'

I am so lost in the conversation that I have forgotten about my food. My gaping jaws are shocked into obedient mastication.

The story of 'that thing' and her bitchiness goes on for another month. We have some episodes with mince, we have some with pilchard curry, we have some with cabbage.

Then one evening we hear that 'that thing' had threatened to beat up the 'whole bladdy factory'. She got fired. Derek and I receive this news with tripe and butter-beans.

Then there's the story about Rachel.

Rachel, a cutter at the factory, is almost caught selling baby clothes during working hours. She hides the clothes inside an unfinished jacket. The jacket is then passed from bench to bench so everyone can have a chance to discreetly inspect the goods on offer.

'And while Lena is looking at these things, won't Mr Nissenbaum come out of his office and walk straight towards her. So what do you think she does? She ever so calmly takes the little bonnets and booties, stuffs them under the lining of a jacket she's working on and starts sewing it closed. Then she gives it to Mr Nissenbaum himself, together with a few other jackets and says ever so casually, 'Ag, Mr Nissenbaum, won't you give these to Wilfred so that he can do the sleeves, please. Thank you.' And Mr Nissenbaum takes the jackets and off he goes.'

Derek and I smile at each other. Some of Ma's stories are just too good.

Then one day Ma comes home earlier than usual. She brings her scissors, slippers, cup, overalls and all the other things she keeps in her locker at work. This can mean only one thing.

'The factory's closed. Mr Nissenbaum says he only got to hear about it last night. Ag, he looked so sad when they came to fetch the machines, he was down, I tell you, down.'

'But what happened?' Dad says.

'Insolvent. Bankrupt. Well, at least he gave us two weeks' wages. We didn't want to take it but that only made him feel worse. So we took the money, not that I minded.'

Ma is at home for a few weeks. It's bad; she's always finding some job around the house for us to do. While our friends are playing football, we're sweeping the yard or cleaning the chimney or going to the shops for a tin of baked beans or something. She also plays fahfee, sometimes betting a whole rand on one number. And we were not supposed to tell Dad about it. But if we do something wrong she soon lets him know.

One evening, while Ma is busy cooking, Dad comes into the kitchen with the newspaper.

'Shirley listen to this. He reads aloud slowly about a Mr Nissenbaum trying to leave the country with too much money. Mr Nissenbaum told the court things were not working out for him in South Africa so he wanted to go back to Israel to start afresh. The case was proceeding.

Ma just says, 'Ag' and Dad says, 'the fucking bastard' and turns to the jobs pages to find a job for Ma.

He finds one that says: Women wanted to start immediately on buttonhole and jumper-basting machines. Must be neat, hard working and have at least five years' experience.

'Cut that one out for me,' Ma says. 'I'll go see them tomorrow. Five years experience? What are they talking about – I've got ten.'

Magic

A Magic Show.
Date: Tuesday the 2nd of February.
Place: School Hall.
Entrance fee: 20 cents.
In aid of: The Seaside Fund.
Come One. Come All!

THE SEASIDE FUND takes a hundred Joburg children down to Durban every summer for one whole school term – three months. It's hard to qualify for this free train trip to a school on the beach, called Transhaven, six hundred kilometres away. You have to be all of the following: starving to death; not wearing shoes to school, even in winter; never bringing lunch to school, and Coloured. Most kids, including myself, were only one or two of these at any given time.

Kendrick Appollis is chosen one year. He's all of the above, plus he never has a hanky. He's been in the same Standard for three years and his mother has been in a bus accident and can't work – in case there's more space on the form.

If poor children who live in Joburg go to the coast, I wonder when I'm a little older, where do the poor children who live at the coast go? Later, I also wonder how a term of schooling by the sea is supposed to help these poor children. The old people claim that a dip in the sea takes away all the bad luck. But, after the three months away, these boys and girls come back to school and back to square one, going around barefoot with runny noses and begging sandwiches during lunch breaks.

Anyway, I ask my mother for twenty cents for the magic show. Whenever I ask her for money she says, 'You really think money grows on trees, don't you?' To which I always want to reply, 'If I did think that, I wouldn't be asking you for some, would I? In fact you'd be asking me because I just happen to be a better tree-climber than you.' But, of course, I don't because that would be the same as saying, 'Don't give me any pocket money for at least a year.'

Ma wouldn't have given me any money for the show, but I reminded her that when the school showed Steve McQueen in *The Great Escape* she didn't have twenty cents for me. Over the years, we had established a kind of financial arrangement: I could have money only for every other school function.

So I get the twenty cents, a grubby little thing with the face of the old prime minister's on it (the one who was knifed to death in parliament and is now dead and buried) that she disinters from a corner of her purse. Ma hands it to me with a reminder that it could've bought two loaves of bread, but what did I care. Bread appears and disappears in our home every day, the Magic Show comes once a decade.

We file into the school hall under the swishing cane of Mr Kelly who, if he wasn't beating us up, was treating us to a dose of his very smelly breath, the perfect atmosphere for his yellow teeth to rot in.

There are no chairs in the hall. If we all sit on the floor they can fit in thirty or forty more of us. So we sit cross-legged in rows from the Grade 1s in front to the Standard 5s at the back. This is supposed to have the same effect as a movie theatre where everyone can see over the heads of those in front. It works up to a point. And that point is me. I find myself behind a boy who has been in the same class for three years so that while his brain is learning the same stuff over and over, his body is growing bigger and bigger. So today I will spend the best hour of the year trying to look past those same ears his teacher accuses him of not having – yes, it's old Kendrick Appollis, the Seaside Fund boy.

But let the show begin!

Three men come strutting on to the stage, laughing and shouting. One is beating a drum, another blows a whistle, and the third man is singing a merry tune. We like it, we like it. The singer stops singing and tells the two players to shut up so that he can speak to us.

He waves a big golden bangle at us and wants to know, 'What's this?'

We break into shouts of 'Bangle!' and 'Ring!'

Our teachers, sitting on chairs along the sides of the hall, smile at all the goings-on.

On stage, the man swirls a finger at his own brain. This means we're all mad. We cheer; it's a refreshing change from being called stupid.

He takes a scarf and asks us: 'What colour is this?'

'Yellow!' On this we're unanimous.

Then, in dramatic slow motion, he pulls the scarf through the ring. It turns green and we, row upon row of excited boys and girls decide to warn this man that things are changing fast right under his nose. Instead of paying attention to what he's doing, he's looking at us and, with mocking bewilderment says, 'What's the matter?' We point four hundred fingers at him and shout, 'Your scarf is green!' He says, 'What?'

'Your scarf! It was yellow now it's green!'

'I beg yours?'

'Green!'

Only after cupping his ear is he able to hear.

He looks down at the scarf – but by then it's yellow again. He confers with his two friends and they all agree: we really are a crazy bunch. Try getting a magician to call you mad. I tell you it's the funniest thing in the world.

There's more magic. He takes a cake tin and points out a girl two rows away from me. She points to herself just to make sure. The magic man says, 'Are you not Belinda Brown?'

'No, sir,' she says.

'Then you're the one I want,' he says.

Wow, does that joke get us slapping our knees and rocking our bums with laughter!

The girl gets up, a little red in the face now, dusts lots of invisible fluff from her gym and steps on to the stage.

'What do you see in this tin?' he says. She looks inside, looks up at the magician.

'Stones?' she says, as if she's not too sure. But with a magic man who could blame her?

'Show them, tell them.' He hands her the tin of stones. 'Rattle them.'

Even though she's a little shy, she shows, rattles and tells.

What is this guy going to do?

'Watch,' he says.

He places the tin of stones on a table and, as soon as his back is turned, his friends cover the tin with a sheet. But no sooner have they done this than he yells at them to 'Mind your own business! Who asked you?' and tells them to take their stupid sheet off his tin of stones. Only now it's … a tin of sweets! Mints, toffees, nougat, coconut. And he gives it all to the girl who isn't even Belinda Brown!

He repeats this trick with a cake tin of mud, which he turns into a chocolate cake and hands to Mrs Petersen, one of the Grade 1 teachers.

I go home that afternoon wondering why he couldn't just have made tins of sweets and chocolate cake for all of us. God knows we had enough stones and mud on the school grounds just waiting to be turned into something tasty.

Well, whenever I think of that magic show, I think about my Auntie Katie.

Hardly a week after the show, just as the talk of magic is beginning to disappear, Ma gives me some news.

'Auntie Katie's coming to visit us today.' This is a Saturday.

Auntie Katie! She's my mother's younger sister, Catherine. She's a replica of Ma, except that she's taller, and wears glasses. Like Ma she's very pretty. Even before I was ready for school she showed me how to hold a pen. Of all my mother's ten brothers and sisters, Auntie Katie is considered to be the cleverest because she's gone as far as Standard 8. Ma and everybody else, it seems, had dropped out in Standard 6, the beginning of high school. It must be all that studying that led to the glasses. Auntie Katie is twenty-two years old.

'And she's bringing her new boyfriend.'

'Really, Ma!' That's all I'm allowed to say. Something like, 'What happened to the old one?' would be seen as *ougat*.

In our little two-bedroomed house there is much preparation – shining the three front steps, wiping the sticky marks off the front gate, dusting off the coffee table in the lounge. Then Ma sends me to the shop to buy a family size Coke and a Fanta. And a packet of Bakers Romany Creams and Choice Assorted biscuits. Usually all we get is one bottle of cooldrink and one packet of Choice

Assorted which is about seven cents cheaper than the Romany Creams – and then my brothers and sisters and I fight over the lemon creams – of which there are only two in each packet.

Auntie Katie and her new boyfriend arrive in the afternoon. They walk in and, from our kitchen, I listen to the adult ritual of how-d'you-do's in our tiny lounge. 'Desmond Domingo,' I hear my father say. 'Related to Peter Domingo who used to play centre forward for Gladiators?'

'My older brother!' I hear Desmond say. And then all four adults burst into polite laughter as if being the brother of Peter Domingo is a funny thing.

'Where's Chris?' I hear Auntie Katie ask. I smile in the kitchen and get up to have a sip of water so that I can look busy when she comes looking for me. Seconds later Auntie Katie is in the kitchen with her boyfriend and I'm surprised at what I see. Desmond Domingo is a short, stocky man – even shorter than my aunt. And in every other way different from what I had imagined. Dark of complexion, a full crinkly beard, big white teeth. His small, brown eyes glint with a mischievousness I usually only see in someone my own age. A hand pops out from a fawn corduroy jacket to shake my little hand. I shake his hand and smile back at him. I like him from the word go. Auntie Katie can see that I like her new boyfriend and beams happily from behind her big round glasses.

But this is only the introduction.

After the biscuits and tea and cooldrink, it is usually the time when children have to disappear. This is when adults talk about who's pregnant, who's still not married, who's pregnant and still not married, and so on. But Uncle Desmond calls for a pack of cards and Ma knows it's safe for me to stay.

He makes me pick a card. This is an old trick and I've seen it done lots of times before by my uncles, Mellvin and Eddie. I pick the three of diamonds and put it back in the pack. He shuffles the pack. He stops. He thinks hard.

'Is this your card?' he holds up the two of clubs.

'No.'

He throws it face down on the coffee table and shows me another card. Again he's wrong. (This is not how the trick usually goes.) He flips that one face down too and shows me yet another card. This Uncle Desmond is so wrong, he isn't even getting the colour of the card right. Now there are three wrong cards lying face down between us.

'But why do you say no, no, no, when your card is there?' (lying face down on the table).

'But Uncle Desmond …' I turn to my aunt who merely arches her eyebrows behind her glasses. Ma laughs, Dad looks bemused.

'That's where your card is,' the short man says, pointing to the three wrong cards.

'It's not.' I have known him long enough to put a little bit of indignation into my voice. This short, bearded, new boyfriend has shown me three cards and none of them is mine.

'OK, what was your card?'

'Three of diamonds.'

'Well, check those cards,' he says, pointing to the three on the table.

I turn them up and there's my card, the three of diamonds! My face must look quite a mixture of amazement and disbelief. I have been tricked. But I can see that my parents have been tricked too. Only Auntie Katie appears unfazed. I ask Uncle Desmond to do the trick again. This time I watch his every move; even when he puts his cigarette in the ashtray and puts down the glass of beer that Dad has poured for him, I keep my eyes on that pack of cards. But again he tricks me. And one more time.

His magic is not confined to cards alone. He shows us how to get a twenty-cent coin out from underneath an upturned bottle – without lifting up the bottle. Then he makes that same bottle (the family size Fanta which is now empty) stand without support in a corner of the room – halfway between the floor and the ceiling. He also guesses correctly the number of matches in a matchbox just by shaking it near his ear – seven times in a row!

A year later, my aunt is Mrs Desmond Domingo. They have a son and she is pregnant again. Uncle Desmond has acquired a house for them on the corner of the street we live in and identical to ours. Moving into a house so quickly was unheard of in those days when the waiting list for houses was so long that people who got married usually only got a place of their own when their eldest was in high school.

I hear my father say, 'Desmond,' in admiration. 'I tell you that one's got connections.'

I'm still very fond of my Auntie Katie. Whenever Ma sends me on my daily errand to the shop for bread, I pop in at her house to see if she wants something from the shop too. Auntie Katie still likes me. But she seems always too busy washing nappies, hanging them out on the line in the bleak and tiny backyard, breast-feeding one baby, spoon-feeding another, changing nappies. Sometimes she's so busy that she can't even remember where she put her purse or what she needed from the shop or to ask me if I had passed my exams. The years go by and she just keeps on having babies.

Whenever I walk past their home on Saturday afternoons, Uncle Desmond is hanging out with his workmates and other friends who have come to visit. And they're forever drinking. The brown quart bottles of Castle and Lion beer, and Richelieu brandy, and Mainstay Cane Spirit are a familiar sight on the coffee table. Music on the turntable – El Ricas, Trini Lopez, Johnny Mathis and the Flames – familiar sounds.

Another sound that grows familiar through the years is Uncle Desmond's favourite word for my aunt: 'Bitch.' Used in the following ways:

'Bring the chow, bitch. How long do we have to wait?' 'We' is himself and his buddies.

'Bitch, gimme more money for beer there. And move that fat arse of yours.' This is meant to be a joke but his friends never laugh as heartily as he does.

'Bitch, the fucking child is crying, go and see what's wrong, Jesus.' Or just: 'Ag, fuck you, bitch!'

Auntie Katie doesn't have another name for him. Desmond is what she always calls him.

One night, no, about three o'clock in the morning, there's a knock on my parents' bedroom window. I wake up and hear Ma opening the squeaking window, and my aunt's voice, also squeaking, with fear. Her children are crying, in her arms and around her legs.

'Ag please, Shirley, tell Nick to come quickly. Desmond's gone mad down there!'

I can hear Dad shake himself awake. He puts on pants, a cardigan. And slippers! I'm disappointed by the slippers. You can't kick a man with slippers. My father goes out into the cold, barking night to see what Uncle Desmond is up to down the road. My father is an ex-Rosebuds goalkeeper. He's tall, athletic, and knows how to kick an object. But has no intention of doing so tonight it seems.

Wide-awake now, and eavesdropping as usual, I piece together the story. First from Ma and Auntie Katie in the kitchen where they drink a cup of tea and try to get the kids to stop crying. Then about half an hour later when Dad comes back and tells her to try and get some sleep – on the couch. It's OK now; Desmond is sleeping it off.

He and his mates had finished two bottles of brandy. His friends had staggered off home at past midnight but he wanted more liquor. He demanded five rands from my aunt. She wouldn't give it to him – 'because I just did not have it,' she tells my mother. So he beat her up. The noise of her screaming woke up the kids and they all cried in a terrified bundle on the bed. He took a bottle of paraffin from the bathroom, went outside and splashed it all around the house. He tried to light a match … 'That's when I grabbed the children and ran up here.'

There were more Saturday night/Sunday morning bangings on the window-pane. Lots more tears. Sometimes Auntie Katie walked about with a black eye for days.

One day she decides that enough is enough. Uncle Desmond comes home late one Friday night, drunk. He bangs on the door. Auntie Katie opens up. He stands there, swaying from side to side. He has a friend with him. Somebody Auntie Katie has never set eyes on before. A woman who could not have been a day older than eighteen, in dirty Levis too tight for her and a tatty, skimpy blouse with her breasts popping out of the top. A mixture of cheap perfume and day-old brandy fumes flutter from her. She is also swaying and, apart from an intermittent giggle, says nothing, shows no embarrassment or awkwardness for what is happening or is about to happen. I don't know how my uncle puts it to my aunt, but he tells her that Carol, his friend, would be sleeping in their bed with them tonight.

Then, so the story goes, my Auntie Katie uses Uncle Desmond's favourite word.

Auntie Katie doesn't say much else to anyone after that. But together with my mother, they plan The Great Escape. Auntie Katie decides to save some money, borrow some more, sell some of their clothes for a few more rands. A few weeks later she goes to Park Station, buys a third-class ticket to Durban (children under seven travel free) where she would start a new life, without Desmond, or any other man.

The day comes. It's a Friday morning and Uncle Desmond gets up and goes to work. This is the day when his wild weekend begins and Auntie Katie's nightmare starts: Friday late afternoon until the wee hours of Monday morning.

Friday's the day most Coloureds get their wages and when a kind of frenzy is ignited. On Monday morning many would not even have twenty cents for bus fare to take them to work. But what the hell; on a Friday afternoon when that first drink cascades down your throat and flows through your bloodstream, its first effect is to make all Mondays disappear from the calendar, together with all the white bosses in the country – from here to eternity.

Uncle Desmond-style weekends were not unique in Riverlea. Take, for instance, the Jardines and the Constances opposite us. Mr Jardine was married to Mr Constance's sister and Mr Constance was betrothed to Mr Jardine's sister, so they were closer than most families. Plus they lived opposite each other. Unlike Uncle Desmond and Auntie Katie, these two couples drank together as a merry foursome, alternating their homes as the venue. They drank, joked, fried meat, drank, sang and became maudlin. Then an argument would erupt, usually from something minor: a spilled drink ('D'you know what the fucken stuff costs?'), the words of a song ('It's regrets, I've had a *few*, not a *view*'), because one of them stayed in the toilet too long ('Have you passed out on the toilet seat again?'). The guest couple then went outside and smashed all the host couple's windows, all around the little matchbox house, with half a brick each. The host couple would then stagger across the road and give that house the same treatment: tit for tat, butter for fat.

But back to The Great Escape. As soon as Uncle Desmond leaves for work, Auntie Katie jumps into action, with an expression of resoluteness that had last been seen two or three years ago, in her pre-marital days.

She washes the kids, packs three or four suitcases with essential things, and fills a Tupperware box with cheese and tomato sandwiches for *padkos*. She comes to say goodbye to Ma – I was at school, Dad was at work. Ma hands her the train tickets that she has kept hidden for her. My aunt leaves the key with a neighbour – to be given to Uncle Desmond when he comes back from work that evening. Another neighbour, Mr Adams, a pensioner, drives her to the station in his old Anglia.

Durban. A new life. Without Uncle Desmond and his drinking and swearing and beating and trying to burn the house down and trying to have three-in-the-bed sex. There are good dressmaking factories in Durban, and an old school friend, who is also now living in Durban, is looking out for a job for my aunt. For now, she stands on Platform 14 surrounded by suitcases and bags with zips that don't work and a child who is hungry, another who is thirsty, and one who wants to pee. The train comes. And out of the blue, like the jack of spades in one of his card tricks, there is Uncle Desmond.

This is such a shock for my aunt that she bursts into tears and says, 'D'you blame me, Desmond? D'you blame me?' taking off her glasses and wiping them clean on the hem of her dress, putting them on, taking them off …

How did he know she was leaving him? But there's another surprise: he whips out … his own ticket to Durban and gets on to the train with her and the kids.

They've been living in Durban for thirty years now, in a slum called Wentworth. Uncle Desmond got work on the docks, refurbishing ships. Auntie Katie worked as a seamstress. They had three more children. Every Friday Uncle Desmond comes home drunk and beats her up. He still calls her a bitch and she still calls him Desmond. Apart from the fact that they all have a Durban accent now, nothing much has changed – most people regard them as just an ordinary Coloured South African family.

Divine intervention

BERNICE SEPTEMBER IS PRETTY. She's dark with long black hair. But that's not all Bernice has going for her. At almost thirteen years old she's one huge bundle of energy; when she's around I always feel like an old man even though I'm about the same age, ashamed that I'm not running or jumping or tumbling as fast as I should for a boy.

There are boys and girls at school who run fast, faster and fastest. And then there's Bernice. Coming first in the 100 metres, first in the 200 metres, first in the relay.

But Bernice has brains too. The first year in high school all the kids are put into one room and given an IQ test. For about two hours we all have to answer questions like this:

Which number follows the following series of numbers:

7 ... 15 ... 23 ... 31 ... 39 ... ?

Or:

Which is the odd word in the following:

bird ... feather ... egg ... glove ... claw ... nest

Well, we all think it's pretty easy stuff. But a few weeks later, when the results come from the Department of Coloured Affairs in Cape Town, Bernice September is called into the principal's office. She's not supposed to tell anybody what has happened there. But, according to her, the principal and a white inspector shook her hand and told her that, according to the results of the tests, she's brilliant. A genius.

Bernice is always everywhere. On the football grounds, the hockey grounds, at the tadpole dam, in the library, in the park, in the street skipping rope. And of course with so much to do she's never home on time. They live in Colorado Drive a street away from us but our back doors are diagonally opposite and sometimes, after dark, you can hear her father calling:

'Berr-NICE!'

One day, Bernice isn't everywhere, she's with me. This wild, energetic, clever girl who's all over Riverlea, is now all over me. When I come home from school, she's there. When my mother comes from work, she's there. She goes home to have supper, make tea for her parents or wash the dishes after supper – and then she's back. This happens every night, for a few summer weeks. She brings me little gifts, like peaches, which she picks from a neighbour's tree – one for her and one for me.

'You don't have to wash it, I've already washed it for you.'

Or a bunch of grapes for us to share. Or a sweet.

My mother says nothing about this sudden, eager visitor, but I catch her smiling mysteriously at us.

We play hide-and-seek with other boys and girls, and Bernice hides where I hide. Even if it's such a small hiding place that only one body can fit in there – in fact, especially if it's a small hiding place.

Well, you may not believe me, but despite all this strange behaviour on Bernice's part, I still have no idea that she has one serious crush on me – that she *smaaks* me *stukkend*.

Bernice realises my ignorance and so she resorts to that system that never fails, the love letter. Bernice has a high IQ. But she's no Shakespeare. She writes:

> Dear Christopher
>
> I like you very much (It's Love with a capital L). Do you also like me? If you want to kiss me you can kiss me because I will not tell nobody. I'll see you tonight.
>
> Bernice September
>
> Underneath her name she puts in:
>
> I.T.A.L.Y. [I trust and love you]
> R.O.M.E. [Remember our moonlight evening]. (I swear there had never been none such, but in those days no self-respecting love letter came without these salutations)
> H.O.L.L.A.N.D. [Hope our love lasts and never dies.]

I read the letter in our bathroom/toilet. My first love letter. Oh, Bernice, dear, lovely Bernice. I wish I could reply to her and say: 'My answer is YES'. But I can never do that. You see, Bernice has a squint. And so do I. And if ever there was a recipe for laughter then this is it.

Both Bernice and I get teased all the time. She doesn't seem to mind these taunts too much, but I do. And being boyfriend and girlfriend together would just invite a fresh attack. So Bernice and I would not be lovers. Never.

'Six-five.'

'Seven-eleven.'

'Cockeye.'

'*Skeeloog*.' (That's Afrikaans for cockeye.)

I hear them all day, every day throughout my childhood. My mother sends me to a friend's home a few streets away. I knock on the door. An adult opens with her little kid in tow.

'Good evening, Mrs Davids. My mother sent me for the white cotton.'

'Oh, of course, come inside, sit down.'

In the meantime, the little fellow is staring at I-know-what. He waits for his mum to disappear and when it's just the two of us in the room, he says softly: 'Hey, cockeye' and giggles, delighted at the freak who has come into their home to provide him with some quick amusement.

In another home, a well-meaning boy says to me, in the presence of his entire family: 'D'you know there's something wrong with your eyes; you're not looking in the right place.'

The entire family go: 'Hey!' out of sheer embarrassment. And of course being Coloured they go, not red but a deep shade of maroon.

I go to the shop and some kids loitering around there, chewing gum, see me and say: 'Hey six-five!' and keel over with laughter. I am their matinee, their entertainment, the freak to amuse them while they chew their Chappies.

It gets worse. Sitting in a car, I stare out the window at a truck of workers. They stare back, spot me, and the game is on. Traffic is too loud for their taunts to reach me, but when words fail, there is always sign language: a crossing of the forefingers, followed by whoops of laughter.

One day a girl at school decides to have some fun at my expense. 'Cockeye, cockeye, cockeye,' she goes until I disappear into the toilet. A week or so later I walk past her house. She stands in the doorway staring at me. Beside her stands her mother – who has one of the worst squints in the world.

'Why do you bother calling me 'cockeye' when you can do it in the comfort of your own home?' I should have asked her, but didn't.

I was born with a squint in my left eye. Before I'm a year old Ma, Dad and I are making monthly trips to St John's, the eye hospital near Baragwanath Hospital in Soweto where I was born. I have my first eye operation when I'm about nine months old, and, Ma says, the eye simply wandered back to the inner corner, where it preferred to stay.

And the visits to opticians and optometrists continued throughout my childhood. Ma and Dad or my aunt Venecia would take me. I know the benches, long, dark brown and gleaming from the hundreds of bums that polished them over the years. Then there are the optometrists/opticians with their white coats and their charts with the mixed-up letters of the alphabet, from gigantic Os and Xs to mere blurs of letters lower down the chart. I can only ever read up to the fourth or fifth row. After that the Es look like Bs and the Ys look like Ts and I'm beginning to guess.

Then they shine their tiny torch deep into my eye, detectives looking for clues, some with minty breath, others with smoker's breath, still others with a bad dose of halitosis. All white men in white coats.

They shake their heads and talk to Ma. She says,

'You know, Doctor, when he was a baby I'd notice that when he drops something on the floor, like a cent or something, he starts looking for it and can't find it. I point to it and say, "There it is, there." It's right under his nose but he can't see it. Eventually I have to pick it up for him.'

The way Ma tells the story it seems like she's trying to tell him I'm half blind. It's not true. What happens is she says, 'There! There! Christopher there! Christopher there!' She gets such a hysterical edge in her voice that I begin to panic and I end up not looking properly. But if I told the doctor this Ma'll say to me on the way home, 'But how can you embarrass me like that in front of the doctor?' So I just say nothing and let the doctor write what he wants to on my card.

I spend many days and nights coming home crying at the taunts.

Dad flies out and finds the rascal who has called me 'cockeye' and gives him a good dressing down. But he grows tired of having to fling down his newspaper and go after them.

'Listen, Christopher,' he says one day. 'If somebody teases you, fuck him up. If he's bigger than you, pick up a brick and throw his head off and run home.'

Ma's advice is more practical. 'Just try to ignore them,' she says.

One day I solve the problem – but don't use the advice of either of my parents.

We're kicking about a tennis ball when a boy called Melvin Langrich decides that he'd like to have a go at me.

'Six-five,' he says.

'Fuck you,' I say.

'Six-five.'

'Fuck you.' I'm tempted to say something about his mother, but there's one golden rule about peer group teasing – which we call *gwara* – and that is 'no mothers'. Besides, he would've said something right back about my mother so what's the point.

Melvin has never been my best friend, but he hasn't been my enemy either. He's one of the guys. He has two bigger brothers and I often go to his home to swap comics with them. I don't know where their ma works but she brings home stacks of second-hand *June* and *School Friend* and *Valiant*.

Melvin has a sister who is the lead singer in a band that has actually cut an album. The Langrich family is one of many African families that have made their way into a Coloured community, to escape the indignities of the pass laws and stay where job prospects are better, albeit slightly better.

A. Morewa of Alexandra township moves into Riverlea and becomes Mr Moore. The Ndlovus become the Oliphants – they change their name but still remain the animal with the long trunk. The Setlares become Grootbooms thus retaining their family tree. The McBaines used to be Magubane and the Masekelas are going around as Maskells. The list goes on and on.

Right now Melvin is the man of the moment. He's, in fact, doing clever things with the tennis ball, which is amazing everyone. And he's having a go at me, which is amusing all the boys. That they are not only his friends but mine too doesn't quite count for anything right now. I'm on the receiving end and that's OK with all of them.

Melvin introduces some variety into his taunting. 'How many fingers do you see?' he asks, holding up one finger.

'One,' I answer foolishly.

'No, cockeye,' he says with a chuckle. 'You see two.'

The boys love it, flinging themselves against the sagging garden fences and slapping hands together.

'How many of me do you see?' Melvin asks me.

A retort comes into my head from nowhere. I take a deep breath and decide to use it. 'I see two of you,' I say, giving the answer he wants. 'But why is it that you are both kaffirs?'

'Oh God, nice!' The boys say, loving the wonderful comeback.

Immediately Melvin loses interest in the tennis ball, letting it roll away from him.

'Sonny,' he says, coming close up, chin to chin. 'Sonny, I'll fuck you up.'

'But that would be unfair,' I protest. 'Two kaffirs against one Coloured.'

I wasn't proud of using that word. But I went home hoping that my tormentor would understand that I had only done to him what he had been doing to me.

On one of my many visits to St John's a doctor comes up with a new plan. He gives me an eye patch to wear over my right eye, my good eye.

'It will force him to use the lazy eye,' he tells Ma.

It's school holidays and I'm spending them at my ouma's in Coronationville. Every morning Ouma makes sure I'm wearing my eye patch before I go out to play with my cousins.

'But I can't see, Ouma.'

'That's just it,' she says, 'we must get you to use that other eye.'

I go outside, sneak around the shed where I'm alone, and switch the eye patch to the other eye. Now I can play without having to grope about.

'Christopher!' Ouma calls me at twenty-minute intervals. I run to her side. 'You're still wearing it. Good boy.'

But my ouma has one last card to play. And this time it's not so easy to deceive her.

Some time later, a man of God comes to Coronationville. A dynamic man, a passionate man. A man called Brother McGregor. He and his entourage find a clearing and pitch their tent, as wide and as high as the Catholic Church. They have come to proclaim that Jesus, the son of God, is alive and well and ready to live in our hearts as long as we change our evil ways and accept the Lord Jesus Christ as our own personal saviour.

Every night for a month, people flock to the tent to praise the Lord. They sing and dance and listen to the word of the Lord, as interpreted by God's great messenger, Brother McGregor.

With every evening that passes, the tent grows fuller and fuller, as more and more sinners come – and come again, wanting to hear more about God and His wondrous work.

And even if you do not go and bear witness, half the township can still listen to the word, thanks to a powerful generator and a set of microphones and speakers the size of wardrobes. So you can be sitting down to supper, washing dishes or listening to the seven o'clock news when the voice of Brother McGregor or the vocal chords of the lusty congregation cuts clear across the summer night calling on you to give your heart to Jesus.

The Anglicans, the Catholics, the Ebenezers, they all have hymns, sombre, serene and centuries old. Brother McGregor's church has choruses. They're lively, bouncy, clap-your-hands joyful. They're hallelujah and loud and get-up-and-dance and Jesus is alive! And amen and praise the Lord!

And with every passing week the township has more and more to say about this new church, this new messenger of God and how the Almighty is working his miracles through Brother

McGregor who, through the Lord, has also come to heal the sick and the infirm.

The stories are legendary. A woman in Fuel Road, who has been bedridden for eight years with backache, was carried by her sons and grandsons to the tent. Brother McGregor laid his hands on her and prayed and prayed and beseeched the almighty God to take away the devil that was causing this lady so much pain. That woman was last seen strolling into the local café and telling everyone how wonderful God is.

Clifford Conley, a boy from Riversdale Street, used to have terrible asthma. Well, he breathes okay now, praise the Lord!

Then there's the story of Oupa Damons, an ex-World War Two soldier. He had a combination of gout, arthritis, alcoholism and heart disease, plus a bullet in his ankle from a German rifle. He spent half his day in the pub drinking wine and getting drunk. Only half his day mind you because he hobbled on a stick and took about two hours to reach the pub – and three to get back home because of the added disadvantage of being drunk.

Well, one fateful evening, Oupa Damons gives the pub a miss and hobbles with great determination to the tent. Brother McGregor prays for him and Oupa Damons leaves the tent with a spring in his step.

For a week Oupa Damons reads his Bible night and day and comes to the tent to give thanks and praise to the Lord. But after that initial hale and hearty week he takes a brisk walk to the pub to celebrate his newfound health with a tiny litre of wine and to say hi to his old friends.

Sadly, God is keeping a very beady and omnipresent eye on Oupa Damons. And the Almighty acts swiftly. For when Oupa gets up to go home, he finds that he's taking such a long time to get out of the pub that the barman is forced to give him another one for the road. He's not only drunk but his afflictions have returned.

Oupa Damons is dead now, but he spent the last years of his life hobbling from house to pub at his old, pre-McGregor pace.

So there I am listening to these tales of the tent and its charismatic Brother McGregor. But unbeknown to me, my ouma is having ideas about getting me closer to the action.

And one day my uncle Mellvin arrives at our home. He has been instructed to fetch me so that I may have the privilege of having God correct my squint through the wonderful healing hands of Brother McGregor.

I stare at my uncle – or stare past him, I suppose – thinking, what now? I love my ouma so much, but this is not a move that appeals to me at all. But even at age thirteen, I realise how complicated this whole thing is. I don't believe for one minute that Brother McGregor, or God, has the power to straighten out my squint. Why, I ask myself, did he give me this thing in the first place? If he had not given me the squint, or Oupa Damons the slow hobble or hundreds of old men and women the cataracts, then we would all have saved him a whole lot of time and trouble.

There is even the thing about Lazarus in the Bible that confuses me a little. He's this guy who was dead. And then Jesus came into their town and someone – I think Lazarus's wife – asked Jesus to please do something about it.

'Like what?' Jesus asks her.

'Like bring him back to life.'

Most guys, even most faith healers, would've shaken their heads and said no, that's not possible. But Jesus says, no problem, where's he? The next thing Jesus tells Lazarus to get up (the actual quote, I believe, is, 'Lazarus arise') and he gets up.

Now my question is: Lazarus was in heaven which is supposed to be such a nice place – no worries, no school, no homework, enough to eat every day, plus the prospect of this going on for ever. There's never a time when God says suddenly, 'Look, this month we're gonna have to tighten our belts a little, so go easy on the condensed milk everyone ...' So wasn't Lazarus cross when he came back? And if he wasn't cross, then why didn't Jesus bring him back to life the second time he died? And what about all the other people in that town who had dead relatives? Didn't they say, 'Hey, what about my dead mother or brother or granny – bring them back to life too?'

Yet, I know that this is not how my ouma sees the whole thing. And if she knew about these thoughts going through my mind, there would be trouble. One does not question God's ways. So I pack some clothes into a packet and off we go, Mellvin and me, heading for Corrie where I have an appointment with Ouma Ruby and Brother McGregor. And God.

While I'm not at all looking forward to what I'm going to encounter in Corrie, I nonetheless look forward to seeing my ouma again. Even the journey to Corrie is always exciting. Mellvin and I cut through a patch of veld past the old mineshafts on the outskirts of Riverlea. Half an hour later we're in Industria, full of factories and railway sidings and Coloured and African workers in blue overalls. We walk past the tobacco factory, the Koo canning factory. When the wind blows southwards, we in Riverlea can all smell the factory. Sometimes it smells of burnt tomatoes and at other times like one great big fart.

Mellvin and I have between us about twenty cents and we go into a café to buy Chappies and Sharps toffees. We still share our sweets, but these days Mellvin is wearing Levis and in his back pocket carrying around a paperback novel swung inside out. The author is James Hadley Chase and there's a white woman on the cover who's wearing a very short red dress and fishnet stockings. Mellvin also used to read the odd Enid Blyton and Hardy Boys but now he reads this stuff.

'What's the story about?' I want to know.

He grabs the book out of my hand. 'Can't tell you.'

'Why not?'

He laughs and looks away, at new furniture in the window of Gossels.

I ask him again.

'Because you're a *laaitie*, sonny.'

I sort of know what people are doing in those books. And as soon as I can lay my hands on one of them, I'll read it for myself. My vocabulary is probably bigger than Mellvin's; I'm aware of this. So there's nothing really stopping me.

Mellvin changes the subject. He tells me he's thinking of quitting school.

'Why?'

'To help the old lady. She's struggling at home there.'

'What kind of work are you going to do?'

'Clerk.'

I've seen the word. It's pronounced the same as Clark Kent, who is Superman in disguise. But that's all I know.

'What does a clerk do?'

'He writes things in a book. His boss comes to him and puts things on his left-hand side and says I want it all done by this afternoon. And then he writes and writes and whatever he's finished writing he puts on his right-hand side. That's a clerk.'

I'm impressed – and even more impressed when he takes out half a cigarette, lights up, coughs and says to me, half embarrassed: 'What?'

I have supper at Ouma's house, while she coaches me about what to do when we meet Brother McGregor.

'When he puts his hands over your eyes, you just close them tight and you tell yourself, when I open my eyes they will be right, because God is going to make them right for me, you understand me, son?'

I nod.

'You do believe in God, don't you?'

'Of course, Ouma.'

I look around at my cousins and young uncles wiping their plates clean with wads of bread and looking at me with empathy and affection – either that or they wish there were seconds. In less than an hour there will be hundreds of strangers staring at me like this.

'Who'll be there?' I want to know.

'Who'll be there?' Ouma repeats the question. 'You don't worry about who's there and who's not there. To hell with everybody else. I'll be there, me, your ouma. I'll go up to the front with you and I won't leave you until he has prayed for you and everything.'

'OK, Ouma.' I put on a brave face and my granny gives my wrist a squeeze and wipes the sweat off my nose with a thumb and finger.

When Ouma and I walk up to the tent, we can hear them starting up, going 'testing, testing, testing' on the microphones and tuning their guitars for those wide-awake hymns of theirs.

We walk into the tent. People are sitting on long wooden benches under bright, naked light bulbs, underfoot is grass. More and more people stream in and there are murmurings of 'brother' here and 'sister' there and 'bless you' all over the place.

We find seats near the front, the easier to reach Brother McGregor when the moment arrives.

A slit in the tent parts and the Brother himself materialises in suit and tie. He takes the microphone and begins, thanking us all for coming and asking us to bow our heads in prayer.

Brother McGregor begins slowly. He smiles at us, he smiles even more when he speaks about the wondrous works of God – 'and maybe our heavenly Father will perform more miracles here tonight' – and my heart drops miraculously into my scuffed Bata Toughies. I have been hoping in vain that just for tonight he would drop that part of the proceedings.

He speaks about Satan and then things really begin to heat up. He's really cross now. Starvation in parts of Africa, the muggings and the killings in the streets, youth turning to crime and cigarettes – I think of Mellvin who is now officially a smoker – teenage pregnancies, wife beatings, drinking. This is because we have all lost the path to Jesus 'Jeee-zus' he says. If he had put this name in a speech bubble in a comic, it would have dozens of hearts around it.

The Brother's preaching is interspersed with sudden bursts of very robust singing and clapping:

> I'm happy tonight,
> In Jesus my Lord
> He has ta-ha-ken all
> my si-hins away
> And that's why
> I'm happy tonight.

About fifteen minutes into the service Brother McGregor begins to sweat a lot – from his screaming at that devil who is forever stalking us, waiting for that weak moment to enter our hearts. I decide there and then that I am never going to look up the rude bits in the James Hadley Chase novels or read the *Post* when my parents are at work. This battle between God and the devil, I realise is a very serious World War. I have known almost all my life that the two were not on speaking terms, but I never knew it was this bad. In our church, in all the churches around the township for that matter, we are really just warned about the devil and his tempting ways. But here is a different story. This Brother is fuming and raging about what a nasty piece of work ole Satan is. The sweat is pouring down his face at the rate of hundreds of drops per second. And when he raises his hands to give thanks to or praise the Lord, I see huge wet blotches under his arms.

An assistant passes him a towel, for which he says, 'Thank you, brother.' This is like a boxing match.

When he takes off his jacket and rolls up his sleeves, well I know we're about to move to another level. This man really goes to town on the devil. The things he says about that guy, I think his ears must've been burning – although I suppose they burn all the time because of that big fire he's got going down there in hell.

Then there's a part of the service called 'Giving Testimony'. People in the audience, if they have the guts, are asked to come up to give their hearts to Jesus. And then they have to tell us all what bad people they've been all their lives. This part of the service is a good thing because it gives the brother a chance to get his breath back.

'Is there anybody here tonight who wants to give their hearts to Jesus ...'. The organ is playing soft music that has this magic ability to ease you gently off your bench.

People get out of their seats, shuffle up to the front and turn and face us. When the Brother thinks he has enough of them, he praises the Lord and says a prayer for them.

Then each of them tells us about their drinking and their smoking and their looking at other men's wives.

'Praise the Lord,' the audience says, and 'amen.' My ouma also utters a spirited 'amen.'

Then it's our turn. I'm in a crowd that includes a woman with arthritis, two women with backache, a man with breathing problems, a deaf baby and a teenage girl in a wheelchair. We are all chaperoned. My ouma holds my hand and squeezes it gently.

The Brother begins to pray for us one by one. I would have preferred a collective prayer, but there's a different prayer for different ailments. Squints are last.

He puts his hand on my forehead and stares into my eyes. His eye is piercing and bright, much like the torchlight that the optometrist uses at St John's. He demands, in the name of the Lord, that the devil leaves my eyes, gets out! Goes away! Leaves now and leaves for ever!

In my mind I say, 'When he takes off his hands I will not have a squint any more, hallalujah!

Afterwards I look up at my ouma. The squint is still there. I will go home to my aunts and uncles and they will see that the squint is still there. I will go home to my mother and she will see that the squint is still there.

They will do what I hate them doing, look and look and look. It's as if the squint has just begun all over again.

Brother McGregor takes down his tent and goes away, to do battle with the devil in another town, another eye. I'm relieved … but only for a while. My ouma says:

'He's doing all the Coloured townships. Mrs Cupido told me he's in Kimberley now. Her daughter lives there and she wrote and told her mother. When he comes back this way he's coming to Riverlea. And when he comes we'll be there waiting, my son.'

She must have seen the shadow of doubt darkening my face, because she says:

'God is testing us, Kuller. He's testing us to see how many of us believe and how many don't.'

Riverlea. God no! All my friends live in Riverlea. I only need for one or two of them to come to the tent and see Brother McGregor try to shake the devil out of my eyes. The next day in school, all those bastards who had grown tired of taunting me would look at me anew and the games would begin all over again.

But God answers my prayers and Brother McGregor never came to pitch his tent in Riverlea.

However, he didn't disappear off the scene completely. About three years later I open up the *Sunday Times* and, lo and behold, there is Brother McGregor making news. He's run off with the wife of one of his fellow pastors … and some church funds.

Praise the Lord – or is it the devil I should be thanking?

Politics and sex

I'VE HAD ELEVEN BIRTHDAYS and just as many Christmases and I haven't stopped hoping that on one of these special days I'll wake up to find a shiny, new bicycle leaning against my bed waiting for me.

But in the meantime I have a plan. In the Comics section of the *Sunday Times*, there between *Blondie and Dagwood* and *Bringing up Father*, is a Chappies bubble gum competition and it says: 'Hey kids! Great prizes to be won!' There are not one or two or three but a whole fifteen bicycles to be won. There are also one hundred consolation prizes of Chappies hampers.

I have to ask Ma what a hamper is. She says it's a parcel of different things to eat. I ask her what's a Chappies hamper.

'I suppose it's enough sweets and bubble gum to give you rotten teeth.'

I won't mind winning the hamper. But it's the bicycle I'm after.

It's not easy getting a bicycle. Rodney Jordan has one but that's because, even though his parents are factory workers like mine, he's an only child so they can afford it. Then there's my friend Alvin. There are four children in his family but he's got a brand new racer because they run a shebeen and the profit from selling liquor is always good.

You ask Rodney for a ride and he says, 'My father says he doesn't want to see every Tom, Dick and Harry on this bike.'

My brother, Derek, says, 'I'm not Tom, Dick or Harry.' That's not because he's witty, it's just because he doesn't understand the idiom.

I say, 'Don't worry, I'll ride where your father won't see me.'

He says, 'No, I'm scared.'

He's not really scared, just selfish. Ma says that comes from being an only child – you don't ever have to share things with your brothers and sisters so you automatically become selfish.

Moms and dads are forever watching us playing our street games. They stand at their front doors or lean on their gates, smoking and laughing at our antics. And now they're watching the game of Rodney and the new bike. And that's why Ma is able to put her penny in the plate too.

Eventually, we do get Rodney to give us a ride by using a bit of psychology on him. We refuse to talk to him, we don't greet him, we don't look at him when he rides past us, and worst of all, we don't let him play ball with us in the street. It's not easy when there's a dozen guys going mad in the street and you're not part of it.

Rodney gets off his bike and says, 'Side?'

'My father's gonna shout if we play with you,' says Derek. This time he is being witty.

So eventually we each get a ride up and down Flinders. But the queue is too long and the work involved in getting to this point is too hard. That is why winning the Chappies competition would be very, very nice.

I need a two and a half cent postage stamp for my entry. Ma gives me five cents and Keith and I take a walk to the Langlaagte post office. It's far – about half an hour there and half an hour back. But that's not the problem; the problem is Langlaagte is in *Boere* territory and those Afrikaner boys don't like it when we come to the post office. They say, 'Hey, bushmen, what d'you want here?' 'Fuck off, you Hotnots!'

But Keith says, 'Don't even look at them. And if I say run, run.'

I buy my stamp from the small window on the side where it says: 'Non-whites/Nie blankes'.

And then we walk back, keeping our eyes open and talking softly as we pass the white people glaring at us from their gardens. We get home safely.

OK, let's see, what else do I need? Scissors. A postcard. A pen. Glue.

There are three faces of Chappie Chipmunk, A, B and C. They all look alike but one of them is different from the other two. I look at their ears, their teeth, their caps … aah, it's their bow-ties. Two of them have striped ties and one has a polka dot bow-tie. I've found the impostor!

Next I have to write, in ten words or less, why I like Chappies bubble gum. This is the easy part because I know I'm good at this kind of thing. First I write on a piece of paper three different ideas. I take it to Ma and Dad's room to ask them which one is the best.

I like Chappies bubble gum because ...

1. the more I chew the more I like

2. it blows big bubbles and lasts a long time

3. it's delicious and lasts all day

Ma likes the first one. But Dad says:

'What's this for?'

I tell him.

'You'll never win,' he says.

'How do you know?'

'It's for white children, these competitions.'

'It doesn't say that anywhere, I read the rules.'

'It doesn't matter whether they say it or not, everything's for whites only.'

'But how will they know I'm not white? I've got a white surname.'

'They'll see by your address. Riverlea.'

'But you fill in *The Star* crossword every week and send it in.'

I even helped him with it once. He was stuck on 3 across and couldn't get the answer. I said, 'What's the question?' and he said, 'You won't know the answer.' Ma told me the question: 'Van Riebeeck's wife's name. Five letters,' and straight away I said: 'Maria'. Dad said, 'How do you know that?' Ma chipped in, 'Because he learned it at school.' She said, 'You went to school too, Nick, but you were probably absent the day yous learned about Maria.'

Dad laughed good-naturedly at the joke. But the truth was slightly more embarrassing. The Navy had recently bought two submarines and they said they would name one the *Maria van Riebeeck*, after Jan van Riebeeck's wife. We'd all heard it the other night on the radio and my father was definitely present.

But now Dad says, 'Of course I send in *The Star* crossword, but I don't put my home address, I put the factory's box number.'

I don't know what to do now, but Ma says, 'Send it away, you never know.'

I don't win a bicycle – or a hamper for that matter. But nor does Dad win the R10 000 in *The Star* crossword competition.

Warnings about competitions and the odd, bitter remark about white bosses and white people in general are about the sum total of political lessons from Dad. For the real story I would have to look elsewhere. He has six children and sends them out into a racist world without any preparation. But our family is not unique in this regard. The whole of Riverlea goes about in this happy or unhappy state of amnesia.

Like I've said before, sex and how babies are made are never discussed in our house – or any other house in Riverlea either. The first time I ask where babies come from Ma tells me an aeroplane brings them. Why? Because it's better than having to tell us anything at all about sex. In the meantime I'm picking up all kinds of information in the streets.

Vickie Johnson lives two doors away; he is three years older than I am and one year above me at school. His family are Afrikaans speaking and, with every visit to their home, my Afrikaans vocabulary grows bigger and bigger.

One day I hear him use the word '*jags*' all the time. He uses it as a synonym for 'crazy', like this:

'Hey Vickie, how about a piece of that sandwich you're eating.'

Vickie: 'Don't be jags, sonny.'

'Hey, bra Vickie, that's my top.'

'Your top? Don't be jags. I bought this top yesterday.'

'Jags', I decide, is a cool word to use and as soon as I get the chance I'll make it pop out of my mouth just like ou Vickie does.

The chance comes that very night after supper. My baby sister, Allison, sees me chewing gum and she stretches out her hand and says, 'Ta.' (That's baby talk for 'gimme some'.) We're not supposed to give her gum so I say:

'Don't be jags, girl.'

Every Van Wyk is in the kitchen when this happens. Dad is sipping tea and a mouthful spurts back into his cup.

'What the fuck did you just say now?'

I get a fright, and so do Derek and Shaun. And Allison begins to cry.

'I said … jags.'

'And he's still got the fucking nerve to repeat it!' he tells Ma. 'Did you hear that, Shirley? Did you hear this fucking … child!'

'Nick, Nick, Nick!' Ma has to reprimand Dad now. 'Where did you hear that word?' Ma says.

'Vickie Johnson.'

'Listen.' Now I have to look at Dad again. 'I don't want to see you with that little bastard again, d'you understand me, you piece of shit!'

'Nick, control yourself.'

I spend the rest of the night in total humiliation and, from then on, everything I do I do in a kind of slow motion. I wash slowly, wash my socks slowly, and take a long time to fall asleep. But I'm also confused and angry. If I'd known it was a bad word, would I have dared to utter it in their presence? Why did they not tell me calmly that it was a bad word and never to use it again? Then there's the humiliation of being sliced up like that in front of my younger siblings. And another thing: how in the world am I going to stop being Vickie's friend? When we spin tops he's there; football, he's on one of the teams; having a veld party, he's one of the planners.

Ma and Dad, in the meantime, have put the radio off early tonight and there's no point in even asking them if I can listen to my serial. And before nine o'clock Dad tells me to 'put off that fucking light!' I don't really mind. I don't feel like reading a book anyway because I know what will happen, I'll just read the same sentence over and over again.

All the lights in the house are out and I can hear the clock in the other room ticking the night away. Every now and then there's a sighing sound in the stove as wood and coal collapse into ash.

I lie in the dark and wish I was dead. What if I ran away? I could pack a few things into a sheet and bring the four corners together and tie them to the end of a long stick – I see this all the time in the comics – and make my getaway. Walk a hundred kilometres in any direction until I get to a nice jungle. At night I would make a fire and just heat a can of baked beans over the coals and eat straight from the can. The cowboys do this all the time.

In no time birds would get used to me and come and sit on my shoulder and rabbits would come and chat to me and I would say to them, 'howdy, pardner' like the cowboys say it.

And then years and years would go by and one day I'd be walking about in the jungle with my spear, and my loincloth just covering my bum like a Zulu warrior. And, of course, I'd wear a mask. So there I'd be walking and then I'd hear, 'Help, help!' I'd run to go and help and I'd see a woman and a man both dangling from a cliff face. On top there's a leopard trying to get hold of them, down below are the rapids of a swollen river. I'd take aim with my spear and I'd let fly and get the leopard in the middle of his forehead. He dies and I pull the man and woman to safety. I'm shocked to see who it is; it's Ma and Dad! I pull them to safety and Dad says, 'Thanks.' But Ma is staring at me, staring and staring. And then she says, 'Excuse me, aren't you … aren't you …?'

But before she can finish her sentence, I'm gone.

Ma and Dad aren't talking in their room as they usually do. Dad must be lying awake thinking, 'How jags we must've been to have him!'

Ma's stomach is so big it looks like she's swallowed a whole watermelon. And her sister, Auntie Linda, has come to live with us, to help when the baby comes. Despite all these signs we are still told about aeroplanes coming to drop off babies.

One afternoon Ma and Auntie Linda have a chat and a cup of tea in the lounge.

'Ag, you know,' Ma says, 'when Mabel's baby was born, the little thing was so small that they had to put it in an incubator.'

'Ag, shame!' says Auntie Linda.

Oh my God, I think, what happened to the poor baby? I'm not supposed to be here in the first place, but this is an emergency and so I ask:

'Ma, what's an incubator?'

Ma gives a little sigh and looks at her sister. Auntie Linda gives an uncomfortable shrug. Oh shit, this must have something to do with being 'jags'. But all I want to know is whether the incubator is good or bad for the child.

After a pregnant pause Ma says:

'If a hen lays eggs, in order to get the chicks to hatch they sometimes put those eggs in an incubator. D'you understand?'

'Yes, Ma.'

'Now go and make me and Auntie Linda more tea.'

'Yes, Ma.' I know, I know, I'm being told to vamoose.

I do understand. What Ma was trying to tell me was that an incubator is a place where a baby who was not fully formed in the womb is allowed to grow. But how pathetic! Can they not just come out and say it: we had sex and now I'm pregnant. That means that there's a brother or sister for you growing inside me and in nine months he or she will be born. And that aeroplane I've been telling you about, well, stop looking out for it.

Anyway, Ma gets fatter and fatter as the months go by. One day she calls me from the street where I'm playing football.

'Ma.'

'Go and call Yvonne for me.'

'Yvonne, Ma?'

'Yes.'

'Yvonne Carstens?'

'How many Yvonnes do you know? Yes, Yvonne Carstens.'

I can see it's no use asking why, so I go and call Yvonne, the girl who lives next door. Yvonne is two years younger than I am but, other than that, there's nothing special I can say about her. I see her on the school grounds during break, I spot her coming from the shops with a loaf of bread under her arm, I hear her singing pop songs in the afternoons. That's it. Actually she really likes my brother Derek a lot and sometimes I see her staring into his brown eyes when they have a chat across the fence.

I go next door and the back door's open but I knock on it anyway and she says, 'Come in.'

I go into the bedroom and there she is with Maisie and Bernice and they're chewing violet-flavoured Beechies and combing each other's hair. I tell her my Ma wants to see her and she jumps up and tells her friends she'll be back soon and follows me out.

We get to our house and to Ma and I wait to hear what all this is about. But Ma turns to me and says, 'OK, you can go play now.'

I turn and go outside. But there's a mystery here. Yvonne comes out of our back door. The straps of her sandals are loose and her hair is bouncy as she runs out of our yard. Five minutes later she's back with a small packet in her hands.

When Yvonne is thanked and she leaves, I go and confront Ma.

'Why did you send her?' I want to know. 'I could've fetched whatever she fetched for you.'

'You couldn't have.'

'Why not?'

Ma is beginning to get impatient and she starts calling me by my full name. 'Ag, Christopher, there are some things you're just … I can't explain … it was women's stuff, OK.'

Yvonne! Yvonne is a whole two years younger than I am! She gets the words of songs wrong. She mispronounces words when she reads out loud. She sometimes says 'is' when she's supposed to say 'are'. And there Ma goes and chooses her to run an errand for her while I'm standing around here as if I'm the one who's younger than she is.

Later that same day Ma goes to hospital because she's bleeding too much. Norman's dad, Uncle Johnny Crowie, takes her in his green Peugeot. Dad visits her in hospital two days in a row and comes back and tells us she's OK.

On the third afternoon Ma's back home and I'm playing soccer in the street. Norman's ma calls me and I walk over to her gate.

'Hullo, Auntie Noreen.'

'Tell me, how's your mother?'

Aha! These are the people who have been feeding us with fantastic stories about babies being delivered by aeroplanes. But now, when push comes to shove, when they become desperate, we are the ones they turn to for information. I rise to my full height and I say,

'She's fine, Auntie Noreen. The labour pains are over and she's just relaxing. The baby hasn't come yet.'

The woman stares at me for almost a full minute and then she flings her gate open. 'I think I'll just go see for myself,' she says and walks across the street to our house.

Stamp collecting

IN 1969, WHEN I'M 12 YEARS OLD, I become a stamp collector.

It turns out that I'm also a word collector. For instance, most people in Riverlea, teachers included, don't even know that I'm a philatelist. Ma and Dad know that I've taken up a new hobby called stamp collecting and they're impressed. But when I tell them I'm a philatelist, well, they're totally blown away. Again I'm paraded before uncle, aunt and friends to proclaim my hobby.

'Christopher!'

'Coming, Ma.'

'Tell Uncle Willie what's that hobby of yours.'

'I'm a stamp collector.' I'm playing a little hard to get.

'No, no, that other word.'

'I'm a philatelist, Uncle Willie.'

'Ungh!' Uncle Willie groans and slumps in his chair as if the word has hit him right there in the solar plexus.

When I leave the lounge there's a tiny bit of chuckling in the room, quiet and with just a tiny hint of derision. But later that week on the *Surf Show 21* on Springbok Radio, Paddy O'Byrne asks the contestant:

'For four hundred rand, what is the rarest stamp in the world?'

This radio quiz show is strictly for whites only. But nobody can stop a Coloured philatelist in Riverlea from shouting out the answer.

'The Penny Black,' I scream, while the contestant goes 'uhm-uhm-uhm'.

If I were white, I would've had four hundred rands in my pocket – about ten times Dad's weekly wages. So who's laughing now about philately?

In the first week I have ten stamps. A month later I have over two hundred. Not only do I learn new words all the time, I also learn the names of new countries, places I didn't know existed, that I would never learn about in the classroom throughout my whole school career. Rhodesia and Nyasaland. British East Africa; Tanganyika, the Gold Coast, Upper Volta. In the top left-hand corner of almost all these stamps is the queen of England, her hair neatly arranged, her crown pertly in place. She's always smiling serenely over a lake or a mountain or into the rump of a buck or a wildebeest, seeming apart and yet part of all that she surveys.

I scour the township for stamps, asking friends and their fathers. My ouma takes out of her wardrobe shoeboxes full of yellowing letters from the 1930s and 40s. When she puts them all back their envelopes are minus a right-hand corner. She doesn't mind. But she's curious.

'What's it for, son? School?'

'No, Ouma.'

'Do you get pocket money for them?'

'No, I just ... I just ... it's just a hobby.'

'You go ahead then and have your hobby.'

I go ahead and have my hobby. I've got over a thousand stamps now and getting more every week. But one day something happens to me at school that makes me stop being a philatelist.

I'm in Standard 4 and Melbourne Kelly is my class teacher. It's Monday morning. We're standing in a half-circle at the blackboard and we're learning maths. Today Mr Kelly is teaching us Tens and Units and he has written a few sums on the board.

'If you minus eight from five you take from the tens, not borrow or lend but take, because you are not going to give it back ...'

Maths is not my strongest subject. I like words. I like pronouncing the names of the countries on my stamps. Czechoslovakia is Ceskoslovenski, Spain is Espana, Ireland can also be Eire ...

'Christopher!'

'Sir.' He's looking at me and I hear the end part of his question as he repeats it. I say, 'borrow, sir, I mean lend, sir ...'

He says, 'Come here!'

The boys and girls stand aside to make a path for me. Mr Kelly bends me over and starts whipping me on my bum with his cane. I think that after three or six cuts it will be over. But he goes on and on and on, screaming and whipping. I scream in pain and I hear the gasps from the class and the pee runs freely down my legs and into my shoes.

The rest of the lesson is a blur.

When first break comes I wander out of the classroom and go and sit – at this stage my poor bum is so numb that I can still sit – far away from the football players and the hopscotch players and the boys and girls who count the hundreds of cars that whiz past the school.

But after a few minutes they come, my classmates, to comfort me. I don't really want them there but they sit around me and chat to me and to each other. A tall, fair-skinned boy called Evan says something to me that makes me even more frightened than Kelly's wild attack on me. He says, 'I counted the lashes, it was exactly one hundred.'

For the first time I look at my classmates one by one. I am amongst the weakest in class when it comes to maths. But I do know something no matter that I am a mere 12 years old. And it is this: Melbourne Kelly's attack on me was not a wild, deranged one. He wanted to see what the effects of 100 cuts would be on a 12-year-old bum. All day in class I'm stinking of pee. Kelly doesn't ignore me. In fact he glares at me from time to time and calls me 'Cockeye'.

When Ma comes home from work she says, 'So how was school?'

'Mr Kelly gave me a hundred cuts today.'

Ma doesn't believe me so I pull my pants down, right there in the kitchen, and show her. She bursts into tears. My bum is a swollen mass of pink and blue welts and bruises. Half an hour later it's Dad's turn to see. That night he's fuming and seething and swearing.

That evening doesn't pass normally for the Van Wyks. Dad is cursing and Ma is sobbing and the radio serials and quiz shows have to wait for another day.

Ma says, 'You sit at work thinking that the one place your children are supposed to be safe is in school. But then look what happens? You come from work to find that your children have been half murdered.'

Dad says, 'Tomorrow I'm going to the newspapers first.' And turning to me, 'I want them to take a picture of that arse of yours – for the front page! Then we're off to Coloured Affairs to get the bastard fired. Then we go to the school to tell the principal why the swine has been fired.'

I say to Dad, 'I don't care what happens as long as I don't have to be in his class any more.' I tell Dad about Mr Roper. He's the other Standard 4 teacher. One week Mr Kelly was not in school so we all had to go to Mr Roper's class. During that week John F Kennedy's brother was killed in a hotel somewhere in America. Mr Roper cancelled normal lessons for the day so that we could ask him questions about the whole thing.

'What's the name of his party, sir?'

'The Democratic Party.'

'Who killed him, sir?'

'We don't know yet.'

'Was he going to be president like his brother?'

'Very likely.'

'Were they having elections?'

'No, they were having their primaries.'

'What's that, sir?'

He tells us. Most of the questions come from me and Mr Roper says to me that I have a curious mind.

He's right about my curious mind. He'd be surprised to know that I've often wondered about his own family. The Ropers own an undertaker's in Newclare. Sometimes I walk past the shop and look at the coffins and plastic wreaths inside and wonder what it's like to work with dead people all the time.

But I like Mr Roper and that week in his class was one of my happiest. I tell my father I want to go to his class now – today.

Even though Dad's plan is repeated dozens of times that evening, the next morning there is a slight change. Our first stop is the school, the principal's office. And as it turns out, this is a bad move.

The principal is Mr G. W. G. Lawrence. He is fat, with a double chin, and he sits behind his dark, shiny desk, hunched over his fancy pens and desk calendar like a bullfrog. He's got a little rubber stamp and stamp pad on his desk for printing G. W. G Lawrence on our report cards every term in purple. There are so many of us that if he signed each report himself, his hand would fall right off his wrist, so he gets his secretary to stamp them instead.

This school once belonged to the Afrikaners of Langlaagte who got tired of it and gave it to us. Looking at Mr Lawrence you'd think they forgot to take their principal with them.

He just sits there staring at the trophies that the school won for athletics and football. I get the feeling that he wants to have nothing to do with us, the scurvied and ringwormed and hungry and rude and smelly and squinty. During assembly on Monday mornings he lets the teachers run the show, getting us to sing hymns and telling us what lowlifes we are.

Once a term he wanders on to the playground to stare at us disdainfully from beneath his whitish eyebrows.

He never gets totally angry – like Mr Kelly – just irritated. Then, if he catches you dropping your lunch packet on the grounds, he says, 'you sausage'.

I think he lives in Bosmont. It's a posh township, nicer than most Coloured townships but not as nice as the white suburbs.

When Dad talks to him he stays hunched in his bullfrog position, listening. After two or three sentences from Dad he says 'excuse me' and calls his secretary and tells her to go and fetch Kelly.

While this is happening, he turns back to Dad and tells him to go on. After a while Mr Kelly comes in and Mr Lawrence tells him and Dad to go and sort out this thing in a room somewhere.

The principal tells me to sit down on the chair farthest away from him. I don't mind, it's the one I would have chosen anyway. My arse is still on fire and I sit at an angle. I hear the air wheezing in and out of Mr Lawrence's fat body. I hear the cars zooming up and down Main Reef Road. In the distance I hear a class chanting in Afrikaans, three times: '*Marietjie speel met haar pop*' (Marietjie is playing with her doll).

I wish Mr Lawrence's big black telephone would ring. Then he could talk to someone and I could listen. I've never in my life spoken to someone on a telephone and I would really like to. The whites have phones in their homes but only one or two rich Coloureds have one. Dr Smith also has one because he's a doctor. If you want a phone and you have the money, you have to write on the form: 'My granny is living with us and she's sick and we have to keep phoning the doctor.'

I'm glad that I'll be going to Mr Roper's class. Mr Roper doesn't know about this yet, but he won't mind one extra. He'll remember my questions about Bobby Kennedy.

After a while, Dad comes back into the principal's office without Mr Kelly. Dad says, 'It's all been sorted out and thank you for your time, sir.' They shake hands.

The first thing Dad tells me when we're outside in the sun is this:

'Don't worry, you're going back to Mr Kelly's class.'

I stand dead still and look at him. He smiles and puts his hand on my shoulder.

'But what must I do now?'

'Just walk into his class and sit down. I'm telling you, it's all sorted out.' He says, 'Don't worry, sonny,' and smiles. He says, 'Go now,' and watches me walk into the classroom.

Everybody looks at me because they know something happened in Mr Lawrence's office. Mr Kelly says to me, 'Sit down, my friend,' as if I'm a newcomer from Rhodesia and Nyasaland. (Isn't it funny: the first thing he asks me to do is the one thing I actually cannot easily do – sit down?)

When he asks the class a question I put up my hand, not only because I know the answer but also because I'm worried about getting another hundred cuts. Kelly points to me. I answer and he says to the class:

'Our friend is right.'

I don't like this 'our friend' and 'my friend' business.

That evening I get to hear what happened between Dad and Mr Kelly. Dad tells the story to Ma but, because I'm the main character in this whole sorry saga, I'm allowed to listen too. He says:

'We went into a little room at the back there. There's this Coke fridge and he's standing up against this fridge facing me. He says:

'Mr van Wyk, please … sir … it will not happen again …. Just give me another chance, you'll see …

I imagine his big, shiny forehead getting shinier as he pleads, his glasses, which he takes off because they're slipping down, his horrible breath as he comes closer and closer begging for mercy.

Over the next few weeks I hear my father repeat this story to all who come a-knocking and a-drinking tea or beer. It's like he's that old Nick van Wyk, back in the goalposts again, jumping high, diving low, making the crowds erupt.

'I tell you, the man was ready to go down on his knees and beg,' Dad says.

This is a great victory for Dad.

But actually it's not. And I should know, I see both warring parties every day. And the winner by far is Melbourne Kelly!

Before that week is over, Melbourne Kelly has grown tired of calling me 'my friend'. Which is a relief because I'm tired of it too, of seeing the whole class turn their heads to see what answer his friend is going to give this time.

Melbourne Kelly says:

'I'll kill the lot of you, and if anyone of you goes crying to his parents ...' And when he says that he looks at me.

We do a test and nobody gets all their sums or their words or their facts right. So we all have to get whipped. He says:

'How many cuts should I give you?'

'One sir!'

'Two, sir!'

'One, sir!'

'Three, sir!'

I don't participate in this circus. He notices and says: 'Van Wyk.'

'Yes, sir.'

'How many cuts?'

'I don't know, sir.'

'Give a bladdy number, can't you even do that?'

I shrug.

He says: 'Fucking Cockeye!'

He devises a unique system of punishment. When he announces it, there is a flurry of nervous excitement all around me. He writes the numbers one to ten on pieces of paper, folds them up and puts them into a bowl. We have to nominate a classmate to draw a number and this will be the number of cuts we will all get. He says:

'Who do you nominate?'

'Evan, sir!'

'Judy, sir!'

'Robert, sir, Robert!'

'I pick Ursula, sir!'

Melbourne's half-bald head sways from side to side as he looks at his charges, grinning, king of the Yellow Teeth People.

Eventually, Evan goes up and draws a three. And when it's over we're all writhing in pain and we could've had two or three more lessons.

When it's only one person who has to be whipped he doesn't use the raffle system, but he does have another game. I see it for the first time when my best friend, Keith, kicks around the lid of a polish tin while Mr Kelly is out of the classroom. Mr Kelly comes in and catches him, 'Playing football in my classroom, huh?'

We were about to do a Geography lesson, but suddenly things have taken a new turn and instead we're going to be spectators to 'The hole in the bucket'.

Keith doesn't know how many cuts he'll be getting. Kelly tells him it's a surprise. He bends over with his bum in the air, facing the class so that he can't see what Mr Kelly is up to. Mr Kelly starts singing:

> There's a hole in the bucket
> Dear Lisa, dear Lisa
> There's a hole in the bucket
> Dear Lisa
> There's a hole…

On and on Melbourne Kelly sings, with his cane in his hand. And Keith waits. Then, suddenly, the cane comes down on him – whack! And again and again, six times in all. For kicking about the lid of a polish tin.

Mr Kelly sees himself as one great wit. When he's giving a lesson and there's a knock at his door, he says:

'Kena!'

This is the Sotho word for 'Come inside' and when he says it he looks around at us as if to say, 'laugh at the funny word'. And the class never disappoints.

When it's a shy girl at the door, he decides to tease her a little. He says to her:

'Ja, jakalas.' The poor girl is so shy, she gives a nervous laugh, her face goes red and one leg crosses over the other one, as if she is standing there dying to pee, but she's just embarrassed.

The first time I hear this 'jakalas' thing, and see and hear how wonderfully funny those around me think it is, I am convinced there is a sequence somewhere that I've missed. Maybe when I was out to the toilet one day or absent from school, an amusing event took place. And now everyone laughs and remembers that day whenever Mr Kelly says the amusing word: Jakalas.

But it's not so. 'Jakkals' is Afrikaans for jackal. And by inserting one more syllable into it, Mr Kelly is poking fun at the pronunciation of African people. That's all.

On cold winter mornings he sends Judy to the staffroom to fetch him a cup of boiling water. He'd never send me because he knows I'd spit in it. Judy brings the hot water and he drops an Oxo cube into it. In no time the classroom has the mouth-watering smell of a canteen. And then, while he sips away, he calls me 'Cockeye'.

The best time in Melbourne Kelly's class is the half-hour before closing on Friday afternoons. He gathers us up in one of his semicircles by the blackboard and lets us sing for him. He pretends that he is a great conductor: He divides us into different voices: soprano, alto, tenor, bass. Then he swishes his cane like the conductors do in the movies. His favourite song, which we sing over and over and over, goes like this:

Jy is my liefling
en ek is so bly
Ja die tyd is verby
en jy kom weer by my …

It's about a young Afrikaner woman who is deeply in love. She lives on a farm and her boyfriend comes visiting once or twice a week. Her little heart bursts with longing for this handsome lover and she sits by the window waiting, waiting, waiting for the sound of the hooves of his horse, and then she hears him and looks and sees him in the distance coming, coming to be with his love.

The song means nothing to me, it's about Afrikaans people, like those who beat us up when we go to the post office to buy stamps, people who are called Fanus and Johannes and Koos and who call us '*boesmanne*'.

But what do I care? I sing as lustily as I can because at the end of it the bell will ring and it will be no more Kelly for two days. The monster that Dad tells everyone he has tamed.

One day Mr Kelly tells us all about ants. He says:

'Who can tell me what is unique about the strength of the ant?'

My hand goes up and he nods my way, giving me permission to answer.

'An ant can pick up twice its own body weight,' I say proudly.

Melbourne flings down the book in his hands and comes towards me, baring his yellow teeth.

'You fucking fool!' he bellows, 'you fucking fool!'

The class, true to form, begin their giggling. The show has begun again, a special featuring The Amazing Melbourne and The Pathetic Cockeye. Cliffie Weideman, two chairs in front, turns around and sniggers. I see his big teeth and his glasses and he looks to me like one of the hamsters he keeps in a cage in his backyard.

Kelly goes into a ten-minute rage before he tells the class:

'The ant can lift many times its own weight, not twice, like Cockeye says.'

Melbourne Kelly believes I am something useless, something to be despised, discarded and spat on. But I'm not. I'm a good reader, I'm a good creative writer, and now I even have a hobby. So one day I get it into my head that if he somehow knows about the hobby, he'll change towards me, he'll like me, he'll stop calling me Cockeye. I decide to do something about it.

I choose my moment carefully, when he's not whipping or swearing at somebody. I go up to him and ask him if he has any old stamps.

'What for?' He doesn't seem at all surprised at this request coming from, of all people, me. But he doesn't look at me, just goes on writing in his register or something.

'I'm a stamp collector, sir.'

He nods. 'I see. OK, I do have some stamps lying around at home.' He flicks his eyebrows upwards to make me disappear.

I go back to my desk and do my writing. I am pleased by the exchange I've just had. And I wouldn't dare remind him about the stamps. If I asked him again in six months, he'd tell me that I was nagging. But now he knows: Cockeye, the one he gave a hundred cuts and called 'my friend', has a hobby. There is a philatelist in our midst. Now maybe my life will improve.

Well, I don't have to wait six months. Not even six weeks. Two days later he calls for our attention. He holds up a white envelope and tells the class:

'Cockeye wants me to give him these stamps. Let's see if he can earn them. Come up here,' he says, curling his finger.

I go up, and the circus has come to town yet again. He explains to his excited audience and to me what he has in mind. 'I'll see how well you know your multiplication table and, if you do well, you can have these ten stamps.'

'Yes, sir.' I nod and smile, but I am numb with humiliation and have no wish to participate. He proceeds:

'Six times eight.'

'Sixteen.'

'Four times nine.'

'Twenty-three.'

'Five times seven.'

I say anything that comes into my head, waiting for the torture to pass so that I can go back to my desk and try to be invisible.

But Melbourne Kelly is having fun and he's not about to stop. When the quiz is over, he asks the class:

'How many did he get right?'

Some say one, others swear that it was two, and so they become participants in my humiliation. I find it remarkable that I got any right at all.

Now it's time for the prize-giving.

He shows me each stamp individually and says: 'Do you have this one? This one? This one?'

I say, 'No, sir, no, sir, no, sir.' And with every 'no, sir' his yellow grin gets yellower and yellower.

He says: 'Who also collects stamps?'

Robert Rhoda's hand flies up.

Mr Kelly calls him up and presents the stamps to Robert, while I look on.

Robert is my friend. But after school he walks home with me and shows me the ten stamps. I wish he'd say, 'Let's go into the veld and make a small fire and burn them.' But he does no such thing.

Today, Robert is a pastor in a church, going about spreading the word of God. Does he ever, I wonder, preach about the parable of the stamps? It could be a sermon that goes something like this:

'… so I took the stamps, my brothers and sisters. I took them not realising that I was participating in my friend's humiliation, in his oppression, brothers and sisters. I did not ask for them, I did not earn them. But I was given them to make Mr Kelly's sadism complete, to humiliate and degrade a friend …'

At home I take out my stamp collection. It has grown to over two thousand stamps. I keep them in a shoebox and they look like square confetti. The flowers and the wildlife and the waterfalls and the monarchs and the heads of state of the world.

Many years later I will understand it all. I will learn the words 'colonialism' and 'freedom' and 'pan-Africanism' and the 'Scramble for Africa' and 'Africa for the Africans'. I will learn about how Europe carved up our continent at a meeting in Berlin in the 1890s and said, 'this is for the Portuguese, this is for the British, this is for the Germans, this is for the French …'

I will learn about a Ghanaian called Kwame Nkrumah and how he said, 'this is not for the British,' how Kenya's Jomo Kenyatta, a meter reader in Nairobi said, 'and this is not for the British' and how the Algerians said, 'this is not for the French,' and how a South African freedom fighter called Robert Sobukwe was jailed on Robben Island and was not allowed to talk to fellow-prisoners, but when he saw them passing by his lonely enclosure, he would scoop up a handful of soil and let it trickle through his hands and let his fingers do the talking.

But I would have to wait until after I finish school to know about Africa. White people write our history books and as far as they're concerned, they are the only ones who make history. For the moment I don't know what's going on.

But this afternoon I begin searching through my box of stamps and soon enough I find them, the stamps I told Melbourne Kelly I didn't have. I have them all and, what's more, I knew I had them when Melbourne Kelly asked me. But every time I said 'no sir, no sir, no sir' I could see how pleased he was. For once I have pleased Melbourne Kelly. I look at them now: Upper Volta, Malawi, Great Britain, Malta, Kenya …

I take them all and go to the coal stove in the kitchen and burn them. They curl up and go black and make the red coals flare up for a while. In less than ten seconds I am no longer a stamp collector. Or a philatelist, for that matter.

Here's a postscript.

Seven or eight years later, I'm out of school and working. My sister, Allison, is now in Standard 4 and guess who's her teacher?

When I come home from work one day she has some news for me about Melbourne Kelly. He said to her: 'Ah, another bloody Van Wyk! You'll see what I do with you.'

The old scars burst open and start bleeding. And a few days later I decide to go and seek out Mr Kelly.

'What do you have against the Van Wyks?' I ask him. Now I have grown a moustache and am bigger than he is, and I will not allow him to breathe his yellow-toothed halitosis on to me.

He becomes all fawning and apologetic. But I remember my father's encounter with him in the little room by the Coke fridge all those years ago.

'Leave my sister alone,' I tell him. But Allison was only a pretext for getting me here. There is something I want to say to him.

'Mr Kelly,' I tell him, 'do you remember that lesson about the ant?'

He stares at me blankly and I explain.

'I know a thousand teachers who would've said, 'Not quite correct, Chris, but you're on the right track.' But you spent the next twenty minutes of the lesson berating me, calling me Cockeye. Why? Why did you do those things to me?'

He shrugs and says, 'Look, I'm sorry,' but he isn't really, I can see that.

Nor is Mr Lawrence. The principal is still there, in bullfrog position, staring at his trophies and his phone and his shiny desk.

I have nothing to say to him. He is still distant, aloof, like the white person who I think he wishes he was. He says something that surprises me:

'I see you've become a well-known writer.'

I nod. He's referring to poems in the newspaper, an interview in *The Star* – not much else. They're poems inspired by Steve Biko's Black Consciousness philosophy, which I've recently discovered.

The next thing he says assures me that he's still the same Mr Lawrence I knew all those years ago. He says:

'I see you're concentrating on the blacks in your writing. Why don't you write about your own people, the Coloured people?'

(Well, here it is, Mr Lawrence, and I hope you like it.)

Kathy

When I go to visit Keith I have to pass 81 Colorado Drive. This house looks exactly the same as all the other houses in Riverlea. The only remarkable thing about it is that another Van Wyk family lives here – no relation to us.

There are three Van Wyk kids, Kathy, the eldest, Gregory and Charmaine. Kathy is my age.

When I first meet her she is a pupil at St Theresa's, a Catholic school in Coronationville. These St Theresa's kids all take a bus from Riverlea in the mornings and the bus drops them off again in the afternoons. I think it must surely be the most exciting thing to go to school by bus every day.

One day I stop Kathy and ask her this and she says, 'It's OK.' And shrugs her shoulders and skips away from me because she's in a hurry.

She's a thin girl. She sometimes wears her long black hair in a ponytail or two pigtails. She also wears a fringe but this won't always lie flat on her forehead so she keeps patting it down.

One day I hear Kathy and her friends chanting a rhyme as they spill out of the bus:

'Sister Nunciata
Eats peanut butter'

On an on they chant.

'What does it mean?' I ask Kathy.

'Ag, we're just teasing Sister Nunciata who's a teacher at our school.'

Silly girls.

One day I wait for Kathy to get off the bus, but she's not there. I go back the next day and wait again and there she is.

'You weren't here yesterday,' I say.

'That's because I go to my granny in Coronationville on Wednesdays,' she says. Suddenly she turns to me and says, 'Were you waiting for me?'

'No, no, no, I just passed the bus on my way to the shop and … D'you sleep over at your granny's every Wednesday?'

'Ja.'

'Why?'

'I don't know,' she says with a pat of her forehead, and then, 'because I like her.'

That's a good enough reason for me.

'Every Wednesday my granny makes spaghetti bolognaise for supper because it's my favourite,' she says proudly.

I think Kathy is pretty and I like her because she seems friendly and ladylike. But one day I have my doubts. Her brother, Greg, comes home crying one afternoon.

'What's the matter?' Kathy asks.

'Arlene hit me.'

Arlene is Kathy's age and they attend the same school. But that counts for nothing, it seems, when family honour is at stake. Kathy dons her fighting garb of shorts and T-shirt and prepares to stick up for her younger brother. She grabs Greg's hand and storms off up the road to where Arlene stays. Kathy walks right in and delivers a couple of slaps to Arlene's face and warns her to 'Leave my brother alone!'

That evening Arlene's dad comes to complain at the Van Wyks.

'Is this true, Kathy?' her father asks her.

That evening Kathy's dad makes his daughter and son move a few dozen bricks from one place in the yard to another. This is punishment for slapping Arlene.

Greg sniffles and complains about what he sees as an injustice but Kathy says, 'Don't worry, they don't realise that carrying bricks around just makes us stronger.'

A few months later, Kathy and her brother do some more misbehaving. A group of friends gather at a muddy dam near the mine dump. Everyone dares Kathy to jump in and she does.

'My mother found out because she found my corduroy dress wet, deep in the washing basket where I hid it. I got a hiding.'

One afternoon at school, during playtime, Kathy's aunt comes with bad news. Her granny has died suddenly. She cries for a few days and I feel very sorry for her. When she cries her fringe gets springy and won't sit flat at all. But she's so upset that she doesn't bother to pat it down.

When she feels better she shows me a trick she does with her tongue. 'Watch this,' she says, then she sticks out her tongue and makes it touch her nose.

Kathy van Wyk will always be Kathy van Wyk. She will never change her name to take her husband's. That's because our long-time friendship will later turn to love and we'll get married in 1980, when we're both a few months away from our twenty-third birthdays.

One day, when we begin going steady I go to my ouma's house and pick mulberries and wish Kathy were there so I could share them with her. I write this poem for her:

confession

i would
have brought
you
mulberries
but
they threatened
to explode
their mauve
corpuscles
all over
my
best shirt
so
i ate them

Burning

My Uncle Mellvin wasn't joking when he said he was quitting school. Because I'm starting high school he gives me his school bag, a haversack with M – V – H in black koki for the world to see who the owner is.

'Here, sonny,' he says. 'All you do is you soak it in some water with bleach and then you can write your own initials on it.'

'Inscribe,' I say.

'Huh?'

'Inscribe my own initials.'

'Ja, whatever.'

That's what I do and now it says C – v – W (I've come a long way since K – F – V). Some boys and girls have brand new satchels, shiny brown or toney red with buckles that wink in the sun. A new satchel sells for about fifteen rands and there's just no way my parents could afford that. They had to buy me a new pair of shoes, a shirt, grey trousers. A blue blazer. Even the monograms, which the school supplies, cost four rand each. It's three Latin words around a chain, which very few people know the meaning of. And it gets more and more fuzzy with every trip to the dry cleaner's.

But I don't mind the haversack. You sling it over one shoulder and away you go, with all the Biology and English and Afrikaans and Science and Woodwork and Commerce in the bag, and which you're supposed to get into your head.

I've got lots to do when I get home. Our domestic worker, Agnes, makes us all tea with four slices of jam and bread each. Then we sit at the dining-room table and do our homework. That's the routine.

But one Wednesday afternoon all that routine flies out of the door.

When I step into the house I hear my sister, Allison, five years old, screaming her lungs out. I drop the haversack and go to see what's happening. She's lying naked on my parents' bed, her hands clawing the air, her body writhing. 'Help me! Help me! Help me!' she screams, begging me. 'Please, Kuller, please!'

Right before my eyes I see blisters appear all over her body, and her skin starts flaking off.

Agnes tells me quickly what happened. Shaun, who is seven years old, came home from school and wanted tea and bread. She told him to wait while she took the washing off the line. But he wouldn't wait. He filled the kettle himself, boiled the water, and accidentally tilted it over my sister's body as she came into the kitchen.

I wrap her up in a blanket and Agnes and I run down Flinders Street and across the football field to the Witsco clinic. It takes us twelve minutes but I know by the feel of the blanket that it's a never-ending journey for my sister. She's still crying and moaning and I try to comfort her. And I wish I could take the pain out of her and feel it for myself.

The nurses at the clinic take one look at the moaning mass of blisters in the blanket and phone for an ambulance.

'Get into the ambulance with her,' they tell me. 'Where's your mother? What's her phone number?'

I don't know the number but I do know the name of the factory. We get to Corrie hospital twenty minutes later. As they wheel Allison into Casualty Ma arrives. Her face is white.

'Christopher, who is it?'

'Allison.'

She lifts the blanket to see Allison's face and she sobs.

A few days later, while my sister is recovering in hospital, Ma is on the bus coming from work. In the seat in front of her she can't help hearing this conversation between two other factory-working women:

'Did you hear about this woman whose little girl was so badly burnt?'

'I heard. Shame!'

'What shame? She should be at home looking after her bladdy children instead of chasing money.'

The money Ma is supposed to be chasing is about R16.00 per week.

Many of my friends have decided to quit school and go chasing money, because it's tough at home.

There's my Uncle Mellvin for instance. He said goodbye to Corrie High halfway through Standard 7. And now he's driving a forklift at Wispeco, where they make steel door-frames and window-frames. He hasn't managed to get a job as a clerk, writing things for his boss, after all. He gives my ouma a few rands every Friday and now there's at least bread and milk most days.

My friend, Allan, has long since outgrown being Tarzan of the backyards, and given up being a schoolboy. A couple of months of high school and he makes a bonfire of those Department of Coloured Affairs textbooks and says, 'that's it for me'.

Allan has joined his dad, carving furniture. And he's just as good. They've moved to a better part of Riverlea, where they have three bedrooms and a spacious carport. This is where they have their workshop. There's elbow-room for two and they blow cigarette smoke into each other's faces and curse and crack those unique Walburgh type jokes.

Then there's Vickie Johnson, Liney Vergie, Vivian Basset, Willie Matheson, Melvin Jaftha. They've all been swallowed up by wood factories in Doornfontein and Industria, where the noise of the machines and the banging of hammers and the white boss shouting and cursing above the racket are ear-shattering. They're biding their time, waiting for a friend to get them into the welding trade, which pays a few cents more per hour and where the noise of the machines and the banging of hammers …

'My father says what's the point of education,' they argue. 'I can read and write a little, and count. That's all I need. Let's take, for example, the fly. Why do you have to know how many legs he's got, or how many fucking eyes he's got. All you need to know is how to chase the bladdy thing away from your food, that's all.'

I laugh but I'm not convinced. They sound to me like boys desperately in need of more education.

They come home from work every evening smelling of wood and glue and sweat and with a white man's abuse ringing in their ears. All they seem to talk about these days is how many bottles of brandy they smashed last weekend, clicking their fingers as they tell the story. Like their fathers have been doing for generations before them, they also complain about the boss – 'my *larney*'. Almost without exception they say: 'I prefer the *Boer* to the Englishman. You know why. The *Boer* hates you but the Englishman tells you he likes you but stabs you in the back.'

This is a piece of township philosophy I first heard when I was about six years old and into my apprentice eavesdropping years. And here's another generation spouting the same ridiculous nonsense.

They swap football scores and stories about knife fights and gangsters:

'Hey, you heard what ou Spotty did again at the Matador last night?'

When they do talk about movies it never seems to go beyond the karate antics of Bruce Lee and Jackie Chan. What's the point of watching a movie, they believe, if nobody is brutally murdered in it?

They never have any thoughts about history, literature, current affairs. They live in a triangle of shebeen, factory, football field – well a quadrangle if you include the sleazy Matador in town that passes for a nightclub. There is no world beyond the township. There is no Europe, no America, no Asia, indeed there is no Africa north of our border.

They are the main *ous* of the township. They go to work with kitbags slung over their shoulders. With a little whistle and an elaborate little jog, they jump on to the bus after it's begun to drive away and jump off before it stops. They walk with a bounce now, and with a roll of the shoulders. At work they have a stub of a pencil behind one ear, and behind the other a half-smoked cigarette.

There are many still at school who watch these young factory workers and their antics, who idolise them. They want to drop out of school too and follow their heroes into the factories and the shebeens and the nightclubs of the city.

Dropping out of school is not for me. For one thing I have these ears that stand far away from my head and won't hold pencils or *stompies*. And then there's the problem of books: I like reading them and talking about them to whoever will listen. And while Riverlea High School is not the ideal place, it is the closest I can get to a bookish environment.

But dropping out does cross my mind every now and then.

We are five children now, me, Derek, Shaun, Allison and Nicolette. And we don't know it yet but Russel will be born when I'm well into high school. The family grows but the house remains the same size. And so Derek and I have to sleep in the dining-room. Every night we have to wait until Ma and Dad have finished listening to their radio shows, The *Surf Show 21* and *George and Rita*. Then my brother and I push tables and chairs aside and the couch doubles into two Siamese beds.

There's no sleeping in on weekends like those brothers and sisters in the real bedrooms. On Saturday mornings an endless stream of people come knocking on our front door: Mr Evans wanting his wood and coal money, the dry cleaner's people, women from Soweto bartering vases and ashtrays for old clothes, an old couple to collect a few rands for a *stokvel* club Ma belongs to ... This continues on Sunday morning when the Ebenezer Church elders descend on our home for their tithe – or whatever we can give, and to chide us for not having been in church that morning.

One day, I tell myself as I blink and yawn in the early morning sunshine in our backyard, I shall have my own bedroom and I shall lock the door and go to bed for a hundred hours and nobody, no mother, no father, no silly church elder, will come and chase me out of bed.

Dad had a car once, when I was about five years old. A small blue second-hand Fiat built in the early fifties, driven around for ten years by some white family and then sold to the blacks. Dad had it for less than a week before he slammed it into a horse near the Uncle Charlie's turn-off south of Johannesburg. And that was the last time the Van Wyks owned a car.

There are about two cars in every street in Riverlea. That's about two *skorokoros* for every forty families. Then there are three more per street that are just hopefuls. Uncle Ron next door has one like that. It's a *19-voetsek* Zephyr or Anglia or Ford. You buy it from a white guy you work with. He says the clutch needs a bit of tightening up, you need to adjust the brakes, she's leaking oil somewhere but it's just a drop every hour and once it becomes a pool every half hour you've got problems, and, of course, she needs a new battery and just file the spark plugs down a bit – otherwise she's fine. R350 cash.

Uncle Ron borrows a set of tyres from a friend, just to get her here. Then he takes off the tyres and puts her on four sets of bricks. And she – all cars are female – becomes part of the front garden decorations.

He spends a few weekends in dirty overalls, half of him swallowed up by the bonnet.

When we, the neighbourhood boys, have nothing to do, we go and stand around watching Uncle Ron probe the car's intestines, waiting for the day when the car will actually become mobile. He tells his son, Gregs, to sit in the driver's seat and 'pump' the accelerator. 'Pump! Pump! Don't stop until I say stop, you *houtkop*.'

When Uncle Ron starts swearing I decide I've had enough and I disappear.

The poor car never rides again. The rains come and the car sinks deeper and deeper into the ground and becomes a car tree. The outside begins to rust and then the inside and the windows don't come up any more and the beading falls off and the seats split open and the foam jumps out.

When we come home from school we play in the car. Yesterday Derek drove and we went down to Durban. Today Gregs will be behind the wheel and we're off to Cape Town.

Then one day we get some cigarettes and matches and, to break the boredom of these long journeys, we light up … and half the car burns up.

One Sunday we are invited to my ouma's house in Corrie for lunch. It is somebody's birthday and so all the cousins and uncles will be there. Of course, because we are going out for lunch, Ma doesn't cook that day.

So there we are dressed and ready to go and we wait for some neighbour to fetch us. Dad has arranged for him to do us this favour in return for about five rands.

We wait and wait and wait, while Ma warns us not to go outside and dirty ourselves up again.

'Jesus, Nick,' Ma says, 'look at the time. Go and see where this man is.'

Dad goes off and now we wait for Dad too. Dad comes back without the man with the car.

'What?' Ma says.

'He's bladdy *tieping*.'

I pretend I'm not listening but I am and Dad has just told Ma that our driver had been drinking and is drunk and sleeping it off.

'Oh shit!' says Ma. 'Why don't you go ask George?'

Dad goes off again. And we wait. And we're getting hungry. And Ma says, 'Just shut up and sit still.' There are four of us she has to watch so it's a constant stream of: 'Take that marble out of your mouth. Don't do that. Leave him alone.'

Dad comes back and I hum along with a tune on the radio to pretend I'm not going to listen to what he tells Ma. He says,

'George says no problem. For ten rand.'

'What! His arse. Does he think we're the Oppenheimers?'

These little financial embarrassments are taking place all over Riverlea, with slight variations on the theme. But there is no way my parents will allow me to drop out of school.

Dad is proud of his intelligent eldest boy. And when his friends come to visit he says, 'This is my eldest son, Christopher, he's in Standard 6.'

'Seven, Dad.'

Most times he just doesn't know. Neither of my parents has ever been to an event at my school: sports days, nativity plays, school concerts, awards evenings. I see other parents in attendance all the time and Ma and Dad's indifference bothers me a little. But they are factory workers with six children and their leisure hours are very limited.

However, they seem to make up for it in other ways. I see an advert in the paper for a set of encyclopaedias. The first one is free, the eleven others will be sent to you later and you will have the option of paying them off. I fill in the card and send it away, and a few weeks later they arrive.

I do all this without Dad's permission. But he doesn't mind at all the monthly payments that place an extra burden on his very limited financial resources.

The encyclopaedias are good for school assignments. But, at the risk of sounding difficult and ungrateful, you know what I'd really like? I'd really like Dad to take me and my brothers to a movie, to tell us who Walt Disney is, why we've had two World Wars, to explain what a terrorist is, why Mandela was jailed. Why are we called Coloureds? Why do I have to use the small counter at the post office? What is a 'non-white'? 'If apartheid is a bad thing why does the government allow it – in fact why did they create it?

He never once takes us anywhere or tells us anything. But there are always the encyclopaedias, A to Z. And he even makes a bookshelf at work for them and my growing collection of second-hand books.

Poetry

LET ME TAKE YOU BACK TO A TIME when I was ten years old. I'm in Ouma Ruby's house. It's school holidays and, as usual, I'm spending them there with my cousins and uncles and aunts.

Everybody's out somewhere in the yard or in the street, playing. I'm looking for something to read. Auntie Venecia's school case, fat and creased, is standing in a corner, where it will gather dust for the next three weeks. I flip it open and start browsing and unpacking. I find a school anthology. It's a hardcover book but it's so torn and worn that I have to hold it tight to keep the inside from slipping out.

I go and lie on a bed and I begin to page through it. I can read the poems but I can't understand them and I get more and more frustrated. There are words that I've never heard before: 'alchemy' and 'lore' and 'forlorn'. And then, to make it harder for me, these poems have the same difficult words they use in the Bible.

But then I see a poem that makes me sit up. The poet's name is Stephen Spender and he writes: 'my parents kept me from children who threw stones.' I read it over and over again.

When I go out into the sunny yard where my cousins and uncles and aunts are playing, I notice immediately that the world has changed. Sharon is sitting flat in the sand with her friends playing *gatjie klip*. Her little frock is dusty and there's a loose strand everywhere you look. Denzil and Neil are on top of the shed. They are both barefoot and Neil has a big safety pin keeping up his hand-me-down shorts. They call me to join them. It's nice to be up there because you can be scared that you're gonna fall off, you see things the way you don't normally see them and, when Ouma Ruby is not at home, you can stand on the edge and pee down on to the yard. Venecia is standing by the fence having a long conversation with her pretty friend, Myrtle. If you don't know, you won't notice anything different about them, but there is: they've swapped Alice bands.

I look at all this and I know two things: that Stephen Spender's mother kept him away from the likes of me and my cousins, my uncles and aunts. And I know that I'm going to be a writer one day. I don't think it in my brain but I know it in my heart.

Years later, I'm in matric and we're in English and ready to hear all about Thomas Hardy's *Far from the Madding Crowd*. But our teacher, Mr Bouah, tells us to close our books and to listen up.

'Especially you, Van Wyk,' he says, 'because you are probably going to end up being a writer.'

My secret is out. I sit up and listen.

Mr Bouah explains that he's about to read from a book called *Sounds of a cowhide drum*. The poet is a black South African called Oswald Mtshali and he used to be a messenger who went about on a scooter delivering stuff from one Joburg office to another.

When Mr Bouah reads the poems I'm stunned by what I hear. There's a poem, no longer than six lines, about a boy on a swing wanting to know why his father was jailed. And another one about a black man in a city street who is amused at how a white woman switches her bag to the side farthest from him as he walks past her.

Until now I didn't even know one could write a poem about being black.

A few weeks later, I bump into Fhazel Johennesse. He's a year older than I am, a swarthy, athletic fellow in glasses who's highly articulate. I haven't seen him in ages because he used to be a boarder at St Barnabas College in Western Coloured Township. But now he's finished school and works in town as a computer operator.

He sees me making my way to the shop and he says, 'Hey, Chris! Just the man I want to see.'

'Hey, Fhazel! Howzit, man?'

'Couldn't be better under the circumstances. You do write poetry, don't you?'

'Uh … ja, I do.'

'I thought so. Can I see a batch sometime?'

'Of course, but what for?'

He tells me he works with two white girls. They're young poets too. They have this idea of publishing a book of black and white poets – together in one book. 'It would make one big bold anti-racist statement in this race-obsessed country of ours, don't you think?'

I say, 'Ja.' And even if I did not agree with him, I would still have said ja, just for the smart way he says these things.

'But we want it to be a foursome and I told them about you.'

'You did the right thing,' I say, and he laughs and I'm glad I've made him laugh because he's so clever.

'So when can I see some of your work?' he says.

'Monday. I'll have to find them, they're all over the place.'

'No problem, man.'

So when I get back home that evening I start writing my first poems.

Mrs Wilson

I'M SITTING IN THE LIBRARY READING A BOOK. I look up and see her legs first. She's wearing our school uniform: royal blue blazer, and a deep yellow, pleated skirt.

The yellow skirt I'm looking at right now goes up and up and up, to reveal thighs that make me feel lucky and happy … and a little unhappy all at the same time. The reason why there's so much to see is because this girl's reaching up to the top shelf for the authors whose names begin with A. And this gives me a perfect opportunity to look at B for *boude*.

In books and in the movies the guy goes up to her and asks her if he can lend a hand. They discover that they both love Hemingway – it's always Hemingway – and of course some Emily Dickinson poetry. One of them recites a poem and the other completes it and they laugh. One of them throws in a pun and they laugh again and they look into each other's eyes and you know, you just know.

Well, there's no Hemingway, no Dickinson, nothing, not even a hullo. She walks out of the library with her books and her school bag and I decide to find out who she is.

Desiree Wilson. Standard 8. And the best piece of information of all: she doesn't have a boyfriend. I can't believe it. Light hair, green eyes, shy smile, decent legs. And no boyfriend?

Every afternoon after school, when Desiree goes home, she makes her way to another school. Her mother is the caretaker of T. C. Esterhuysen Primary School, the very school that I had attended not so long ago. I know their house well. It's on the school grounds, a tiny red-brick affair made up of a row of about three rooms next to each other.

Now I have to get to know her. The way most guys do it is to send a passionate letter pouring out their hearts. But this is a dangerous thing to do. Take the case of one Trevor Simons, an Afrikaans-speaking matric boy. He sends a letter to a girl in my class, Denise Carelse, confessing that: 'I have a unstoppable love for you.'

Denise shows the letter to Rose, and they have a good laugh. Then they show it to Kathy, Stephanie, Debbie. The next thing, poor Trevor is taking a brisk walk towards the woodwork centre with a dozen or so classmates when someone waves to him and says, 'Howzit, Unstoppable'. Instinctively, poor Trevor knows that, not only would he never win Denise's love, but that she has been waving about his ungrammatical passion for the world to see and now he is being made to look the fool.

So, much as I like putting pen to paper, and despite the fact that I can probably do it better than most in the school, I decide not to go there.

I know a guy called Claude whose family is friendly with the Wilson family.

'We go to the same church,' Claude tells me. 'And sometimes Desiree comes over to visit on Sunday afternoons.'

'When is she coming again?'

Claude makes sure that she's there the following Sunday. Claude and his two teenage sisters join us in the lounge and we spend the afternoon drinking tea, playing records and chatting. I make puns, crack jokes, sing the songs on the turntable before the bands can do it themselves. Actually I'm showing off big time, and between Trevor 'Unstoppable' Simons and myself there is no doubt who is the bigger fool.

Later, just before sunset, we all walk Desiree home, taking a shortcut through the veld past the old mineshafts. Claude and his two co-operative sisters walk on ahead so that Desiree and I can casually chat. I don't quite come out and tell her about an unstoppable love, but by the end of the day, she knows that she has an admirer. She has also promised to be at the library next Tuesday.

'What for?' she says.

'So that I can watch you take books off the top shelves.'

Her cheeks light up.

On Tuesday afternoon she's at the library and we chat and I touch her hand. I'm officially her boyfriend now and she's my girlfriend. We're going out.

'But my mother must never know,' she implores, shaking her head as she contemplates the consequences of her mother knowing.

'Don't worry,' I say, and kiss her when nobody's looking. I hear somebody flutter the pages of a book.

We bump into each other on the playground and swap sweets. Once, in the English class, we're all quietly getting to grips with a comprehension exercise, when there's a knock on the door. It's usually a pupil with a message so I don't even bother to look up. But my friends nudge me and one or two make that hissing sound that we boys are so infamous for. It's Des, whose face is a dark red.

Going to movies, a restaurant or on a picnic, those things are obviously out of the question. Her mother would never allow it. And neither of us could ever afford it. But we try to see each other whenever we can.

Desiree helps her ma clean the school – the classrooms and the principal's office. Sometimes, when I have a ten-cent piece to spare and the public phone by the rent office is actually working, Des and I arrange that she will be by the phone in the principal's office at a certain time. Then we whisper three minutes of nice things in each other's ears.

One afternoon I decide to be bold.

'I want to come up there and visit you,' I say to her in the library.

'Don't even think about it,' she says. 'Please, Chris. My mother has warned me a thousand times not to go near boys until I've finished school.'

'You mean she knows what I want from you?'

'Uhm-hm.'

'She's perceptive. She doesn't even know me. OK look, let me call you later today in the principal's office. Then you go and ask her if I can pop in and say hullo.'

'But I just told you.'

'That way it would look spontaneous, unplanned. Like I just phoned and the idea came into my head just like that. And we're friends. I'm in matric, you're in Standard 8, you once asked me to help you with some English homework.' With so many kids dropping out of school many parents are impressed to know that so and so is in matric. And I hope this applies to Mrs Wilson too.

Des nods, but she warns me not to get my hopes high.

Later that day we put our – or rather, my – plan into action.

Desiree runs to ask her mother. I wait. Within minutes she's back, breathless. 'My mom says it's OK, come.'

'You serious?'

'Just come before she changes her mind.'

So I take the road back to my old school where Des is waiting for me at the gate. She's nervous.

'We're just friends, don't forget.'

'Hey, don't worry.'

We walk across the playground towards her home, making sure, as we do so, that we have more than the usual space between friends. But her mother is no fool. She's waiting for me. Not pretending to be doing something else while waiting but deliberately waiting. Watching me approach her home, looking at me, my legs, my hands, mostly, of course, my face. I stand still a few feet from her and smile and greet her:

'Good afternoon, Mrs Wilson.'

She says hullo, but continues her inspection of me, her hands on her hips. The message is clear: You want my daughter so I'll decide whether I like you or not no matter how long it takes me.

I don't find this rude at all, I find it funny and I grin. Of course, this also gives me a chance to inspect her in return.

She's taller than her daughter, and her long black hair has not yet gone grey. Everything about her conveys strength. A strong jaw, strong shoulders. Strong arms and legs that scrub classrooms and clean toilets and shine the principal's desk and the trophies in his cabinet. Strong piercing eyes that say: So what? Look at me, a struggling maid at a school, earning next to nothing, but I'm proud.

Eyes that probe me now, searching for something. Then it seems as if she's found what she was looking for. And even more than she had expected – or less, if you like. She breaks into a warm, welcoming smile. She holds out her hand and I shake it. She tells Des to make tea – three cups – and we sit down in their tiny lounge and drink and talk.

Actually, it's not so much a chat as a friendly interrogation. Mrs Wilson wants to know my mother's name and maiden name, my father's name, where my parents lived when they were young. I had already passed her approval test and this was the normal string of questions adults asked. Grown-ups often knew each other in a former life, got married, left the township for another township twenty kilometres away or another city in another province.

In a day or two I get to meet the entire Wilson family. A 13-year-old brother, Shane, and a 9-year-old sister, Janine. Shane teases his sister, Desiree, now my girlfriend, almost non-stop, whether I'm around or not. But I like him anyway. He's living in an age that I have recently evolved from; he has great dreams and plans and schemes.

He wants to build his own bicycle. He's forever zooming off to Zone 2 to see a boy who's brother has a friend who has a front wheel that he wants to sell, and a boy in Zone 1 who has a back wheel. And another who has a frame hanging from a nail on the wall in the backyard.

He does his homework quickly, shouting over his shoulder to anyone who can help him with a synonym, the answer to a maths sum or how to spell an Afrikaans word. Then he tells me something about his sister's past that he knows will embarrass her. And then he's gone, eating his lunch – two slices of bread and jam slapped together – as he skips out to wherever he's meeting his friends.

There is also a Mr Wilson. He's a drunk. He works at Afcol, a furniture factory less than fifteen minutes' walk away from his home. When he isn't working he sits or lies down in a room, alone, drinking. He goes for the cheapest alcohol available, because he's got no choice, wine that cost sixty or seventy cents a bottle. As soon as he gets thoroughly drunk he begins his ravings against the family. Sitting in the lounge two rooms away from him, I try to make out what the man is saying. It's all one long string of incomprehensible invective, with key recognisable common or proper nouns.

To me all of this is much like baby talk; outsiders can never make any sense of the baby's toothless gurgling syllables, but a member of the family will turn to the child and say, 'No, you can't have any more sweets.' Shane laughs at his father's noises, Desiree gasps and Mother Wilson shakes her head in disgust.

One day Desiree and I are sitting in the lounge chatting while the drunk Mr Wilson is cursing the afternoon away in his dark parlour. A month has gone by and my status has gradually changed from 'stranger who likes our daughter' to 'frequent visitor who will surely one day marry Des'. I have, in the meantime, become accustomed to the drunken ravings from two doors away and it has the same effect on me as the constant traffic on Main Reef Road nearby or the sounds of the birds in the trees – I just stop hearing it after a while and it becomes background noise.

But obviously this is not so for the Wilson family. One Saturday afternoon I'm telling Desiree about how badly our History teacher teaches History:

'For the entire double period he reads aloud to us from our History textbook, the word is 'dictates', and we have to write it all down, word for word. I don't see the sense in that ...'

Des stares at me with her large green eyes, horrified. If I could get others to feel this way about bad teachers, I could start a revolution at Riverlea High. But it's not at all about anything I've said. She bursts into tears, jumps out of her chair and runs to her mother.

'Mummy, Mummy, go and talk to Daddy,' I hear her sob in another room. 'Tell him to stop saying those nasty things.'

What nasty things? I wonder. Mrs Wilson drops her rags and brushes and flounces into Daddy Wilson's den to sort out 'that stupid man'.

Desiree won't tell me what he said because if I haven't heard, then it's less embarrassing. But I want to know and I insist and eventually she tells me. He said, in Afrikaans:

'That little fellow sitting there in my lounge courting my daughter should just get it over and done with now and take her to bed and make her pregnant and marry her and get done with it. Hallelujah!'

My translation gives it respectability. But even in its crude original Afrikaans, I still find the whole thing funny.

'Hey, Des, don't worry about it. He doesn't even know what he's saying; I'm telling you, it's that wine that he's drinking in there.' Not to mention that this wine should have been bread, rice, *mealiemeal*, tea and sugar for the family.

Once or twice Mrs Wilson asks me for a loan. 'Just a rand or two if you have, please Chris.' I'm desperate to help this woman but I never have money. A rand rarely finds its way into my pocket.

One Thursday afternoon Mrs Wilson comes to chat to me in the lounge. She has a look in her eyes that tells me this is an issue that has been on her mind for a few days.

'Chrissie, you coming around on Saturday?'

I'm puzzled but I answer yes. I always come to visit Des on Saturdays.

'Then I'm officially inviting you to supper on Saturday,' she says.

I'm still puzzled. Since coming to date her daughter, I've always been made to feel very welcome here. Bread and jam with tea, coffee, black or white, a plate of food on those odd days when I'm there until late. So what's the difference? It's made clear in her next sentence.

'On Saturday I'm cooking the Wilson special.'

I glance at Des for a clue. She's sitting back in her chair smiling, but giving away nothing.

'The Wilson special?'

'Trotters.'

I get it now. This woman is under the very mistaken impression that the Van Wyks have never eaten soul food. Well, I have salivated at many a dinner table over pap and *morogo*, samp mealies and beans (affectionately called Cowboys and Crooks), tripe and butter-beans, even, once or twice at my ouma's, a bowl of rice sprinkled with cinnamon and sugar when there was nothing else for supper.

'Jislaaik! I can't wait.'

Mrs Wilson gives me the warmest smile, and squeezes my arm as she passes me on her way out.

One day during break at school, Des comes up to me.

'If you come up this afternoon, bring your poems,' she says.

'Why?'

'My mother wants to see them.'

Why? I wonder. I'm wary of showing my poems to Coloured people over thirty. They come in two categories: those who cannot understand what I'm getting at, and those who get the message immediately but don't like what I'm saying and advise me not to get involved in politics or I will end up on Robben Island.

But I walk into the Wilsons' lounge with my file tucked under my arm. Mrs Wilson appears a few minutes later, taking a break from sweeping classrooms. She greets me and asks, before anything else, 'Did you bring your poetry?'

I hand her the file, but she shakes her head and refuses to take it from me.

'I don't want to read it, I want you to read it to me.' And she plonks herself in an armchair opposite me. I have no problem reading my poetry to anyone who cares to listen. I don't have to suck a sweet first or drink some water or clear my throat or try to get my hands to stop shaking. The poems are filled with, if not a hatred, then at least a sharp loathing for white people. My poetry is brash and full of black consciousness pride. There are little puns and show-off words and jokes.

To my pleasant surprise Mrs Wilson is in neither of the two above-mentioned categories. She laughs and gasps and smiles and even calls for an encore of one short poem:

The Chosen

Some people it seems
Have to carry their crosses
For the rest of their lives.

Others think they can
Get away with it
Simply by throwing theirs
Into ballot boxes.

'Couldn't have said it better', she says, smiling proudly. 'Keep it up.' And then she goes back to her dusting and scrubbing.

The more I see of Mrs Wilson, the more I like her. Her strength in dealing with her desperate circumstances, her cooking (not so much cordon blue as 'this'll have to do'), her patience with the drunk in the parlour, who growls all day long and probably stinks too.

But there is something about Mrs Wilson that I know I'm never going to get used to. Her love for the Church. It's the New Apostolic but I don't care how new the thing is, I'm just not interested.

On their sideboard, in a smart frame, is a portrait of a white man. Why a photo of a white man? This is, after all, apartheid South Africa where whites have pictures of whites in their homes, Coloureds of Coloureds and Africans of Africans. This white man watches me kissing Des and trying to put my hands where she keeps telling me I shouldn't.

'Who's this guy?'

'He's our apostle ... of our church.'

I look closer. There's a name underneath. Van Biljon or Visagie or Van der Merwe. An apostle? It doesn't make sense to me. My idea of an apostle is a guy with a long, grey beard, in sandals, who lived near a well with lots of daughters a long time ago in the Bible. This guy is clean-shaven and very likely uses 'Whites-Only' toilets and entrances to shops and government buildings and lives in a white suburb in South Africa.

'Are you serious?'

Desiree clicks her tongue but I want to pursue this subject. I ask a string of questions like:

D'you like him? He is after all a *Boer.*

Have you ever met him?

What does an apostle do?

What would he do if a black and white couple fell in love? It's against the law remember?

In the end I take the photo of Apostle Fanus Visagie (or whatever) and place it in such a position that he can have an even better view of what Desiree and I are doing when her mother is out scrubbing the classrooms.

Mrs Wilson gets it into her head that I need to get involved in the religious aspects of their lives. One day she asks me to accompany Des to church. There's no way I can get out of this one so I agree.

I wake up early Sunday morning, wash and take a walk up to their house. Des is ready and waiting for me. We have some coffee and she and I take a brisk walk to the train station, which fortunately is not too far away from Des's home. We board a train and get off in Bosmont, twenty or so minutes away, and make our way to the New Apostolic Church there.

When we eventually sit down in our seats, three hours have elapsed since I woke up. I could have been eating a *koeksister* and drinking coffee, I think with a yawn. But, for this brown-haired, green-eyed, scented, God-fearing creature sitting beside me I would do anything – for her mother.

The service is much like most services: we listen, we read a verse or two from the Bible. The pastor explains what it all means. We get up at certain intervals and sing songs of praise to the Lord, we sit down and listen some more. We pray. I get fidgety, Des frowns at me, I try to pay attention, my mind drifts, I look at hats, napes of necks, haircuts. A child on a mother's lap, judging by his own pushing and pulling, has also had enough of this.

After an hour and forty minutes, the sermon comes to a glorious end. I made it! I smile at Des. God loves us, she loves me, I love her. Outside the sun is shining.

But something's wrong. Nobody's getting up to go! Then I see why. Some elder has appeared on the stage and tells us that the sermon will now be presented in Afrikaans, 'for the benefit of our Afrikaans-speaking brothers and sisters.'

'We understood everything,' I whisper to Des. 'Let's go.'

But she shakes her head and tells me, in a desperate whisper, to shush.

Three months later I break up with green-eyed Des. Maybe to avoid one day getting married in English and Afrikaans – by an apostle from Boksburg.

Des is so tearful that I just want to get away. She says, 'Why, Chris, why?'

'I'm in matric, Des. Exams are around the corner.'

'So, can't we continue going out after the exams?'

I don't want to answer that. Instead I turn around and make my way home.

The enterprising Shane has, in the meantime, built his bike. Two days later he rides over to my home with a letter in his pocket for me.

> Dear Christopher
>
> The break-up between you and Des came as a shock to me. It broke my heart to see my daughter's heart broken in so many pieces. You were my son, my friend, and you did this to our family. I believed that you were from a decent family, I thought the world of you. But I was deceived, totally deceived.
> Exams, hah! Tell me another one.
> You have hurt people. I hope that you learn one day how wrong you have been.
> I wish you good luck in your exams, and with your new girlfriend.
>
> Yours sincerely
> Mrs Wilson

A gentleman

FOR MY LAST TWO YEARS OF SCHOOL a teacher called A. P. G. Kirk teaches us Afrikaans. During these two years I never once see this man laugh or smile or crack a joke. Or encourage or praise any of us.

During this time I see him every weekday, and every single day he wears exactly the same clothes, light grey pants and a slightly darker grey jacket.

He has curly hair, always cut in a short-back-and-sides. He is always clean-shaven. He stands in front of the class, pigeon-toed and *stokstyf*, giving his lesson. He allows no discussion, no jokes, no debates, no interesting little anecdotes. He sticks resolutely to the curriculum as supplied by the white apartheid government to the Department of Coloured Affairs.

One day during a poetry lesson he mentions, because he has to, a group of Afrikaner writers called Die Sestigers (The Sixty-ers). My hand flies up. He says, 'Ask your question.'

'Why did they call themselves Die Sestigers, sir?'

'Because they wrote their poetry and novels in the sixties.'

The class swallows up this crap, but I don't. At this point in my life I've just begun to write my first poems and I know one or two things about the Sestigers. What sets them apart from their literary peers is not *when* they write but *what*. They are, in fact, a group that rejects the Afrikaner government's racist apartheid policies and they say so quite clearly in their prose and their poetry.

The poet, Breyten Breytenbach, is one of them. He leaves the country in the early sixties and goes to live in Paris, where he meets, falls in love with and marries a Vietnamese woman. One day Breyten tries to bring her home to South Africa but the government refuses to let him because she is not white. In 1975 Breyten comes home without his wife, but he comes disguised as one Christian Galaska. He has set up a clandestine organisation called Okhela, whose aim is to overthrow the government and he has come to set his plans in motion. But he is arrested (in the very year Kirk teaches me Afrikaans) and sentenced to nine years in jail.

Andre Brink is another Sestiger. His book, *Kennis van die Aand* (Looking on Darkness) is the first Afrikaans novel to be banned – obviously because it deals with issues of apartheid and this makes the Afrikaners uncomfortable.

Then there is the late Ingrid Jonker who, the story goes, walked into the sea after her father had disowned her for her anti-racist stance in her poetry.

When my first efforts at poetry appear in the *Saturday Star*, many of my teachers, such as Mr Bouah, encourage me. But one Monday morning Kirk – while glaring at me with loathing, in a unique show of emotion – tells the class that there are dunces all over the place who want to be poets and just who do they think they are?

I've always thought that the school was the one place in our bleak and monotonous township where one should be encouraged to do creative things, such as dance, play a musical instrument, write poetry. Kirk obviously doesn't think so. For many years I asked myself why he was so angry at me for penning some verses. But I know now why: I was spitting at his gods. His white Afrikaner gods.

Kirk is a good, obedient Coloured teacher who carries out orders to the letter. He probably has a BA or BEd and has studied some Nederlands, the Dutch that the Afrikaners read when the English do Latin or Shakespeare. He's looking forward to becoming a principal one day, and finally a school inspector. He will have a housing subsidy and will buy a new car every two or three years. He will drive around to the various Coloured schools. He will make sure that the principals have mounted on their walls the government-issue portrait of the latest president. He will make sure that no Bantu poem is sneaked into the curriculum or any mention made of that terrorist, Mandela.

If there should ever be a medal for *amperbaasskap*, for carrying out the white man's orders with diligence and pride, it should have Kirk's *aan die vrek* face embossed on it. On the other side it could have his arse being kicked by a white foot – or my foot, if the master is too busy.

One day Kirk has an announcement to make to the class. He stands before us and in his usual deadpan style (this includes face, voice, and clothing) he says the following, in Afrikaans:

'On Monday I want each and every one of you to bring me twelve rands. With this twelve rands I shall buy thirty Afrikaans dictionaries. One for each of you. The Department of Coloured Affairs cannot supply us with these dictionaries so we shall simply have to buy them ourselves.

'I know what half of you have already decided to tell me on Monday morning: "Sir, my mother's broke, sir, my father's unemployed, sir, my mother says is it OK if we pay it off at two rand a week?" I want to hear none of that. All I want is to see twelve rand times thirty on my desk on Monday morning.

'And just so you know, these dictionaries will be used by those matrics who come after you and those who come after them etc. That means they will become the property of Riverlea High School. You may leave.'

My utter loathing for Kirk knows no bounds. On the way home from school I ask my classmates what they think about his ultimatum. Alvin doesn't really mind bringing the twelve rands. His family runs a shebeen and this weekend will see many notes and coins of all denominations filling his mother's kitty. Kathy, my girlfriend, is from a family of only three kids. Both her parents work and her father has a fairly cushy job at an insurance company. And so on and so on.

I come from a family of six kids. We don't go hungry, but twelve rand is over half of my mother's weekly wages. We run out of toothpaste on Thursdays, we wash with Sunlight laundry soap most days of the week, we wipe our arses with newsprint from about Wednesday, we butter only one slice of the bread in a sandwich – until we run out of butter altogether. We have bread and jam for lunch every single day …

Twelve rand for a stupid dictionary is going to put an even bigger strain on already scarce resources. For a dictionary that next year's matrics will get free of charge.

I convey Kirk's ultimatum to Ma. She shuts her eyes and shakes her head and says, 'My God!' But in the end she hands over the twelve rand. The alternative is that I will face the next few months until the end of school being maligned by Kirk.

At the end of the year though, I have my revenge – sort of. I steal back my dictionary. It is an injustice that my dictionary should become the property of Riverlea High School.

But I don't use this dictionary very often. It sits on my bookshelf at home full of its Afrikaans words and definitions – *met n bekvol tande* (this is an Afrikaans idiom 'with a mouthful of teeth', which means sitting there with nothing to say). The one definition of a word that it's going to take me a long time to forget goes something like this:

Heer: *(n) wit man.*
Translation:
Gentleman: a white man.

And for this my parents had to pay twelve rands.

One of my first encounters with a gentleman happens like this. One day I'm sitting at our dining-room table, reading a book. My brothers and sisters are probably lying down in the room, or are out in the street playing some night-time game under a lamppost or somewhere at a neighbour's home.

Ma is lying on her bed reading a novel. Dad is in the bathroom washing. From where I sit I can actually hear the splashing of the water. I can smell Ma's smoke from her cigarette as it drifts out of her bedroom. And, because our front door is wide open, I can hear noises in the street, familiar voices laughing or calling out names of neighbourhood children I have known all my life.

I hear a car screech to a halt outside a gate. Because our houses are so close to each other, it could be any one of six neighbours about to get a visitor.

Our gate swings open. That screeching car and the slamming car door are connected to our house, to 13 Flinders Street. From gate to door is a mere five seconds. And then he materialises: a white policeman in his blue uniform. He is young, blond and red in the face.

He flies into the lounge and demands of me, in Afrikaans: 'Where's Van Wyk?'

Technically all the Van Wyks living in this house are Van Wyks. But I know what he means and I'm not going to slow down his important mission.

'My father's in the bath,' I reply in Afrikaans.

Before I can say anything else he goose-steps his way to the bathroom door and bangs on it loudly with the flat of his hand, for maximum volume.

'Van Wyk, get the fuck out of the bath now!' he says. At the same time, he glares at Ma, who is now sitting up in bed in her room, gasping in shock.

'Who's there?' Dad calls.

'Constable Vermeulen.'

'What's the problem, sir?' Dad inquires, amid hurried splashing and the thumping of feet jumping out of the bath.

'Just get out of the fucking bath, man!'

In a minute my father is out of the bathroom, dressed, but his hair still wet. The young Boer, shorter than Dad, looks up at him and exclaims: 'Oh fuck, you're not fucking Sergeant van Wyk!'

He goose-steps out of the house. As he passes me, I burst into derisive laughter. But that is really all I can do to register some disgust.

There is a Sergeant van Wyk who lives five doors away from us. And, of course, he is, like my father, a Coloured. Not a white man and therefore not a gentleman.

I hated all whites, gentlemen or not – and this is really just the beginning of a long relationship of hatred. We're about seven months away from June 16 1976, when this hatred will spill out in the form of violence never before seen in our country.

The apartheid government has thrown all African people into a ditch, a hellhole, a cesspit. The Coloureds, on the other hand, have been thrown into that selfsame cesspit, but upside down with our faces submerged in the shit and the whites are holding us by our little brown ankles saying: should we or shouldn't we? The Coloureds are holding on for dear life saying, we may not be white but we're not quite down there with the blacks. So, by their Coloured logic, they're in the middle, a unique position of 'not quite as good … but slightly better than'.

Coloureds come in all shades, from black as pitch to white as milk, and they go through life seeing each other in these little colour variations. They say things like: 'He's dark-skinned but quite handsome'. 'She hasn't got straight hair but she's quite pretty. Actually her hair isn't that bad, it's sort of on the straight side.' 'They're getting married, but he's dark and she's dark so imagine what their children are going to look like.'

Racism is of course not unique to the Coloured community. A domestic worker who lives in Soweto gives me an amusing perspective. When people there – neighbours, friends, relatives – have an argument and start smashing up each other's property, a bystander might remark that 'they are fighting like Coloureds'.

But the racial remark I find the most telling is when Coloureds are called *amperbaas* – almost the master. An Afrikaans word, used by Africans to describe Coloureds.

Books and more books

I'M FREE! I FINISH SCHOOL AT THE END OF 1975 AND I'M FREE. There's no money for college or university but that doesn't bother me at all – I'm free! I'm free of the Kirk and Kelly life (the KAK life). The life of 'no long hair in my class', of 'no talk of politics', of 'don't ever think you'll be a writer', a world where the men and women call each other *meneer* and *juffrou* and bow to the racist flag and sing lustily the racist national anthem and accept all the lies in the history books and love being a Coloured.

In a way, my real education begins now. And despite what Kirk and others have said, I am determined to be a writer.

I comb Joburg's second-hand bookshops buying frayed and tattered copies of a world that fascinates me with every page I turn. In J. D. Salinger's *The Catcher in the Rye* I watch Holden Caulfield watching the adults do very adult things and I cannot believe what we both see.

In Bernard Malamud's stories in *The Magic Barrel* and in *The Fixer* I see joy and sadness turn into one blurry emotion.

Albert Camus's *The Outsider* makes me uncomfortable with its unflinching honesty.

I even read books that I only half-understand: Dostoyevsky's *Crime and Punishment*, *Voss* by Patrick White. But I'm no less fascinated.

These are names and titles and fictional worlds never once mentioned by my teachers. Why?

The Johannesburg Public Library is now open to all black people (Coloureds, Indians and Africans) and I become a regular visitor, smelling the books, old and musty, a familiar smell to many white people I imagine – though many smelled these books when they were new and apartheid was fresh.

I make a fascinating discovery: some seats, once reserved for white bums only, are in fact time machines and this is how they work: I fill in a card requesting a title that is not on the shelves. I hand it to one of the white women in glasses and flat slippers and off she goes. I remain seated in my time machine but I imagine that she goes down, down, down into the cavernous underground warrens, where once white rabbits, but now hares of all colours, have built an alphabetical order of underground rooms.

There the fleet-footed, flat-slippered one finds what I want to read. I page through *The Purple Renoster*, then I read *The Classic*, *New Coin*, *Izwi*, *Contrast*, *Wurm* (Worm).

These are all South African literary magazines from a bygone age. I've never seen any of them in our home, on a teacher's desk, in our local library. But lately I've been reading about them in books and modern literary magazines. And I'm dying to find out what's in them.

The stories behind these magazines are as interesting as the ones inside them. *The Classic*, I learn, was started in the early sixties by a young journalist/writer called Nat Nakasa and other writers from Soweto. They get together one Sunday morning and decided to launch a magazine. They're not sure what to call it until someone says, 'Let's name it after this place where we're sitting in right now.' This happens to be a dry cleaners called The Classic. But others dispute this. The Classic, they say, happened to be a shebeen, but was jokingly referred to as a dry cleaner's by the regulars. When asked by your wife or children where you were off to, it was better to say, 'Just popping in at the dry cleaners.'

Nat Nakasa would know the right version because he was there. But he's no longer around when I first encounter his magazine. On 14 July 1965 he jumped out of a seven-storey, New York building and plunged to his death.

The New York police investigating the incident found in his possession not a passport but something called an exit permit – a creation the likes of which very few inventive writers could have dreamt up. In 1964 Nakasa had received a scholarship to study in the USA. The apartheid government refused to give him a passport. But they did confer on him this exit permit, a document that, in effect, said, 'Get out of our country and don't ever come back.'

The pain of knowing that he could never return to his beloved country became unbearable for the young writer. So he decided to die instead.

He was 28 years old. I was eight.

These magazines have on their pages the first words of many a South African writer who would become famous in the years to come. Here are some of the first short stories of Nadine Gordimer, who would go on to win the Nobel Prize for Literature in 1991. Alan Paton is here, already famous for that epiphany of a novel, *Cry the Beloved Country*, about black people and white living in pain, finding it in their hearts to forgive. Athol Fugard, whose plays will travel to the world even as they go to the heart of apartheid. There's Peter Abrahams, author of several novels. He grew up in the famous township of Fietas but has long since left South Africa, driven out by apartheid, and living in Jamaica.

And while we're in Time Machine mode, may I skip ahead about eighteen years to the 1990s.

I work for the South African Committee for Higher Education (Sached). We develop and publish educational material for black students who have been denied access to education because of apartheid.

To advertise these materials we decide to produce a poster, which we plan to put up in schools, bookshops and other places where young people gather. Rap music is all the rage and the best of all the rappers is a Cape Town-based band called Prophets of the City. This gives me an idea for the poster. Prophets of the City prancing about in their colourful costumes in a typical classroom singing a rap song about books and the value of reading and learning.

'Yebo!' My colleagues all love my idea and I am tasked with getting the Prophets and a photographer into a classroom.

The Prophets are up in Joburg and they say no problem. The photographer says no problem. Now to find a classroom; the easiest part of my assignment – or so I think.

I phone my old high school and the secretary puts me though to my old principal. I tell him who I am and, despite the fact that my poems have by now appeared all over the world – including the set work anthology that his current matrics are studying, he shows no recognition. All he says is *ja, meneer*, and I feel my stomach turn. I tell him that I'd like to use one of his classrooms tomorrow afternoon for one hour.

'We're promoting reading in the schools, Mr Snell.'

After a long pause he says, 'I'm not sure if I can allow that, sir. But if you come and see me next week, I will let you fill out an application form, which I will send to the Department of Coloured Affairs. And if they say you may use the classroom, then I will let you do so.'

'How long do they take, Mr Snell?'

'Only about six weeks. Not too long.'

'Did you hear me say I need it tomorrow, Mr Snell.'

'I'm sorry, sir ...'

'Never mind.'

When I put down the phone Mandela has been released, I've been beaten up by cops, I've been to the Soviet Union, France, Germany, Nigeria, Holland. I've been in fights about sexism and racism, I've fallen in love and got married and am raising a family and, in a few years, I will see the dawning of a new South Africa. But in a place where I spent twelve of my formative years they haven't moved at all.

Sleeping on the ninth floor

I AM OF THE 1976 GENERATION OF POETS.

In the 1950s there was a school of writers known as the '*Drum* school', so called because almost all of them had, at one time or another, written for *Drum*, a monthly magazine that catered mainly for black readers – probably the only one in a world of apartheid where everything was produced for the benefit of white people.

These writers included Can Themba (famous for his shocking psychological thriller of a short story called 'The Suit'); Es'kia Mphahlele who wrote the autobiography *Down Second Avenue*, which is still worth reading today, Casey Motsisi, Bloke Modisane, Henry Nxumalo, Richard Rive.

These writers – except for the sensible and respectable Mphahlele – spent their days boozing in Sophiatown shebeens, making merry and hurting terribly inside from the pain of apartheid and the *babalaas* of the brandy, and writing passionately about both.

Their writing was brash and boozy and filled with the heady smells of shebeens and fast living and open sewers and the horrible, decades-old stench of racism.

In 1960 the apartheid police shot dead sixty-nine anti-pass protesters outside a police station in Sharpeville near Johannesburg. I was a few months away from my fourth birthday.

The government banned the ANC and the PAC. It also banned the writers and their books. Mphahlele left the country to go and live in Nigeria – from where he travelled the world. Can Themba died from too much drink in nearby, but faraway, Swaziland. Bloke Modisane died in the eighties in Germany. And so on and so on.

From 1961 the writing had not quite died but had certainly dried up. Then comes 1976. And with the fire and the blood in the streets of Soweto, the ink begins to flow too. Suddenly there are writers everywhere you look. And among them is one Chris van Wyk, learning, struggling, just a part of the crowd.

There are poetry readings everywhere. I read my poems at schools, I read them at homes in Soweto and at the Regina Mundi Church there, in community halls in Lenasia. Black consciousness poetry, shouted out from stages with the clenched fist salute as a kind of customary punctuation mark.

At about this time I write what would become my most famous poem. I have no recollection of actually sitting down and writing it. But I do recall that I write the poem on the same day as I first read it. And I read it at a poetry evening at the United States Information Service in Commissioner Street, Johannesburg. The small auditorium is packed with poets, playwrights, painters and lovers of literature and the arts, as well as the disciples of Steve Biko, the father of black consciousness. For many, this gathering at the USIS has become a regular occasion. For me, not yet twenty years old, it is brand new and exciting.

There is a good, positive buzz in the air. The simple fact that there are black and white people together means that we have already committed a South African sin. And then there is still the poetry to come: anti-racist, black consciousness, anti-government, screams from the heart against all and everything the National Party has worked hard and jailed and killed for.

I read three poems and the new poem is one of them.

The audience reaction unsettles me. First they shift uneasily in their seats, then they sit back gasping as if they are not sure what they're hearing. Then they decide that they know what they've heard but that I might want to withdraw what I just said. Then giggles and laughter and shouts of 'Viva!'

Even at this stage I feel the poem is incomplete and decide to work on it some more later on. But before I know it the poem is published in some literary magazine and I'm advised by writers and academics who know better to leave it as it is.

Months later I discover an interest in the poem from an unusual quarter: the police are a captive audience.

I'm unemployed and smoking cigarettes and drinking beer, months, years after having finished school, in what I believe is an ongoing celebration of being free of that tightly knotted noose called the school necktie.

I come home one afternoon from visiting friend and fellow poet, Fhazel, who lives in Bambesi Street, twenty minutes' walk away on the eastern side of Riverlea. Waiting for me on the dining-room table is a note from the security police, the first of many. It says:

> Chris van Wyk, please come to John Vorster Square tomorrow 14 July at 12.00 noon. Ask for Captain Sons.

What to do now?

I know all about Captain Sons. He's a Coloured security policeman, based at John Vorster Square, in Market Street. The security police, as their name implies, deal with cases of state security, such as those terrorists and communists who are planning to overthrow the government (which lately I have begun to call 'the regime'). At the moment I'm planning no such thing. In fact, at the very time that I'm wanted at John Vorster Square I have an appointment with my friends, Keith, Roland and Fhazel. Beer and a few games of darts at the Fountains Coloured and Asiatic pub, two kilometres outside Riverlea in Langlaagte.

The cops, it seems, have anticipated that I would choose to go somewhere else for the day rather than spend it in the company of Captain Sons. Detectives Harendien and Harrypersadh come to fetch me as I'm putting new flights into my twenty-two-gram darts.

'So we got you, Van Wyk,' one of them says as they drive me to John Vorster Square. 'You do realise, now that we have you, we can do with you what we want?'

'Mm-mm,' I say, not at all scared.

Fifteen minutes later we drive into the underground parking at John Vorster Square, a huge, fifteen-storey, glass and concrete building on the edge of the Joburg city centre. In 1971 Ahmed Timol returned from Moscow to help build the freedom movement in South Africa. In October the security police arrested him and took him to John Vorster Square. A few days later he came hurtling to his death from one of its ninth-floor windows into the street below. The fall was so severe that it gouged out one of his eyes, crushed a testicle and dislodged all his fingernails.

Timol's death and that of other anti-apartheid detainees, inspires this poem.

In Detention

He fell from the ninth floor
He hanged himself
He slipped on a piece of soap while washing
He hanged himself
He slipped on a piece of soap while washing
He fell from the ninth floor
He hanged himself while washing
He slipped from the ninth floor
He hung from the ninth floor
He slipped on the ninth floor while washing
He fell from a piece of soap while slipping
He hung from the ninth floor
He washed from the ninth floor
He hung from a piece of soap while slipping

'You know which floor you're on, Van Wyk?'

Although I can guess, I shake my head.

'The ninth floor.' He gives me a long, serious look, waiting for something to click. But I don't let on. Instead I shrug. He leads me to the windows. There are dozens of squares of windows, all burglar-barred, plus they are given an added sieve of wire so that the street down below and the Chinese restaurants, barber-shops and scrapyards are all shaded out.

The cop puts his fingers through the mesh and tries to rattle it.

'Tight, hey?' he says.

I nod.

'So why then,' he turns to me, 'do you write poems about people falling from the ninth floor?'

I think for a moment, as if I have no idea what he's talking about. 'Oh, you're talking about that poem of mine?'

'You remember now?'

'That's *fiction,*' I tell him, glad to be able to clear up this misunderstanding. Now he can take me home – or better still, drop me off at the Fountains where my friends are getting more and more drunk.

No such luck. He leaves me in the room and locks the door. I suspect that this little move is to get me to shiver and shake a little and to mend my poetic ways, to think twice before I put pen to paper. But I do none of this. The room is an office, a rather drab office. A table with loose papers and documents spread out haphazardly on it. An office chair on either side. A couch right under the window. I curl up on the couch and in a few minutes I'm fast asleep.

My friend Harendien comes to wake me twenty minutes or so later. He's neither peeved nor amused that he has found me sleeping.

'Come,' he says, 'the captain wants to ask you some questions.'

A few minutes later we're in another office and I come face to face with the famous Captain Sons – famous in a Coloured way. All the terrorists and communists and anti-apartheid activists who are African or white don't know this man. But we Coloureds, we know him, we've heard about him. In the apartheid way, there are entrances to shops for each group, townships, schools, churches and of course even a Special Branch detective.

He's tall and bald and has a big sparse face. It gives me the feeling that he has space for maybe another couple of eyes or a much bigger nose. One thing he has more than enough of is a sneer.

'Van Wyk,' he says.

I nod.

'So Van Wyk, you've been out of school a few years.'

'Ja.'

I notice that he's got a file open in front of him and he's checking his facts against it. I have a file at the cop shop. Special Branch Division. I've barely got matric, I'm jobless. But I've got a file – what they call a dossier in those cop books I read. If only

I wasn't so damn short-sighted, I could lean forward and see what it says about me.

'Riverlea High.'

'Ja.'

'And you're looking for a job?'

'Yes I am.'

Long pause. 'You go to church?'

I don't. But if I tell the truth I would be a Communist, which I know the regime hates more than any other kind of person. Besides the Communist Party was banned sometime in the fifties and all communists go straight to jail.

'Yes.'

'Which Church?'

I tell him.

He shakes his head and sighs. 'Why are you getting involved in this … politics … black consciousness?'

'I'm not involved in anything.'

'Reading poems everywhere, even in Soweto. Van Wyk, do you know what will happen if these blacks take over?'

The one thing I know for sure is that it will bring an immediate end to apartheid. I can't see Mandela saying, 'OK, leave all those 'Whites Only' signs right where they are' But I shrug.

'There'll be trouble. Of that you can be sure. In any case, do you know what they think of Coloured people?'

'Who?'

'Africans.'

'Oh, I thought you meant whites.'

He gives me another long stare. Behind me there are uncomfortable movements as his boys shift around in their chairs. Our captain probably earns as much as a white constable and it's against the white man's law for him to go about arresting white criminals. My remark must have caused some of this to flash through his brain.

'Do you have a girlfriend?'

'Yes.' But I'm not going to discuss my girlfriend with him. I decide that if he asks for her name, I'm going to make one up: Eleanor Petersen, I'll say. But he doesn't ask me.

'You're a nice young man, you're clever, you got your whole future ahead of you. Don't get involved in these things, Mr van Wyk. You understand me?'

I nod.

He gestures to his boys and they jump to their feet and one of them says to me: 'Come.'

But first Sons has something to say in conclusion, an afterthought prepared even before the interview:

'If you have any problems, you can come to me.'

This interrogation has suddenly turned and gone down a dark path.

'I can help you, Mr van Wyk.'

The root of all my problems is with white people.

'If you hear anything, see anything, people trying to make trouble, come and tell me. You don't have work, we can help you with some cash.'

I do not respond at all to this.

After a moment's uncomfortable silence, he repeats his gesture to his underlings and they tell me to come.

The sunlight feels wonderful; warm and new. I feel the same thrill as I did when I walked out of school for the very last time.

Sitting in the back seat I do something audacious. I ask my two security cops to drop me off at the Fountains where I have some serious drinking to do, and a story to tell.

This will not be the last time I meet these cops. Indeed, there are about five or six encounters to go, of which one was more amusing than this one and another was one of the most terrifying experiences of my life. I'll tell you about them when the time comes.

The Night of the Killer Kangaroo

ONE EARLY WEDNESDAY EVENING there's a knock on our front door. I open and there's Themba Miya. He's a dark, six foot two, giant of a man, a Soweto-based poet and one of the gentler souls you'll ever meet.

We bump into each other at poetry readings all over Joburg: Soweto, the city centre, Braamfontein. Themba's poetry, when you first hear it, sounds like much of the one-dimensional 'I hate whitey' cries. But listen closely and you'll hear that the words and rhythms come not from another angry, black voice but from Themba Miya's soul. When I listen to him read, I sense a vulnerability that gives his poetry a warmth and humanity.

He's no coward, Themba. For one thing, he never carries that hated pass-book, which apartheid has demanded that all blacks keep with them at all times. He beats up any cop who dares ask him to 'produce'. And if there are two or three of them, he makes a dash for it, running down streets, jumping high fences. His emotions are never far away and many's the time I've seen this giant of a man weep out of anger at what apartheid is doing to his family, his people.

'My brother,' Themba says, 'I need a special favour from you.'

'What, Themba?'

He tells me. And this doesn't sound at all like a favour. It sounds instead as if the writers and artists of Soweto have conferred on me the Freedom of Soweto for my dedication to the Arts and Liberation – which so far has been the sum total of about twenty angry poems.

After the 1976 Soweto Uprising, many black writers' and artists' organisations spring up all over Soweto and indeed in townships all over the country.

A group of writers and artists led by Themba, and artists Fikile Ngudla and Percy Sedumedi, started a writers' group, Medupe (soft rain), and an arts group, Soarta (Soweto Arts Association).

Medupe, Themba explains, is planning to run poetry workshops once a fortnight, on Wednesday evenings. And the honour bestowed on me is:

'We would like you to come and run these poetry workshops for us.'

I say yes immediately.

But like many such projects at the time, Medupe does not last very long. The underlying problems are too many police everywhere and too little money.

As the season of Medupe nears its end, I invite them to my home one Saturday afternoon: Themba, Percy and Fikile. For the occasion I buy a bottle of brandy and six quarts of beer.

The guys arrive at about 2.00 in the afternoon. They have come by train, disembarked at Croesus Station and walked the rest of the way, a distance of about two kilometres. There is nothing unusual about this; about not having a car or having to walk a few kilometres to visit friends. It is unusual having a few Soweto friends over for the afternoon though – Coloureds are meant to stay in their own townships, Africans in theirs, while the white masters rule us all from their pretty leafy suburbs.

Riverlea is as it always is on a Saturday afternoon. Front doors are flung wide open, TVs (a recent phenomenon in the country) are blinking, radios are blaring, shebeens are jumping, the streets are full of kids playing, or just passing by.

For a while we sit outside in the yard on a small patch of grass. As the sun sets we move into the lounge, where the boys begin to have intense conversations with my father, who listens quietly and watches bemused as we all get more and more drunk.

Now the brandy begins to wash away some of the chronology of events. But I think what happens is that Themba gets emotional, as usual, gets up, staggers to the door and declares that he is so tormented by the white man that he wants to go home. It's the brandy talking now.

We tell him this is not a wise move. Riverlea, like most townships, is teeming with people who have knives and even the odd gun on their persons. But we turn our attention away from Themba and, the next thing we know, he's gone.

I remember him saying he would go and follow the railway line that cuts through Riverlea as this would obviously lead him home. We – Percy and Fikile and I – get up to go and find him.

On our way down Colorado Drive there is a braai happening at the Garcia home. It's a Young Lions Football Club fund-raiser. Bones Garcia and I were at school together. Outside the Garcia residence there are cars parked on the pavements, clusters of boys stand around the cars smoking and joking and showing off. Music blares from the lounge. Somebody sees me with Percy and Fikile.

'Hey, Kuller. You looking for your bra!'

'Ja. You know where he's gone?'

'He's gone in there,' he points at the Garcia house.

Themba might've decided to go in here, attracted by the music, the smell of meat, the laughter. I don't know and never asked him afterwards. Fikile, Percy and I walk into the yard to fetch our brother.

There's a car in the driveway with three or four people in it. I don't know who these party-goers are and I don't care. As we pass the car a window slides down and a voice shouts from inside, 'No kaffirs allowed here!'

Without hesitating I go over to the window and say, 'Whoever made that remark, come out and come face me. Let's see if you've got the guts to say it again.'

Very casually the three men get out of the car and one of them steps forward, smiling, and stands in front of me. He's about my age, maybe slightly older.

'Are you gonna withdraw that remark or are you gonna fight me?' I ask him.

He smiles and says again, 'No kaffirs allowed.'

The crowd forms an instant circle around us and from it I hear a loud collective sigh and someone says, 'Oh shit. Poor Kuller!'

I'm twenty years old. This is the first street fight of my young life and I have decided to have a go at one Cameron 'Kangaroo' Adams. He is the Transvaal middleweight champion and well on his way to being world champion. He is formidable in the ring. His nickname comes from his habit of bouncing about energetically before suddenly slicing his fists through his opponent's defences. His fists are lethal weapons and he has decided not to limit their use to the boxing ring. Like his professional reputation, his fame as a street fighter is legendary. Every weekend dozens of men in the streets, dance-halls, nightclubs, shebeens and house parties are left unconscious and bruised by Kangaroo and his henchmen. This evening it's our turn – Percy and me.

But at this stage I don't know who my opponent is. I put up my fists and he slices into my defences. My lights go out ... and then I see Mr Garcia standing over me and I hear his voice, concerned, telling me to wake up. Cameron Adams denies that he's touched me and nobody in the crowd dares tell him that he's lying. Percy gets up and I get up and there are Themba and Fikile, unscathed. We walk away from the crowds, through a dark veld towards the railway station at Croesus. My Saturday afternoon guests are headed for home and I'm going with them.

The Saturday night adventure has just begun. But everything that happens next takes place in a haze and it will all trickle back to me in a few days in raggedy bits.

At Croesus Station, Fikile becomes the next victim of an unnecessary assault. As we wait for our train to arrive he chats to a friend he's spotted in a train about to pull out. As the train picks up speed, an unknown passenger leans out and delivers a smack to the face of the artist, sending him spinning at least one full circle.

We don't know what to say. It is sad but also very amusing. The snot and the tears and the absolute futility of it. So far there are three casualties among us and not one white person has been involved in any of them. This is what the government calls 'black on black violence'.

The next day, at a shebeen in Soweto, we all laugh about the incident. But it isn't all laughter, all the time.

At the end of the year, Medupe throws a party for all its teachers. It's an informal, low-key affair in a Soweto shebeen; no banners and certificates and guest speakers in the civic hall. That's the stuff of normal societies. This is lots of beer and brandy. We chat about the struggle and the arts. Themba hands around to everyone sealed envelopes containing a small cash amount, less than a hundred rands, but we're all grateful because it's enough for a carton or two of cigarettes. Benjy Francis is there too. He's a theatre director, a South African 'Indian', originally from Durban and also recruited to give theatre workshops.

Midway through the evening, Fikile says something in Zulu and suddenly the mood and the tempo and the flow of liquor and everything else changes.

Well, apart from *mfowethu* and *woza* and *shaya*, and a couple of vulgar words that I used to shout out down mine holes as a kid, my isiZulu doesn't come too isi.

Themba turns on Fikile and replies with an angry volley. Before I know it there's one helluva argument going on.

'Hey, what's going on, brothers?' I ask. It is most disconcerting not to know what the fight is about.

'It's about us,' Benjy whispers in my ear. 'Me and you.'

'*Us?*'

He nods. 'Fikile doesn't like us being here. We're not black enough. Coloureds and Indians, he says, are not black. And Themba and the other guys are feeling embarrassed.'

The other guys insist that Fikile apologise to us. But he says he will not, and he doesn't.

Later, Themba drives me home and apologises when he drops me off in Riverlea.

'What for?' I ask him. 'You were not the one doing the insulting.'

Themba, Fikile and Percy hang out at a flat in downtown Joburg. The little apartment belongs to a white man, an architect called Piero. Piero is an Italian who speaks with a heavy accent. I pop in there from time to time to visit my friends and I have a chat with Piero. He's always the same: untidy beard, warm handshake, wearing a polo-necked jersey underneath his jacket whether it's winter or summer.

The flat is always filthy and stinking, there being no regular cleaning going on there. But a lot of drinking.

Piero is a self-styled patron of the black arts. He's a well-meaning man but, Jesus, does this man live in filth!

One day I have to go there to seek out, of all people, the one who likes me least. Who am I fooling? Fikile loathes me.

This is how it happens. In 1980 I join a progressive publishing house, Ravan Press, as the editor of the literary magazine, *Staffrider*. Apart from the magazine, Ravan publishes novels, poetry collections, children's books. One of Fikile's artworks appears on the cover of one of the books we publish, a collection of poems by Ingoapele Madingoane called *Africa My Beginning*. Later we also publish an excellent collection of stories by Njabulo Ndebele called *Fools and Other Stories*. A British publisher buys the rights to *Fools*. They have seen the Fikile illustration on *Afrika My Beginning* and like it so much that they want to commission him to illustrate their edition of *Fools*. I get a phone call all the way from London and an editor gives me all these details. She also says:

'We are prepared to pay Fikile fifty pounds in cash for an illustration.'

When converted to rands it will be about five times what Fikile gets for a commissioned artwork. I'm happy to be the go-between, but there is one serious problem. Fikile is drunk most of the time and I somehow don't believe that he is going to be in any mood to produce a nice picture to attract the British book-buying public to *Fools*. There's also the other problem between me and Fikile, namely the colour of my skin or, I suppose, my claim to being black. If I should tell this British publisher that she is not likely to get a cover out of Fikile on account of him being drunk in a flat all the time, word would get around that I've stabbed a brother in the back. Or Fikile might get to hear of it and say to his detractors, like Themba, 'You see what I mean?'

So two or three weeks later, the fifty-pound note arrives from the United Kingdom – with the queen's face on it, waiting to give old Fikile her royal smile. I take it and head for Piero's place in town. I run up the broken stairs getting ready to hold my breath because of the stink. And, of course, I'm not disappointed.

There, sits Fikile, exactly where I saw him two or three months ago, slumped in a broken kitchen chair. I know exactly why he's slumped – he's drunk, that's why.

I say, 'Fikile, Fikile. I say, Fikile.' Because of our strained relationship I can't call him 'brother' or 'bra Fiks' so it gets pretty boring saying Fikile all the time. I take a break and look around the room: there are dirty cups, empty bottles, a dishcloth crawling with ants. Outside there's sunshine for Africa: it's shining on hawkers and ripening their bananas, glancing off the thousands of windows of Joburg's skyscrapers, it's everywhere. But my friends prefer to be stuck up here in this gloomy filthy flat waiting for the next drink.

On an easel near the slumbering Fikile is his latest offering to the art world and the oppressed masses. It's a great big black and white pencil drawing: a black man in profile (the lead from many HB pencils has made sure that he's not some half-caste like me). Out of his head float thousands of petals as if he's had a serious collision with a Wits Rag float. I gaze at the drawing trying to work out what Fikile is trying to tell us (maybe not me because he never has much to say to me, but black people in general, and Piero, who seems to be OK despite his obviously white skin). Maybe this guy in the drawing is a gardener and has been a gardener for so long that the flowers are literally oozing from his brains.

I give up and go back to Fikile. I say again, 'Fikile, Fikile!'

He stirs and looks up. He sees me and there is a painful expression on his face. I tell him why I'm here and I take out the fifty-pound note.

'So this is for you if you agree ...'

In a swift move he grabs the money out of my hand, slumps forward and shuts his eyes.

The Brits never did get their cover, but they ended up using another Fikile illustration. And my guess is that when Fikile rose from his drunken sleep and found fifty pounds in his hands, well, he just went and bought more booze.

About a year later, Kangaroo Adams's gloves were hung up for him. He killed a policeman, was arrested, sentenced to death and hanged.

Three packed into one compartment

WHEN I'M ABOUT TWENTY-ONE I decide to go down to the Cape to write a book. I have got it into my head that my first novel should be a family saga and my own roots could be found in the arid dust of the Karoo, that famous semi-desert in the Cape, in a little *dorp* called Carnarvon.

I first go down to Cape Town for a week. How can one travel all the way to the Cape without a trip to the most beautiful city in the world. Table Mountain, the train ride from Simon's Town to the city, meandering along the beach, the beautiful Coloured girls with their lilting sing-song voices?

Then I travel to Hutchinson station in the heart of the Karoo to be picked up by my paternal grandfather's younger brother, Henkie. A bigger version of my grandpa. Uncle Henkie's other difference is that he has mischief in his eyes where my grandpa has only brooding shadows.

Then follows an hour's drive to Carnarvon on one long, hot, dusty potholed road, past waving poor people on foot or pushing bicycles, carrying bundles of wood or things wrapped in newspaper.

Carnarvon is a place in the middle of nowhere where nothing happens. Simple breakfasts, lunches and suppers are linked together by chains of cigarettes and conversations consisting of long, trailing life histories, which make the old men in their elbow-patched jackets stammer and squint into the past from behind their thick spectacles, as they dig up stories from their dry riverbeds of history.

What a wonderful thing it is listening to those minutely detailed stories. But after two weeks I'm bored out of my township wits. The novel can wait, I decide, as I pack up and am driven back to Hutchinson station. The train from Cape Town – the very same one that had brought me there two weeks before – slides into the station. I bid Uncle Henkie goodbye with a promise that I will feature him prominently and truthfully in my novel.

When the train slithers out, I turn from the window to look at the other passengers in the compartment with whom I expect to spend the next sixteen hours or so on the way to Johannesburg.

There are three young men, two bearded, two chubby. (If you think I can't count remember the riddle of the two fathers and two sons who each shot a duck. Only three ducks were shot. Why? Because one was a grandfather, another a father and the last a son. The man in the middle was both a father and a son. Got it?) All youthful and exuberant, they are drinking beer straight from the can and their conversation is full of the hammers and nails of their trade and punctuated with laughter and good-natured arguments. None of them swears and they all flash smiles at me, accepting me into their circle with an easy friendliness.

'You been to Cape Town?' one of them enquires.

'Ja,' I say, shoving my bag into the space above the door among their bags and parcels.

'Then you must've got your quota of ten girls,' he says with a wink.

Of course I know exactly what he's talking about: it's a well-known fact that in the Mother City there are at least ten girls to every boy. I give my train friend a supercilious nod, hoping to convey the impression that I had certainly got my fair share. The truth is very different. All I can truly claim is a brief encounter with Marina, a nurse from Tygerberg hospital. She had allowed me to kiss her in the back seat of her cousin's car, but my beer breath had proved too much for her and after administering a violet-flavoured Beechie, she bade me goodnight and told me to come and see her in the morning.

There are two other passengers in the compartment. They are not as friendly as the trio from Cape Town. They sit huddled in a corner, muttering in undertones and casting sidelong glances down the green SAR leather seat at me and my new buddies. They appear to be brothers, as they have identical features: sandy hair that has been cut so short that the hairs grow in sharp italic spikes. They both have dark, brooding eyes and thick pouting lips. They are both wearing khaki shirts and pants.

Try to describe people you see on a bus or train it says in the writer's manual that I have at home. I slip a blank sheet into my mental typewriter and do as the manual says:

> They sit huddled in the corner of the compartment, bent so low in their conniving that they almost stick to the green SAR leather like two unsightly stains. They are identical but for the fact that there is a two- or three-year difference between them. Juveniles in khaki, they look like fugitives from a boy scout patrol, runaways not prepared to abide by the rules of the Lord Baden Powell. Stripped of their badges, their epaulettes, their scarves, banished to ride forever second-class on the Trans-Karoo.

As I said, I was only twenty-one at the time.

I turn away from them and back to the three big men who are chatting to me as if I am an old buddy. I'm surprised and pleased by this unexpected attention and friendliness. One of them glances at his watch from time to time and stares out of the window at the scrub that makes up the dry, desolate landscape of the Karoo. They ask me about my trip down to the Cape. They all seem genuinely interested. One of them slides a can of beer across the little panelyte table and they all sit forward to listen to what I have to say. I pass my pack of cigarettes around to my three new friends and we light up. Then I begin to tell a story which I have already tested on my uncle in Carnarvon. There, among seasoned storytellers, it had gone down well so I know I have a winner.

On my way down from Johannesburg there was only one other person booked into the compartment I was in. He was a Capetonian. He travelled in a flamboyant, striped, yellow and white suit. Every time he spoke he injected an air of drama into the compartment, and when he was quiet he seemed all the time to be sizing me up. I remember his name, Georgie Abrahams, from Elsies River.

As the train started out of Johannesburg station on its long journey, Georgie began to tell me how he had once killed a man. Where? In a compartment exactly like the one he and I were sitting in now, facing each other. Why? Because, Georgie was very eager to explain, this now-dead *skelm* had tried to steal some of Georgie's possessions. Food, money, an expensive watch, perhaps, I can't remember exactly what it was, but Georgie caught him in the act, beat him up, and, in Georgie's own words, sliced him from his greasy, fat neck down to his *klein gatjie*.

He threw the remains of the dead man out of the window in the dead of night and wiped the blood carefully from the window-pane, the green leather seat and the floor. When the conductor questioned the disappearance of the passenger, Georgie merely shrugged and uttered a melodious, 'How should I know? Nobody asked me to take care of him.'

But even as Georgie was relating the tale of theft and murder in all its horrific detail, I knew it was a lie. This was simply Georgie's way of warning me to keep away from his luggage! And the story had quite an amusing ending. When we reached Cape Town station, a toothless woman in a lopsided jersey, stretched to twice its original size (which was probably XL), was waiting for him. She welcomed the murderer home with an unceremonious slap across his face, while I looked on together with a brood of his startled children, who didn't know if they should laugh with delight at their papa's homecoming or cry for the humiliating welcome he was getting from Mama.

'Ses maande en djy skryf niks, phone niks, nie 'n blerrie woord van djou!' (Six months and you don't write, don't phone, not a bladdy word from you!)

My companions chuckle, at my Cape Town accent as well as my story, I think.

I take a peep at the two sullen boys in the corner. They had followed the entire story but did not laugh once. So what? It hadn't been for their amusement anyway.

But then my trip takes an unexpected turn. An hour or two into the journey, my three companions get up, stamp the pins and needles out of their feet, straighten out their clothes and begin to gather up their luggage. They shake hands with me, slap my back and say goodbye. And at the next station they're gone. It all happens so quickly that I'm a little stunned. Here I was thinking that we were pals all and going to Joburg together. How foolish of me because between Cape Town and Joburg there are dozens of stations.

Now it's just me and the khaki kids. And then a strange thing happens. Suddenly, I know why these two are dressed in khaki. They're from a Cape Town reformatory, on their way home to Johannesburg. Why have I not realised this obvious fact before? The answer is simple: I had been far too preoccupied with my new friends to pay proper attention to these boys. And, besides, there were no guardians in sight. But now that I'm alone I focus my attention full square on these two and, in an instant, I realise where they're from.

In the meantime, the two juvenile delinquents also seem to be undergoing some kind of transformation. They no longer mumble but speak loudly, spicing their conversation with four-letter curses (three-letter when they switch to Afrikaans). And, just in case I haven't noticed them, they take up more than their fair share of the compartment, stretching their stocky legs along the seats, putting their luggage everywhere, littering the floor with clothes and greasy food packets.

Then they begin a conversation that freezes my blood. It turns out that their older brother, the leader of a street gang, has been murdered, as recently as yesterday, by a rival gang in Coronationville. They're on their way home, having been given a week off from the reformatory in Ottery, to attend the funeral. They'll bury their brother like the hero that he was, but will, they vow, avenge his death before the soil on his grave has hardened. They even argue as to how this murder should be carried out. A slow cutting of the throat is the younger one's suggestion. No, no, the elder brother disagrees, stab him about a hundred times, but from the ankles to the neck.

As these plans are being discussed, they both stare fiercely at me from time to time as if challenging me to say as much as one word in protest. Each time I look away.

The train, meanwhile, is riding into a scenic sunset as if it has only contented passengers on board. A cool breeze replaces the stuffy heat – and the grim brothers pull up the windows. A pity, but I say nothing.

Now I have a problem. How can I spend an entire night in a pitch-black compartment with two little low-life gangsters who have nothing but murder on their minds? Maybe I could go off in search of the conductor and ask to be moved to another compartment. But if I did that my two little gangster friends would know instinctively what I was up to. Besides, it would also mean leaving my luggage unattended for a while. With these thoughts going through my head, I pull down the top bunk and get up on it to put myself as far away from them as possible. I look down from the bunk and catch the elder brother staring at me. Oh God, he knows what I'm thinking, I'm sure!

Soon it's dark outside and we turn on the light. A noisy caterer slides open our door and reads the menu for supper. The two boys order steak, buttered bread and potato salad. For some reason, I have no appetite. The caterer leaves and I hear him whistling down the corridor and rattling open the next compartment door. Again my companions give me one of their looks, as if they know why I haven't ordered a meal.

On my way down to the Cape, Georgie Abrahams had joked about committing murder. This time there was no such threat – on my life anyway. But, for every dark kilometre to Joburg, I feel that my home city is moving further and further away.

'You!'

I look down from the bunk. It's the elder brother who is demanding my attention.

'Ja,' I answer as casually as my voice would allow.

'I know you.'

This is how the trouble starts, I know it, I just know it. 'Me?'

His brother, also looking up at me, chuckles.

The elder brother continues. 'Why you make like you don't know us when you do know us?'

'But …'

'Aren't you Auntie Ruby's child, grandchild, something like that?'

I cannot believe my ears. Auntie Ruby is my very own ouma from Corrie.

'I knew it was you when I saw you,' he says, not smiling but with some friendliness in his voice. His brother, sitting beside him, stares up at me in the same way.

'You're that clever boy who used to read lots of big books.'

'Yes! But who are you?'

'Me and him, we're Auntie Louisa's grandchildren.'

Auntie Louisa is my grandmother's sister!

'Then we're cousins!' I say. This isn't entirely true, but I'm desperate to be as closely related to them as possible.

When their food arrives they insist that I join them, and I do, for suddenly my appetite has returned.

When I get back to Joburg I forget all about my chance encounter with my delinquent relatives, until about four or five years later.

I open a newspaper and read a story about rampant gang warfare in the streets of Western Township and adjacent Coronationville. The report describes streets running with the blood of gangsters, the death of innocents caught in the crossfire, the unending tit-for-tat revenge killings between rival gangs, the desperate poverty that is the root cause of it all, the futility.

The writer pays particular attention to the two brothers who were stabbed to death on the same day and who now lie in the same grave as their older brother killed four or five years before.

Three packed into one compartment.

A short obituary

FRANK VAN WYK IS DEAD.

That's my paternal grandfather. The short man with the crinkly hair – completely grey at the time of death. The man with the high cheekbones and the narrow eyes. The Khoikhoi from the Karoo.

He leaves behind his peach trees, which he never wanted us to go near. And his Volvo, which he hardly ever let us ride in. Somewhere there is a sack of old coins, which he said I could have when he died but which I don't think his daughter, Stella, will ever pass on to me – not that I want them any more. I became a coin collector and grew tired of it without getting my hands on that ancient stash, so what? He had sold his dry cleaner's shop.

For three or four Christmases in a row he took my father with him down to Carnarvon without ever once asking if we – me, Ma, Derek, Shaun, Allison, Nicolette and Russel – would like to go and meet the other Van Wyks. Not that I would ever have wanted to spend a Christmas with the stingy old bushman. It would've been: 'don't play on that', 'don't do that', 'don't go there', 'don't fill your mouth like that' the whole bladdy day, jabbing his little rum-and-maple-flavoured pipe in our frightened little faces.

He's dead. He coughed and coughed and coughed and died.

One day I open up a book and I read about the Khoikhoi. These ancestors of ours spoke a clicking language. Well Grandpa Frank clicked his tongue at me often enough, I'll tell you that.

I also read that they could survive in that blistering hot desert on barely a tablespoon of water – the dew left behind on a leaf. That makes sense. But, if they were anything like Grandpa Frank, they'd need a bottle of brandy with it as well!

These bushmen were such amazing trackers that they could chase after a buck even if it took them a week. Well, as far as tracking goes, I think old Frank was an exception: his *bokkie* –

Mrs van Wyk – left him and he tried to find her but she had vanished into thin air.

The most interesting thing I read about the Khoikhoi is about their cosmology. They believe that when they die they become a star in the heavens. So I gaze up at the sky on some evenings and I say to the stars, 'Which one of you is Frank?'

They never tell me, so I end up having to guess. And there are two possibilities: a metre or two from the Milky Way there's this star that radiates very little light, not because it has no light but because this mean little light is all that it's prepared to offer the cosmos. And then there's one much closer, north-west of the moon. It's the strangest looking star. It shines brightly enough, but it has this brown tint, as if it was once dipped in a cesspit in a time of war.

The A to Zeke of black literature

ONE DAY MY OUMA RUBY TAKES OUT HER PHOTOS to show me. In dozens of books and movies, characters are heard joking about these things: 'So the Hendersons took out their photo album and their whole life passed before you, hahahaha.'

My ouma's album is anything but boring. There are dozens of photos of uncles and aunts and cousins and friends and even my ma when she was a little girl.

'But who is this white guy in the photo?' I ask.

'My father,' she says.

This is not good news. I am black. I write black poetry. I am a follower of the black consciousness philosophy of Steve Biko. And here's a white guy in the family messing up my past and my future. For God's sake, white people are the enemy, I don't want the enemy in my family. Shit!

To tell the truth, I've heard about this white ancestor before; both my mother and my ouma had told me about him. But I decided that he wasn't really white. Coloureds have always had a knack for bragging about the white people in their family, but totally ignoring their African relatives. But this oupa was definitely white, no doubt about that. And a handsome guy too.

But I decide to put this problem on the back burner. For the moment, the revolution has begun and there are important matters to attend to.

It's now 1980 and Kathy and I are married and living with her mother. My friend, Fhazel, comes to me one day and says, 'We have to start a black publishing house.'

The last time I saw Fhazel we pooled our small change for a packet of cigarettes to share. We're better off now financially, but we still have only about eighty rands between us. But somehow he convinces me. And mere weeks later he leaves his job as a computer operator – in the days when computers were as big as wardrobes – and I resign from mine at Sached where

I've been working as a writer of literacy material for new literate adults.

We publish two issues of our literary magazine called *Wietie*. 'Wietie' is township slang for talk, talking, to have a discussion, to chat, to communicate, to exchange ideas.

Wietie is what Fhazel and I do plenty of during those months as publishers. We run the magazine from my mother-in-law's home. The poems and short stories and artwork come and fill up our letter-boxes. We read them aloud to each other. We deposit subscription cheques in the bank, we post our magazine to subscribers. We attend and participate in poetry readings and writers' seminars. In and out of Fhazel's brown Volksie, chatting and chatting and chatting. About writing in general. We swap books: Richard Wright's *Black Boy*, terse and searing, and I wonder if I'll ever be able to tell my own life story with such craft, indeed, whether I even have a story worth telling; the Chilean Pablo Neruda's poetry flowing with revolutionary blood and beating with verses of love, the most beautiful you could ever let into your heart.

About South African writing. The 1950s had seen a Golden Age of black writing. Es'kia 'Zeke' Mphahlele and his famous auto-biography *Down Second Avenue*. I will never forget the little boy Zeke in Marabastad in the 1930s. There he goes down Second Avenue with a bundle of clean washing from his granny to take back to the white man's. Here come his friends to take him to a movie. They cannot go without him because the movie has sub-titles and he's the only reader among them. The writers of *Drum* magazine. Can Themba and his short stories *The Will to Die*; Casey Motsisi, the Damon Runyon of Soweto; Bloke Modisane, who watched as his father was searched for his pass by an eighteen-year-old Boer cop. The scene stayed etched in Bloke's memory all his life – and in mine.

About black consciousness: We are black, not carbon copies of white people. We reject the term 'non-white'; when we are forced, for whatever reason, to use the term 'Coloured' we make two little double quotes in the air. We write poems inspired by black consciousness. One of mine goes like this:

Coming Home

Rising
from a bed
of aberration
and coir
I greet
the
blinding white dawn
with pride
far deeper
than
the pores
of my skin
saying
I
am a black man.

We speak of Africa. Not only had the apartheid government separated the various race groups, they have also sliced off South Africa from the rest of the continent. Nigeria, Uganda, Kenya, Liberia, Ethiopia, The Ivory Coast, Mozambique, Zimbabwe. Nkrumah, Kenyatta, Samora Machel, Frelimo, MPLA. Black Power, Negritude. Names, concepts and events never mentioned in our history books. Often I feel as if my education is only just beginning. Our teachers had told us nothing about Africa and I hate them for it.

We argue about language and words. Fhazel hates nicknames and slang. He was called Spike at St Barnabas College. He refuses to call me 'Kuller', which is the nickname everyone else uses for me. Fhazel prefers to call me Chris or Christopher.

When my son, Kevin, is born and we begin calling him Kevs and Kevzo, and Fhazel says, 'But why did you bother then to name him Kevin?'

'We live in a township, it's part of township culture.'

He shakes his head, unconvinced.

He and I are sitting outside the local café one day, drinking Cokes.

Fhazel nods discreetly but disdainfully at a shop loafer in his takkies and his baseball cap and his slouch, the odd scar, the missing tooth. 'If one of these, comes up to me and says: *'Heita, my bra'* to me, I'll respond by saying: Good afternoon, my friend.'

This is so ridiculous that I actually don't know what to say.

And yet Fhazel loves it when he first hears me say, 'I've got five boys (rands) for beer.' And when we get the beer: 'There's no glasses, we'll just have to bugle it.' (drink from the bottle).

And irony of ironies, my bra Fhazel, you were the one who named our magazine *Wietie*, remember?

One day, in 1977, we read that Es'kia 'Zeke' Mphahlele is coming back home after twenty years in exile. How exciting! Who is Zeke Mphahlele? It was a good question to ask since he and his books were banned twenty years ago – exactly at the time when Fhazel and I were born.

The newspapers are not allowed to quote him or quote from his books. But they give us an update anyway. But I already know everything about him. He was born in Maupanang in the north of the country way back in 1919. He was a shepherd spending his early days taking care of his grandmother's sheep. He grew up in Marabastad, a Pretoria slum. He sat in classrooms of up to eighty kids trying to learn to read and write. He became a teacher. He taught in Soweto in the fifties. He left the country when he joined the teachers' protest against the government's inferior Bantu Education – which he said was preparing black children for slavery. The government retaliated by taking away his job. He left the country and went to teach in Nigeria. Later he went to lecture as a professor of literature at universities in the USA.

How do I know all this about him? Because he's one of my heroes. Because I read his *Down Second Avenue* – a tattered copy, which I keep hidden far away from the security police. Because I want to write like Zeke one day. And because his life experiences and his own philosophy tell me that this is indeed possible.

And now he's coming home!

But the youth of Soweto say, 'Stay where you are, Zeke, don't come home.' Their reason: The *Boers* are going from bad to worse and Soweto is still smouldering from the evidence. Avalon cemetery has hundreds of fresh mounds. Now one of our literary fathers is coming home and his return would say to the world: 'I've travelled the world, but home is best.'

'Not so,' Zeke responds. 'Whether good or bad, my home is my home, and I am going back there to help make a difference.'

I want Zeke Mphahlele back home and I have a better reason than all these intellectuals and activists. I want to shake his hand and say, 'I read your book. I want to write a book like yours one day.' I want to say, 'You are my literary grandfather, I look up to you. Thanks, Oupa Zeke for the stories about our past.'

Everywhere in the world young writers write because the generation before them has written. The American writers of the seventies wrote because of the Baldwins of the sixties and the Faulkners and Hemingways of the fifties and forties all the way back to a granddaddy called Mark Twain. Don't even talk about the English; they go back hundreds of years to a fellow called Charles Dickens, and then another couple of hundred or so to old Shakespeare himself. But we South African writers, well the *Boers* came along with an axe and chopped off the flow, right there in the early sixties. One heavy cut that severed the artery that would have allowed the blood to flow between the writers of the fifties and those of the sixties, between Zeke Mphahlele and Chris van Wyk.

Zeke's return is announced in the press, in between the harrowing stories of the still ongoing township battles that began in June 1976. He has lots of catching up to do, lots of old, almost forgotten friendships to renew. Publicly Zeke is feted everywhere, speaking at libraries and universities and seminars.

One Saturday afternoon Fhazel and I attend a meeting at a venue somewhere in Braamfontein, a seminar or something. The hall is packed with writers, black and white. Everybody is reading out papers and saying things about literature that I didn't even know existed: negritude this, black consciousness that, Achebe this and Ngugi that, discourse this, of course that. Colonialism, liberation, Frantz Fanon. I don't know about Fhazel but my feeling is this writing is harder than I thought. But I'm so happy to be here. Real school has finally started for me.

Zeke is there too. And because he is still brand new and because he still has luggage labels stuck to him that say Paris and Denver and Accra and Lagos and the fifties, he's feted yet again.

'Come up to the stage, Zeke, come and tell us all about it,' The MC says.

So Zeke Mphahlele comes on to the stage to warm applause, and has an informal chat with us all, while Fhazel and I shift in our seats looking from Zeke to each other, Zeke to each other, Zeke to each other.

In *Down Second Avenue* a five-year-old Zeke tells us how he would put leaves into his hands and call the goats to come and nibble and it's so ticklish that it makes him laugh. Well, who was eating out of Zeke's hands now and making him chuckle!

A grey-haired, old white lady shoots up an arm eager to say something. Zeke turns to her and nods.

'I'm Fanny Klenerman,' she says. I don't know if you'll remember me but I owned Vanguard bookshop down in Commissioner Street, and I remember a young Ezekiel coming into my shop to buy second-hand books.'

Zeke is speechless. 'Of course I remember,' he says, a lovely smile spilling out from underneath his spectacles. Then he thinks for a moment. Lots of other hands go up wanting to ask questions, but Zeke is not done with the bookseller. 'In fact,' he says, 'a couple of times I walked out of your shop with one or two of your books stuck under my shirt.'

'That's OK,' the lady chirps, 'look where it's got you.'

A few weeks later Fhazel and I hear that Zeke is going to speak at Wits University. We haven't had enough and we go along.

This is a more intimate gathering; literature students and teachers and writers, about 150 people packed into a lecture room.

Zeke reads from his autobiography. Then the hands go up. Why did you decide to come back? You've been advocating the study of African literature at universities. What will become of European literature? Do you believe that the root cause of the ongoing unrest in black schools can be traced back to the Bantu Education, which was partly the cause of your choosing to leave back in the fifties? What was it like to work with Can Themba and Nat Nakasa in the 1950s?

I've seen Zeke described as magisterial. He is. But he's also pleasant, friendly, and very knowledgeable.

Another hand goes up.

'Professor Mphahlele, what do you think of the new writing that has emerged, the post-1976 writing, as it's already being called.'

'Very exciting, very exciting indeed. Especially the poetry. Writing that is being written in the heat of the moment as it were …'

He's talking about *us*. About *my* generation!

'The name of one of these poets comes to mind. I've been following his career, even from far away in Denver. His work is vibrant, exciting, cutting edge …'

I can't believe what I'm hearing. The great Zeke Mphahlele has been reading *my* poetry and he's about to tell all these people around me! And he's never met me and he doesn't even know I'm in the audience. This is going to make me very uncomfortable. But that doesn't mean I don't want him to say it. Go right ahead, Professor, say it out loud.

'The young man's name is Fhazel Johennesse.'

Here's a little footnote to the Fhazel/Chris friendship.

When Kathy and I get married on 12 April 1980, we have the reception at The Cathedral Place, Doornfontein. Band in attendance: The Silhouettes. We invite all our family and friends – including of course Fhazel and his wife Cassandra. But they don't come. My best friend and he doesn't pitch at my wedding!

I'm deeply hurt and I confront him. And of course, being Fhazel, his reasons are classic.

'I couldn't bear to see my best friend hanging himself by getting married,' he says.

This isn't new philosophy. For months Fhazel's favourite pose has been the chin in the hands, the deep sigh, the chain smoking, the shake of the head.

'Marriage is killing me … When my wife speaks to my daughters she refers to me as Daddy.'

'My God, Fhazel, how cruel!'

'It's not a joke, Van Wyk.'

'Well, what would you like to be referred to as?'

'Don't you see, I'm losing my identity. I've become Daddy and Cassandra's Mummy. It's … it's debilitating.'

I can't see the point nor can I see the point of arguing.

And so he says to me, 'There is nothing wrong with Kathy, but there is something wrong with the institution of marriage. And I just couldn't be there to bear witness to this, to toast to it, to dance to it.'

'OK.'

A few months later Fhazel got divorced.

And a year or two after that he got married again.

Africans and Sons

'I CAN'T WAIT TO SEE MY FIRST ANTHOLOGY, to hold it in my hands,' I say to Stephen Gray, a friend and fellow-writer.

'Collection,' says Stephen. 'An anthology contains the work of several different poets. A collection contains just one person's work.'

Well, what d'you know. Here I am at twenty-one and about to have my first book published and I don't even know the difference between a collection and an anthology.

The publisher is Ad Donker, a tall Dutchman from Holland who has come to settle in South Africa (not a new thing with Dutchmen). Donker attends poetry readings all over the city. One day he phones Stephen, who in turn phones me and gives me the good news. Donker already had a poetry series going and has published Mongane 'Wally' Serote's *Yakhal'inkomo*, Sipho Sepamla's *Hurry Up to It*, Mafika Gwala's *Jol' inkomo*. These were my heroes, writing about the struggle for freedom, the suffering of black people under apartheid. And next in the series would be Chris van Wyk with a collection entitled *It Is Time to Go Home*.

Fhazel, in the meantime, would be published by Ravan Press and he had chosen to call his collection *The Rainmaker*.

While we wait for our books to come out, we sign contracts and read proofs and final proofs and can't stand the wait. And while we wait we have another of our profound little literary debates. It concerns the dedication page of our coming books.

'My poetry comes from my experience with the people,' I say. 'It's about their suffering and our fight for freedom. For that reason I am going to dedicate my book: 'To all the people who are dying for change … and to all the people who aren't." I sit back and wait to hear him say, 'Wow.'

He gazes at me through his tinted spectacles. 'Poetry is a highly personal affair. A matter between the poet and his soul. I shall dedicate my book to my wife.'

Maybe it's these very different attitudes to poetry and the struggle that cause the security police to keep visiting me and to ignore Fhazel completely.

It's time for my annual visit to John Vorster Square.

This time they phone me at my work at Sached in town. They ask me to come to their offices. It's my old friend Harendien from the last time. And of course Captain Sons wants to have a word with me.

I'm not going to run and hide. They can come and get me if they like. But I do tell my colleagues where I'm going to be tomorrow morning just in case I disappear for ever.

'Van Wyk,' Captain Sons says by way of greeting. He doesn't shake my hand and for that I am rather grateful. I don't like him, this Coloured who wants to remain a Coloured lackey of the whites all his life. Who thinks that I believe that he's one very important somebody sitting there behind his desk, with his manner that says: no shit from you OK?

I nod, because I cannot get myself to call him Captain.

'You still writing those poems of yours?'

'Yes I am.' I'm nervous and he can see that.

He glances down at my file. My eyesight hasn't improved and I don't even bother to even try to see what he's looking at.

The small talk is over and he gets down to the nitty-gritty.

'Do you have any friends in Botswana?'

Uh-uh! The land of the exiled ANC. After 1976, hundreds, maybe thousands, of young South Africans crossed the border into Botswana to join the ANC and take up arms against the apartheid government.

If he does a quick flip through my poetry book, he'll see that I have quite a few South African friends living in Botswana. The poet Mongane 'Wally' Serote lives there as well as Thami Mnyele, a former colleague at Sached, who in fact illustrated my poetry book. Both are in exile and work for the ANC.

Actually, if they're tired of my poetry, they could just page through my passport and see that I visit these friends quite often. But if I told him that I know members of the banned and much-feared ANC, I might never get out of here alive. So I say, quite emphatically:

'No, I don't.

He looks up at me. 'Listen here, Mr Chris van Wyk, I want you to talk the truth not lies, do you understand me?'

'Very clearly.'

'Let's start again. Do you know anyone in Botswana?'

I do not know what this is all about. But I begin to have a theory about these security cops. They seem to believe that if you write the words 'I would like to be free one day,' that you must surely be getting this from Nelson Mandela and his cousin, the dead Lenin, the living Lennon (from his song 'Imagine' and from the dead Kwame Nkrumah. The desire to be free cannot possibly have come from your own heart. 'I do not. Why would I lie? Take me to Botswana and show me to every person there and ask them if they know me. They will tell you they don't.'

His underlings shift uneasily in their chairs behind me.

Sons smiles faintly and I smile too.

'Who is A. F. Rickensen?' he says.

'I don't know such a person.'

'Come come, Van Wyk. Think.'

I actually do think. But this does not mean that if I suddenly remember such a person I'm going to share my thoughts with him.

'How d'you spell the name?' I ask him.

'A. F. That's the initials. Then R. I. C. A. N. S. O. N.'

Oh God! With every visit to this place we move to a different dimension. The last time was the ridiculous, today we have the sublime. There's something else I should be telling you about Fhazel and me. When we're not writing poetry, we're engaged in something as subversive as doing crossword puzzles. Not the ordinary ones like: End of a prayer (4): [Amen]. We do the cryptic ones like: For a walk on the beach move the sand please (10) [Esplanade] Here's another one: gegs (9,4) [Scrambled eggs].

Now, here is Coloured Captain Sons asking me if I know somebody called African Son, and he doesn't even realise it. My natural instinct, after over a decade of school, is to throw up a hand and shout out the answer. But I realise that this would be folly. If I said to him: that spells African son, he would say, 'Well, how the hell did you know that?' I would say, 'It's obvious,' or 'Because I went to school'. He would either feel insulted that he did not come to the same conclusion as I did even though he too had been to school. Or he would believe that I had some revolutionary code in my head. So I shake my head and say:

'Sorry, it doesn't ring a bell.'

He's very suspicious. 'We're watching you, Van Wyk,' he warns me. Then he lets me go.

My theory, as I walk out of John Vorster Square, is that one of my friends in Botswana wrote me a letter referring to some or other mutual friend as an 'African Son'. And that letter, having been intercepted, is now in the hands of Captain Sons.

On 14 June 1985 a contingent of South African Defence Force soldiers sneaked into Botswana and shot dead my friend Thami and several other members of the ANC.

Smithie and Cappie

ONE LAZY LATE MORNING I'm sitting on my mother-in-law's stoep drinking Old Brown Sherry with my friends, William Smith and Caplan Block. It's a scorching day but we're under an awning so it's nice and cool. The pedestrian traffic is very sparse, just the odd man or woman passing by. This is because it's a weekday and everybody, including my mother-in-law, has gone to work.

It's 29 January 1981. This I know because in 24 hours I'll be a father. We're drinking as a premature celebration. We'd rather be drinking brandy and Coke or beer. But it's going to have to be sherry and Coke with ice because we're all three unemployed and broke. But we're happy and we're bothering no one.

Both these friends are new. We've known each other for only a couple of years. Caplan lives in Riverlea, but on the other side of the railway line, where they don't have electricity or inside toilets and bathrooms. I'd seen him around but we'd never actually chatted. One day I walk into Fhazel's house and he's there, chatting to Fhazel's older brother. It turns out that we have one thing in common: we've both been picked up by the security police in the last three months or so. We walk home together swapping our cop experiences and, the next thing we know, we're visiting each other every day.

Caplan was questioned for having done community work with one Zephaniah Mothopeng. Mothopeng, one of the leaders of the Pan Africanist Congress, has recently been freed from a long prison term on Robben Island.

The Block family hail from Prieska in the northern Cape.

Caplan says: 'Mostly we were very poor. But the neighbours shared with each other. Some evenings my mother would call me and say, "Here, take this bowl to Auntie Tienie. It's just a little mutton and carrot stew. Tell her if I had more, I would give more but tell her from me to enjoy it."

'So off I go into the dark with this delicious-smelling food in my hands. Ma knows exactly what I'm thinking and she stands on the stoep and tells me to sing *Vader Jakob* over and over again.

The reason for this is so that I won't stuff some of the stew into my mouth.

'Well, chaps,' he says proudly, 'today I can sing *Vader Jakob* perfectly with a lamb chop stuffed into my mouth.' And he demonstrates by stuffing a whole slice of bread into his mouth.

He tells us another story about his childhood. There were six children in his family. When they brought home their reports, his father would read them one by one, making little grunting noises, nodding and shaking his head. But he could not read and they knew that.

These are about the only two funny stories Caplan tells. The rest are sad and even a little repulsive. He tells of the church services that went on for hours and hours on end in the searing, oppressive heat of the northern Cape. The dreary singing of hymns and the priest telling them for what seemed like hours that, no matter what, they would remain sinners in the eyes of the Lord for ever and ever.

'Every now and then there's a shuffle somewhere. You know what it is? Somebody has fainted. It's now obvious that this sermon must come to an end. But not as far as that fucking pastor is concerned. He just goes on and on and on.'

Caplan remembers all of this and the rumbling in his stomach and the dark, pious faces in their darker, raggedy clothes and the crackle of the zinc roof, knowing that when they get home they would first have to wait for an hour or two to be fed while the adults stuffed themselves.

One oppressive Sunday turned into an even worse nightmare. A family friend had come to visit for the day in his old Ford car. Six-year-old John, Caplan's younger brother, sat in the car and started playing with the steering wheel, pretending that he was the driver. Somehow, little John tampered with the brakes and the car began to roll backwards, down the path. Poor John was terrified. Brothers and sisters ran screaming after the car until it came to a halt in a ditch.

John was not hurt and the car was not damaged at all. But the adults came out of the house to see what was the matter. Caplan looked from his father to his little brother and shut his eyes to keep out the vision that was about to play itself out in the next few minutes.

And sure enough, Mr Block, suddenly angry with everyone around him, ordered that his whip be fetched.

'Come here!' he called to John and, there in the street with everyone looking on, meted out a whipping that left the boy bleeding and screaming in pain and humiliation.

Mr Block worked in an asbestos mine. Every day he got up and walked to the mine, a mere kilometre from their ramshackle home. He went into the earth and brought up asbestos for the white man, leaving behind just enough in his lungs to ensure an early death.

One day, in about 1969, Mr Block decided to pack up his meagre and rusty possessions and head for the City of Gold. He hired a rattling truck and, Block, stock and barrel, they trekked north to Joburg, with Mr Block and the truck competing to out-cough each other.

They found a house in Riverlea Extension, so poor and dilapidated that it was christened Zombietown mere weeks after it was built. Mr Block died soon after arriving here. But Caplan has one more profound story to tell, in this new setting and before his father's death.

'My father would sometimes bring home from work a packet of fruit. He'd sit down in the middle of the lounge, right there on the floor. Then he'd call to my mother, 'Come!'

At this signal, Mrs Block would appear carrying the fruit in a dish. There'd be bananas, oranges, naartjies, apples and pears. Mr Block would attack the fruit with a sombre relish, eating and peeling and munching and spitting out pips.

'And your share's in the kitchen?' I ask him.

'No, no, no. What my father is eating is all that he has brought. It's all there on the plate being devoured. So now we smell the fruit because it fills our lounge with its delicious fragrance. And we can't help ourselves so we peep our heads into the lounge. He knows we're there but he doesn't look up. After a while he burps. There's maybe two bananas left, an apple, a half-eaten orange. He calls my mother and says, 'I'm finished, give it to them.'

'But why didn't he share it with you, his children?'

'It's our custom. Adults first.'

'Are you serious?'

He nods.

My mind goes back about fifteen years to when I'm about eight years old. We're three kids: me, Derek and the baby, Shaun. Ma comes from Roy, the fruit and veg hawker down the road, with a big hairy monkey's head in her bag.

'Whaddis?' Derek asks, 'pumpkin?'

'You're a pumpkin,' Ma says. 'It's a coconut.'

Shaun says, 'Jislaaik!' and we all laugh.

I thought I knew about coconut. It's the tiny white flakes that Ma sprinkles on to cakes. This must be coconut's new disguise.

Derek shakes it. 'There's water inside,' he says, his freckles sparkling.

'What are we gonna do with it?' Shaun wants to know.

That's the biggest joke for Ma and she laughs and rubs his head. Ma plucks the monkey's hair off him until he's bald and looks less menacing. She says, 'Look, eyes,' pointing to two distinct black spots. Ma explains that she will have to pierce through one of the eyes with a star screwdriver to get at the milk inside. 'And only one of them works,' Ma says.

I like this. We haven't eaten anything yet but it's all so exciting and interesting.

'Got him.' The screwdriver sinks in deep. 'OK, who's first?'

'Me.'

'Me.'

'Me.'

Ma puts the coconut to Shaun's mouth and he sucks at the hole and swallows. Then it's Derek's turn, then mine. I can't believe how sweet it is. We all smack our lips.

'Jislaaik,' says Shaun again.

'Like tietie?' Ma asks Shaun.

Shaun says yes but I say no. Ma says:

'Why no?'

'Because I never sucked *tietie*, I don't know how it tastes.'

'Ha! Never sucked it? *Die tieties het jou groot gemaak.*' She makes to pop one of them out and says, 'Come here and have a suck.'

I say, 'Ah no, leave me alone!' and run out of her reach.

We all laugh.

Ma takes her heavy brass pestle (the old stamper) and cracks the monkey skull open. The inside is pure white. She knocks it into little jagged triangles and squares and divides it up among us and we chew and laugh because it tastes so good.

So now, when Caplan says 'custom' I turn to him and I say:

'There's no such custom I know of. I think your father was just a glutton.'

The minute I say it, I realise that I may have overstepped a mark. That I've hurt him. But he looks at me for a long time and sits back in his chair and thinks. Then he says:

'You know what, Van Wyk? You're right.'

What the hell was this all about, I wonder. Maybe he'd been waiting patiently for years for someone to say that to him. I wish I could fathom it, understand it, and then write a profound poem about what's just transpired now. But I can't. Later on I do write a poem for Caplan. It's much simpler than the one I want to write. It goes like this:

Candle

Read, brother, read
The wax is melting fast
The shadows become obdurate
and mock pantomimes of you
laughing through crude cement
in silent stage whispers.
Read, brother, read,
though the wax lies heaped
in the saucer
and the silhouettes of gloom
grow longer.
Read brother read.
Only the wick shines red now.
But it is not yet dark.
Remember, brother,
it is not yet dark.

Caplan likes the poem. He's quite thrilled, like a little boy – even though he's about twenty-six at the time. But first he wants to know, 'What's pantomime?'

I tell him.

'And obdurate?' Caplan has a little stammer, which turns into a bigger little stammer whenever he gets excited or drunk.

I tell him what obdurate means. Then he says:

'One day you'll be a famous poet and people will ask, "Who's this Caplan guy who inspired you like this? You know what that means, Chap?"'

'What?'

'It means I'm immortal. It means that even when I die (which happened about eight years later), my name will still be said by people over and over again.'

Actually the poem is like preaching to the converted. When Caplan arrived in Johannesburg, he spoke only Afrikaans and knew hardly a word of English. And even when he did begin to learn to speak the language, he was too self-conscious to have a conversation. He began to read, by the light of those candles I've just mentioned. He read Graham Greene's *The Quiet American* and Joyce's *A Portrait of the Artist as a Young Man*. He read biographies of Karl Marx and Fidel Castro.

I remember especially the banned books because one day the cops come a-looking for me and Caplan and I decide it's time to hide our books for a while. We put them in a box and go around to Mr Cater, a sympathetic neighbour, who had offered to keep them hidden until the cops have come and gone.

A few weeks later we fetch our books. Mr Cater hands them back to us but Mrs Cater confronts us hysterical with anger.

'If yous wanna read this fucking shit, don't bring it to my house when the police come for yous, d'yous hear me?'

By the time Caplan is in his last year of high school he speaks better English than everyone, not only his Afrikaans-speaking classmates, but also the English-speaking families in Riverlea.

But he's anti-racist and a communist and goes about Riverlea sounding too much like a freak. Except when he's with friends like William and me. Then we all go about the township sounding like freaks. But at least it's not so lonely any more because now there are three of us.

When the three of us get together in shebeens and the Coloured and Asiatic bars, the regulars taunt us.

'Hey guys, here come the ANC!'

'So you *ous* reckon that Mandela will one day be president?'

(Lots of laughter)

Before I meet Caplan he has a white girlfriend – Love in the Time of Apartheid. She's a Jewish girl and her name is Jean. I don't know how long the relationship lasted but from what Caplan tells me (and of course William and I want all the details), it's quite exciting, for various reasons.

They met when Jean came to do charity work on behalf of Wits University's Witsco, with a bunch of white students from the northern suburbs. Caplan's conservative church-going sisters don't like her. For one thing, they say, she never dresses properly.

Jean would come a-visiting in a pure white mini dress – with absolutely nothing underneath. It's funny how something that can make a man so happy can make your sisters feel so disgusted. And then, just in case he hasn't noticed how skimpily she's dressed, she waits until they're alone in the bedroom or lounge then she stands and hoists her dress up to her tummy and shouts, 'Ta-ra!'

'Jesus, Block!' William and I exclaim in unison.

When he's looking for a job she buys him cigarettes and gives him the odd ten rand to help him through the week. She also sometimes loans him her car for the afternoon. He finds it in the Wits students' parking bay, with the key always in a secret place that only the two of them know about.

The cops sometimes tail them but, to give them some credit for a change, maybe they decide that they have better things to do with their time.

A big joke for Jean and Caplan is Jean's parents' reaction – if not to him then at least to his name. Sometimes he phones her home and asks to speak to her. If she's not in, Jean's mother or father takes a message.

'Jean dear,' they say, 'a Caplan Block called for you. Said he'd see you tomorrow at university. Nice name Caplan Block.'

'They just assume you're Jewish!' Jean laughs.

They're stinking rich, but streetwise they are not. Jean often smokes pot in her bedroom, puffing away contentedly. Her mother calls from downstairs, 'Are you OK, dear, there's a strange smell coming from your room.' 'Oh don't worry about that, mum, it's incense, I got it from my Indian friends at varsity.' 'What's it for, dear?' 'It's to make me happy, mum.' 'Is it working?' 'Like a charm, mum.'

So this is how we're whiling away the time. Sitting on the stoep and talking about the white people and the black people and how, in fact, in this beautiful country of ours, we sometimes get on but we mostly don't. And we're sipping away at our Old Brown and Coke on the rocks and minding our own business, and talking about the child Kathy and I will soon have. And then another story in our lives unfolds.

A police van comes to a halt across the road and a white cop, bulky and sweaty, hauls himself out of it.

Now what?

He makes his way across the road with his eyes fixed on the three of us in the shade. But he chooses the gate next door and enters. He stops by the fence close to us, in the shade of my mother-in-law's peach tree, which is hanging heavy with ripe peaches into the neighbour's yard. He says, in Afrikaans: 'I'm looking for the Booysens' house, am I at the right place?'

It is customary to end such a request with 'please' but he doesn't.

'You're in the right place,' I tell him, with more politeness than all three of us have ever had from an Afrikaner.

He doesn't thank me but nods, a kind of diluted form of thanks. He takes a long indulgent look at the three of us: our faces, our clothes, the glasses in our hands, the label of the bottle under my chair.

'So this is how bushmen while away their time,' he says. 'Getting drunk, doing nothing all day, every day. This is exactly how I know you people.' He laughs.

Before we can react he turns on his heel, walks up the path and knocks on the Booysens' door. A woman opens and he hands her some document or other and he is on his way back towards us. Again he stops by the peach tree and now says:

'I'll just help myself to some of these peaches while you bushmen get drunk, if that's OK with you.'

William pulls the specs from his nose and puts down his glass of Old Brown. He leaps out of his chair and walks towards the fat policeman, his finger pointing.

'Touch one of those peaches and you're a dead Afrikaner. Fuck off while you're still fat and alive, you ugly bastard.'

'D'you know who you're talking to? I'm Sergeant ...'

'You're spitting on my peaches, fuck off to your police station. You come here and insult us and then you expect us to let you have some of our peaches. Didn't your *Boer* mother teach you any manners?'

'I'll get you, I'll get you,' the sergeant says, very flustered and angry and redder in the face now than the ripest peach. He trots off to his car and speeds away.

'Smithie!'

'What if he comes back with back-up?'

'Fuck back-up. Where's that bottle, Van Wyk. My throat is full of dust.'

William and I meet through his mother, Vesta. Ma Vesta, as we call her, comes from a proud and secret tradition of anti-apartheid struggle and we were once colleagues at Sached, where I used to work. The first time William sees me, he thinks, 'Oh God, what a conservative-looking man. A priest, must be a priest. My mother's always introducing me to old ANC stalwarts and to priests. This one's definitely a priest.'

Vesta tells us one day that in the late fifties she would often be waiting for a bus from Noordgesig, adjacent to Soweto, to take her to town, when a friend from Orlando West, in Soweto, would pull up in his car and say, 'Come, Vesta, let me give you a lift.'

'Oh, hi, thanks Nelson.' And Mandela would give her a ride to town while they talked about the Defiance Campaign, he and Winnie's new baby or how his law practice was doing.

The orange Volksie parked outside our door is William's.

Like Caplan, William is also older than I am, by about four years.

Before the orange Volksie – and before we became friends – William used to drive a Kombi. One Saturday evening the

Kombi's packed with his girlfriend and friends and they're doing some serious shebeen crawling in Soweto. They're driving down a street in Soweto when kaboom, the kombi crashes into a horse.

William hits his head against the windscreen and suffers a zigzag gash on his forehead for his troubles. In a daze and in some pain, he and his friends take a walk to the local police station to report the accident.

The cops drive him back to the scene of the accident – except that the scene has changed considerably since the last time he was here. Now there are women all over the place armed with dishes, axes and knives, helping themselves to horsemeat. When the place clears, all that's left is a smashed Kombi and a horse's head.

William knows all the drinking holes in Noordgesig and Soweto. Each one has its own name and unique atmosphere. Among our favourites is the Black Widow in Orlando East, so called because the shebeen owner is a widow. Also in Orlando East there is the Round Table – and no matter how drunk you are, one look at the lounge table and you know why it's called that. In Noordgesig itself there's Foxy's, owned of course by Foxy.

On a Saturday evening, after the soccer matches have been played and there's nothing much to do, there is always Foxy's to go to and cool off in. You're bound to find the guys there, and if you're lucky you might even find Potsy regaling all with his tall stories – which he swears to be the truth. Everybody knows Potsy to be the biggest liar in Joburg. But, what the hell, the man's got a great imagination. And, in the absence of a good movie, Potsy's the best. So the guys fill their glasses, light up, and gather round Potsy Boy.

Of course, Potsy's glass has to be filled too before he begins. One story goes like this:

'I get to work one morning and the staff are all looking worried. 'What's wrong?' I ask them. They just shrug and tell me the boss is waiting for me in his office. I go in there.

'What's the matter, boss?'

He says, 'Ah Potsy, I'm glad you've arrived. You are the only one who can help me now.'

'Well, tell Potsy the problem and Potsy will see what Potsy can do.'

'There's a consignment of sixty helicopter engines down at the docks in Cape Town. They're from Czechoslovakia and I have to deliver them to a customer here on Wednesday.'

'Who's the customer, boss?'

'Potsy, that I cannot tell you. But all I can say is that the order is worth a million rands to me if I deliver on Wednesday. And worth nothing if I deliver even a day late.'

I say, 'Boss, the longer we talk the less time we got.'

I go into the workshop and tell the boys to get the truck ready and filled with diesel. I work it out. Eighteen hours to Cape Town, ten hours to load, eighteen hours back. I say to my boss, 'Don't worry, boss, I'll be back on Wednesday around this time.'

Off I go. One man, to Cape Town, 1 000 kilometres away. The road is long but I get there eighteen hours later, just like I planned. Next, I go to the docks and I hand over the papers and the workers start loading. They tell me 'Hey, why don't you take a nap while we load?' but I tell them no, Potsy's fine.

The packing takes ten hours, just like I planned. And now I have to drive back again. But, I tell you, I get behind the wheel, I switch on and there's trouble. Of all the gears only the reverse gear is working. So what do I do? I adjust that rear-view mirror and I reverse that loaded truck 1 000 kilometres all the way to Joburg.

Potsy has dozens of these fantastic stories where he saves the day for his boss. What amazed me though is that, despite his fertile imagination, he never once tells a story in which he's the boss and the white boss is his employee.

No freedom yet

On New Year's Day 1985 we head for the hills.

This is an unplanned trip taken on the spur of the moment and in a festive spirit. We make up four carloads of men and women, all in their twenties.

Into the boots of our cars we have packed swimming gear, watermelons, wine, beer, sandwiches, roasted chicken.

Some of us have our children with us. Between Kathy and me sits our four-year-old son, Kevin.

We drive in convoy for over two hours, mostly through conservative Afrikaner suburbs, whose inhabitants are mostly quiet and moving about leisurely on this public holiday.

It's warm and sunny; a perfect day for water and laughter.

Nobody knows for sure where we're going. But this is no problem because the outskirts of Joburg are just one great big picnic spot.

And, indeed, after a while the car in the lead pulls off. At first we smell the water, then we hear the sound of it as people jump into it laughing. Then we see it. There's a huge swimming pool and thatched roofs and patios and people jumping in and out of the water, eating, drinking and laughing. Radios are blaring and on it South Africans are wishing each other a happy new year and the DJ is pleading with everyone to be careful on the roads …

In mere minutes we're in the pool and it's hard to tell the difference between ourselves and the other guests.

Kathy and I are in the baby pool with Kevin, who is splashing about breathlessly.

But then management comes to break the spell.

We are sorry to disappoint you, they say, but this resort is for whites only. This has happened to every one of us before. Mostly you get thrown out. But, as in cases like this, you get asked politely to leave. This is probably because some manager believes he is actually not a racist, just forced to abide by the law of the land.

We gather up our belongings and make our way back to the cars, muttering about whitey under our breath. Kathy and I are walking with our son, in his still-wet trunks and his body still dripping. He suddenly pipes up:

'Mummy, Daddy, I want to stay here! It's nice here. Why are we going?'

'Because we don't have freedom yet, Kevs.' I explain.

He considers this for a few seconds and then he says to me:

'Then let's go and get the freedom!'

This was, in fact, what we are all trying to do when we were not looking for a picnic spot. The group of people I am spending the day with on this New Year's Day are actually all comrades in the United Democratic Front.

In 1983, after pressure from the international community, the apartheid government decides to play a trick on the world. President P. W. Botha announces that Coloureds and Indians will be included in the country's parliament and will have voting rights.

His plans are very complicated, but they work something like this: Coloureds will now have elections and vote for their representatives in a house of representatives. Indians will elect their leaders in a house of delegates. White people, however, will as usual still vote for the house of parliament and will continue to be in power.

And the blacks? They will be accommodated in their various homelands, where they will prosper and be happy.

ANC president, Oliver Tambo, calls on people inside the country to resist these racist shenanigans. Hundreds of church, women's, sport and youth groups, and trade unions throughout the country answer Tambo's call. And the young men and women who have just been turfed out of a holiday resort make up an organisation affiliated to the UDF.

For months – possibly years – we work at getting our freedom. We spend almost every weekend of our lives attending public meetings, writing and printing pamphlets, designing and putting up banners, gathering up signatures for our 'Release Mandela' campaign. (I sign about twenty times, my own name and a good few aliases.)

We also get chased by police, by thugs who believe we're up to no good, by police dogs, by township dogs.

It's mostly exciting work. But the state resists us with all its might and many among us are banned and jailed. And sadly there are also regular funerals of comrades killed by police bullets.

At some of these public meetings I am called upon to render a poem or two in between the speeches.

This is one of them:

My Mother

My mother could never carry me
While they used the warmth of her womb
To forge their hearts into hatred

My mother could never wean me
Because they dried her out
Until her breasts were arid tufts of drought

My mother could never embrace me
While she kept house for them
Held their children

My mother is a *boesman meid*
A kaffir girl
A coolie auntie
Who wears beads of sweat around her neck
And chains around her ankles

But defrocked of her dignity she
has broken free of the heirlooms of oppression
And dresses in the fatigues of those
Grown tired of serving evil gods

Now my mother is dressed to kill.

At about this time the UK magazine, *New Internationalist*, asks me to write an overview of events in the country. It appears, all nicely edited by one Chris Brazier and, quite frankly, making me look smarter than I actually am. Here it is:

Breaking the Spirit

South Africa's record for state terrorism is well known. But it is also guilty of another kind of violence. United Nations figures show that its people's life expectancy fell by eight years between 1981 and 1985. Chris van Wyk receives the news in his own black township.

Acknowledgement: New Internationalist

Riverlea, where I live, is a 'coloured' township clustered around a huge yellow mine dump just outside Johannesburg. The dump tapers sadly skywards like a huge, depleted breast: having weaned white people into the brave new world of a modern industrialised economy, it is of no use to anyone now. Certainly none of the inhabitants of Riverlea, who live in its shadow, have ever laid claim to any of its gold.

Riverlea is one of the forgotten townships. Too small and too quiet to have become a household word across the globe, like Soweto. But it is a suitable enough vantage point from which to view South Africa. *The New Internationalist* tells me that South Africa has the world's sharpest decline in life expectancy in the last few years. This doesn't surprise me – it is the good news which surprises after all these years rather than the gloomy. The black population here is certainly growing faster than the white, which means that each year there are proportionately more people in poverty, more lives lost before their time.

Even the official figures prove this. My wife and I have just had our second child. As a 'coloured' baby my son has a six percent chance of dying in his first year of life. A few miles away – in the world of white suburbia, in the house my next-door neighbour goes to clean every day, a baby has less than a quarter the risk of death. While in an 'African' township, such as Soweto, the risk goes up to eight percent.

Riverlea has always had its share of squalor, crime, unemployment and alcoholism – the natural consequences of apartheid. Unemployment is high. Every weekday morning the buses that take the more fortunate to work run the depressing gauntlet of unemployed people, who hang listlessly around on the streets. Out of long habit, these people rise early each morning. Perhaps this helps to keep them going, keeps them linked to a working class of which they were once a part.

Illegal shebeens and drug dealers have, as you may expect, prospered as unemployed people turn to them for solace. But alcohol and Mandrax don't come cheap. So there are more burglaries now, and muggings. But it is our own homes which are affected rather than those in the white areas which are protected by high security devices. So the quality of township life is made still poorer as we caught up in one of the downward spirals with which the poor the world over are so familiar.

Faced with such terrible inequalities, you might expect Riverlea to be a ferment of protest and political activism. It is not. The only time it even approached such a state was in 1984, when my township probably saw more political activity than it had in all the rest of the 25 years of its existence. This was because in that year 'coloured' and 'Indian' people were finally offered the vote – though for our own separate parliaments rather than on the same electoral roll as whites. Apartheid was to be further institutionalised.

To Riverlea and all the other 'coloured' and 'Indian' communities the government brought its latest offering. Along with other activists I warned people that the new parliament was not the Messiah. How could it be when among numerous other faults, it excluded the African people who comprised 74 percent of the population?

In the end most people did not vote. They were suspicious. Why was the Government suddenly asking them to get involved in politics? Politics! The very word that had for years been synonymous with police harassment, detention and treason ...

Amid all the pamphleteering and the police harassment, two of our comrades fall in love and we are invited to a wedding in Bosmont. They ask me to write a poem to read at their wedding. A wedding poem! A happy poem for a change. I take up the challenge with glee and my offering goes like this:

The wedding

Today two of my best friends are getting married
Lynda, the woman with the bursting laughter

And Ally, who talks to the people who inhabit his dreams
Are getting married today, to each other of course

And all their friends come to wish them happiness
And to dance in all the sunshine
Look, there's Kathy and Eddie and Jenny
And Cyril and Therese and Venita

And William probably got the date wrong in that
Ugly grey prison and will start dancing next week.

And for once we're dispersing confetti not pamphlets
Because Lynda and Ally are tired of separate
Development and want to live together as
Husband and wife.

This is magic
The sun shines through the church windows
And Ally takes just one golden ray
Twirls it into the most golden circle
And slips it onto her finger

And people spill out of their houses and flats
To come and see for themselves
All the love that bursts from the church
From the heart of Ally and Lynda

And those who can't come out to see
Because they have babies clinging to their breasts
And are linked to their pots by chains of salt
Watch from their windows and look like mosaics.

Now Ally and Lynda are one and before the sun
Sets Ally will laugh in his dreams
And Lynda will giggle at all the love
All the love, so much love.

The boys at the Fountains

At one point in my life I just cannot keep away from the Fountains. It's a pub about ten minutes drive from Riverlea and, ironically, in a very conservative Afrikaner area called Langlaagte.

Actually, it's a huge, spacious pub where the Afrikaner boys meet. And attached to this is a pokey little joint for the likes of 'Coloureds and Asiatics' – that's what the sign above the tiny entrance says. The 'Asiatics' refers to Indians and Chinese. But all the Chinese have been given 'honorary white' status and so you never really see them boozing with us.

What a messed up country! And when Kathy wants to know why I'm drinking so much, I tell her it's all these things: Coloured this and Asiatic that and you can't do this or go there. It's this lousy P. W. Botha driving me to drink, I say.

Inside is a small pool table, a dartboard on the wall, and an L-shaped bar.

Even though Kathy has never set foot in this place, she hates it.

I meet the most unusual men at the bar, starting with Uncle Philip himself, the man who sells us the liquor and watches us get drunk. He's of the Asiatic variety – Indian, dark, bespectacled and grey-haired. About sixty-five, he's been a barman all his adult life. But Uncle Philip has never tasted a drop of alcohol.

'Not even a beer?'

'Never,' he says. 'Beer, whisky, rum. You name it, I pour it, but tasted the stuff, never.'

I go to the pub with Fhazel, William, Keith, Caplan. Sometimes we're a threesome, a twosome, sometimes we're there all together, running up a tab that will make us feel more miserable than the *babalaas* the next day.

I don't blame Kathy for hating the Fountains. A lot of women, wives and mothers, appear at the door and swear at their husbands. They say things like this: 'Look at the time! Look at the time!' 'So you tell me you're going to buy potatoes!' Or when they're really angry: 'Jesus, but you're one big fuck-up!'

The poor man leaves, humiliated, with his shirt hanging out, leaving behind a beer getting too warm to drink. And, of course, the next time he puts in an appearance, we all go: 'Jesus, but you're a fuck-up!'

The women never come right inside. They do their swearing and scolding from the threshold. It's as if they all once attended a secret meeting somewhere where they took an oath: 'We will never enter that Coloured and Asiatic pigsty called the Fountains.'

They do have a point. The jokes are so ugly that you have to be drunk to take some of the filth out of them. And try repeating them to sober people the next day and they'll say you need to have your mouth cleaned out.

Neville is a regular. I swear that if he stopped drinking for six months he'd still smell. He's a piles sufferer and the more he drinks the worse the piles get. One day the pain is so unbearable that Neville, still drunk from the night before, goes up to his father, a frail man in his seventies, catching some sunlight in his backyard. Neville pulls down his pants, bends over and implores his father to blow some cold air on to his bum.

'Blow, Daddy, blow.'

Then there's Jerome. He gets so totally pissed every single night that we have to carry him into his friend's car ... The next morning his wife wakes him up for work.

'Why didn't you give me my supper last night?' he wants to know from her.

'Aw, Jerome, I gave you your supper last night and you ate it.'

'So why is there no meat stuck in my teeth?' he wants to know.

Bevan is another regular. He's an alcoholic who actually does not believe he's one. He runs an art school in town and because of his job he has to attend dozens of education workshops and seminars all over the country. Whenever he's invited to any of these, he reads the agenda very carefully and arrives, whether by plane or by car, at the precise moment when cocktails are being served and the meeting is over. There's something about liquor in every story he ever tells (and liquor in him when he tells it).

When he finished high school in the late sixties, his parents sent him to London to do some course or other. While studying he got odd jobs cleaning the homes of Londoners.

'While I vacuum I look for the liquor cabinet and the keys to it. So while the madam is in the bedroom, I'm taking a good few slugs of her whisky. But the trick is not to turn off the vacuum, otherwise she'll know you're up to something.'

Bevan's stories are interesting but they come to you at a great cost to your personal hygiene. He's a spitter, one of those who sprays you wet when he says hullo to you. And to make matters worse, he insists on standing right up against you when he's having a chat. The only time he moves away from you is when it's his turn to buy a round.

For one or two short weeks Bevan gets it into his head that he has to go around in a long beard, a kaftan over his big, fat paunch and sandals. Kids in the street run after him calling him Demis Roussos (the big, fat Greek pop singer often seen on TV) and that puts paid to that little fashion statement.

Desmond is an undertaker. His stories are full of coffins and dead people. But if you're into black humour, he's your man. One of his classics goes like this:

'On my first day of the job the boss sends me to fetch two corpses. The first corpse is a man who tried to cross a railway line and was knocked to pieces. My colleague and I go and we pick him up – about twenty different bits – head here, half an ear there, arm here, thigh there. We put it all in the back of the van and off we go. Our next stop is another body in Hillbrow. This fellow was happily driving behind a lorry that was carrying a load of corrugated zinc. The lorry goes up that steep hill in Nugget Street and one of the zincs slides off and cuts off the man's head.

'We pick up his corpse and throw it in the back of the van where the other corpse is and off we go to the funeral parlour. On the way there we both suddenly realise we're going to have one serious problem when we get to the office – we won't know which head belongs to which body. So to this day there are two graves that just might have the wrong heads – or the wrong bodies.'

I myself am not much better than any of the above. William and I get so hopelessly drunk sometimes that he phones me the next morning.

'Van Wyk?'

'Ja.'

'Tell me, how did we get home last night?'

'You dropped me off, in the Volksie … I think.'

One day William and I take a walk down the road from the bar because he wants to show me something interesting.

'What's it, Smithie?'

'Just follow me.'

There's an old movie house called the Broadway. It's falling apart but surviving because of the kinds of movies it shows. William points to the posters advertising the latest offering.

'What d'you think?' he says.

I don't know what to say. Currently showing is a porn movie and, according to the poster, it has something for everyone: whips, breasts, bums … and it promises that there are no shy girls in the movie. The coming attractions are just as lewd.

'This is porn!'

'That's what it is,' he chuckles.

'Do the *Boere* know about this?'

He shrugs. 'I don't think they care any more. They're leaving it to Mandela to sort out when they let him out in a couple of years.'

'This is a plot to kill Mandela,' I say. 'They couldn't kill him in the sixties so they'll kill him now. We must inform the UDF about this.'

'Do you think we should go in, just to see what a porn movie is all about?'

'What if the cops come?'

'Ag, these guys are giving the cops a cut of the profits, Van Wyk.'

'Man, I don't know …'

'Hey, you're a writer, man. It's for experience.'

'Ja, OK, let's go.'

Smithie pays at the dingy little box office. We disappear into the dark auditorium, Smithie leading the way.

An usher shines his little torch on us and says, 'Ah, Smithie, how you doing? I see you've brought a buddy.'

The Fountains has probably been around since the prohibition was lifted in about 1964. Mr Flusk is a teacher who has been drinking here since then. He remembers one amusing confrontation. He and his teacher colleagues came over one afternoon to sink a few beers.

'We get out of the car and there's a *Star* poster declaring: "Barnard Transplants Heart". There's a bunch of *Boere* schoolkids, teenagers, also reading this big news. I turn to them and I say, "So now we can put a black man's heart into a white man."

'One of them says, "True, but remember it's only a white man who can do it."'

Almost twenty years later, my encounter with the *Boere* at that pub would be very different.

On 11 June 1986 Keith phones me at work. He suggests a beer and I say OK. He says he'll pick me up at about 5.30, and what about those posters I promised him? I say I'll bring them. He's seen our promotional posters for all the books we publish. There are posters announcing our history series: all the history that apartheid has kept hidden away from us. There are posters about workers' struggles, religion, children's books, new South African literature.

It's all very normal promotional material. But in South Africa it looks like the work of revolutionaries, terrorists, communists.

But I roll up a couple for Keith. He picks me up at 5.30 and off we go.

At the pub we drink our beer and play our darts and at one point I unfurl the posters and show them around. This is not the most appreciative of crowds. They're mostly drunk and indifferent and ninety-nine per cent of them are quite happy to see the Afrikaners kick them around for ever.

At about 9.45 we roll up the posters and off we go. Kathy's waiting for me at home and I'm working out what to tell her this time. We get into the car and Keith drives no more than fifty metres when we hear the voice on the loudhailer telling us to stop the car.

But before we can get out, three very big *Boers* and one tiny one yank us from the car. Each one of them is carrying a huge rifle. They pin us against the car and frisk us. They find the posters and then all hell breaks loose.

They beat us with their fists, they kick us, they spit in our faces. The three big ones are meticulous, they swear from time to time. But the tiny one is completely mad, weeping with hatred and rage. 'You fucken bastards want to take our country!' he keeps screaming. 'Why? Take my country and give it to the fucking kaffirs. Why?'

He keeps asking me this, begging me to tell him.

I wish I had an answer that would make them stop, but I don't.

They ask Keith, 'Where's your fucking jumper cables?'

He says he doesn't have any.

Four more big cops pull up. They have jumper cables. They tell Keith to drop his pants.

'Why?'

'So we can clamp them on to your fucking bushman cock and give you a boost!'

They give him another slap in the face and seem to forget about this weird plan. But only until one of them actually does find jumper cables somewhere in Keith's car. Then they start laying into him again.

In the meantime, our friends have spilled out of the pub and are watching all this in total shock and horror.

Some colonel fellow pulls up. They crowd around him and tell him what they've just caught. He too is a small fellow with the customary moustache. He says to me:

'Your face looks terrible, what happened?'

'These men beat me up, sir.'

'Oh please, don't talk shit. We don't beat people up.'

'I'm sorry, sir. I bumped my head as I got out of the car.'

'That's better.'

His underlings double up with laughter and he joins in.

They take us to John Vorster Square. Keith's in one cop car and I'm in the other, we're both bleeding and in pain. They have a race to the police station, swearing at each other through their open windows.

'*Fok jou*, Fanus!'

'Pasop man, jou fokken doos!'

They are P. W. Botha's young, white soldiers enjoying the last days of their rule on the southern tip of Africa. But even as they're having fun, they're going mad because they see it slipping away, changing hands, changing colour.

They drive into the basement of John Vorster Square, a place that is becoming all too familiar to me these days. They order us to wash the blood off our faces at a tap. A few of them disappear into the huge building.

And what do you think these guys tell their womenfolk when they get home? Well, they don't have to tell them anything because the women know very well what their men are doing and, what's more, they approve.

I know this because, while Keith and I are shivering there like sheared sheep, a bunch of about five blonde, female cops appear. They stop and stare and start laughing at us.

'Have you boys been naughty?' one of them asks, and they do that one-foot-in-the-air thing that girls do when they're having a good time.

The big cop, who's probably got my features imprinted on his fists, comes down to the basement.

'Van Wyk!' he shouts, 'you've got a fokken file here and you don't tell us!'

What can I say, I'm a modest guy. I'm convinced that the beatings are going to start again, but they don't. Instead he asks me the most ridiculous favour.

'Would you consider becoming an informer for us?'

Only if I survive this beating, I feel like saying. I say I'll think about it – what I didn't explain was that every time I thought about it I'd say, what a shit idea.

Later they decide they've had enough of us and they drop us off back at Keith's car. We are so shocked that we don't know what to say to each other.

But the ANC hears about my ordeal and a few months later I am flown to Amsterdam where I appear on Dutch television. I tell the world all about my bloody night, a blow-by-blow account. And it's not the version that made the colonel laugh so outrageously when I said I'd bumped my head getting out of the car.

'I will return'

WHAT WAS THAT POEM I WROTE about my ouma the other day?

Ouma's hair is turning silver
as the stars drop their tears on her head
begging her to come and live among them
in their own version of paradise.
Ouma has been resisting for so long now
But soon I know she'll give in …

Quite lyrical, even if I say so myself. I especially like that image of the stars dropping their silver on her head as she slowly dies …

But what nonsense!

Ouma Ruby is still very much alive. In fact she's … Wait, let me tell you the whole thing.

In 1985 two South Africans made important announcements. One was Ouma Ruby and the other P. W. Botha, president of white South Africans.

To my shame, I was paying more attention to Botha than to Ouma Ruby. You see, Botha says in parliament that he's willing to release Mandela, but on certain conditions. He has to renounce violence. This from a man whose apartheid has been killing us for decades!

Mandela thinks about this. Then he writes a letter that he sneaks out of Pollsmoor prison in Cape Town. On 10 February 1985 all of us, the beaten up, the spied on, the tortured and the still-to-be-tortured, the fugitives from apartheid police, we're all there under the banner of the UDF to hear what Mandela has to say about the matter.

Mandela's daughter, Zindzi, reads the letter. It's longish but basically it says to Botha, 'Get lost.'

There's a message for us too. He says: 'I will return.'

There is so much excitement and tragedy and apprehension in South Africa that for a while I don't pay too much attention to my Ouma Ruby. But I will go around to see her one of these days, I keep saying to myself, I will, I will.

Then one day I hear that my ouma has decided to move to Cape Town.

She says, 'I'm old, nobody visits me any more these days. There's a nice old-age home there …'

But why Cape Town? Her family's up here in Joburg. Eleven children, almost fifty grandchildren. She'll die of loneliness down there in Cape Town, where she has no family except an old cousin or something, a woman called Joey. Has she made up her mind already? Yes! She's going. Ag, no! I feel bad. But I will at least go and say goodbye.

But I put that off for a day, and then a week, and a month and, the next thing I know, she's gone.

This is bad. My seventy-year-old ouma's gone off to die in Cape Town. A few months go by. Silence. Then up here in Joburg, somebody's phone rings. It's Ouma Ruby. She says:

'I've fallen in love … I'm not joking … he's my age … Theo Galant … Elsies Rivier … we're going to get married … Too many questions. We're coming up to Joburg and then all of yous can meet him.'

They come up in 1987 and I like my future grandfather from the word go. In fact, when they come up, it's to get married here in Joburg, in the Ebenezer Church in Corrie, my ouma's old place of worship for decades, and for my entire childhood.

Ouma has found a new soul mate, a quarter of a century after the death of my grandfather. And what a grand-looking item they are. Ouma Ruby in elegant two-piece pastel-coloured suits, he in a suit and tie always. And, very important later in this story, a hearing-aid dangling from one ear.

Mere minutes after we've been introduced, and without any prompting from me, he tells me about his courtship. I sit up; this I want to hear.

His previous wife died only a few years ago and, with kids all grown up and out of the house, he's a lonely man. He spends his days tending the church's garden. He's a *kerksmens*, a staunch churchgoer, and a teetotaller – not for him those late harvests and dry reds and semi-sweet whites that the Cape is so famous for all around the world. Some nights he takes a walk down the road to visit an old neighbour three doors away, Josephine, or Joey as everyone calls her.

One evening he walks into Joey's house and there's this beautiful woman he's never seen before.

'Good evening.'

'*Aangename kennis.*'

'How d'you do?'

Usually he's as chirpy and noisy as the sound of cups and teaspoons. But tonight ... well, tonight he adjusts his hearing-aid and positions himself in a chair so that his better ear can hear everything this lady from Joburg is saying.

And it's my wife died in 19-this and my husband died in 19-that. I'm sorry to hear that and I'm sorry to hear this. *En hier te lank en daar te kort.*

And that night Theo Galant finds that he just can't sleep, and it's not just because of the five cups of tea he's had at Joey's place.

And the next evening he's back at Joey's place again. And the next and the next. Lately, Joey is discreetly excusing herself from these conversations, which carry on late into the night.

One late night Theo gets up to leave. He lives a mere three doors away but Ruby says, 'Will you be safe?'

He says, 'Huh?' because the battery in his hearing-aid is weak.

'Will you be safe, Theo?'

He says, 'I'll phone you when I get home.' And four minutes later he's on the phone. They chat for another fifteen minutes. Then he says:

'Goodnight. Pptt, pttt pt.'

Ruby says, 'Did you hear that?'

'What?'

'There was a funny noise on the phone, like a bird or a cat or something.'

'No,' he says, 'that was me ... I was kissing you goodnight.'

Meeting Mandela

IT'S A SUNNY DAY IN JOBURG, 11 February 1990, and the four Van Wyks, Kathy, Karl, Kevin and I are all in Corrie. We're at a party celebrating Kathy's granny's 83rd birthday.

Up to two years ago she was still a grand old lady who read *The Star* and smoked half a pack of Peter Stuyvesant every day.

But news is no longer an important item in her life. Senility has taken care of that. It's a strange disease; one day her mind is clear and she's talking about a conversation she had with a shopkeeper yesterday as well as the miner's strike of 1946.

But right here at the party, while we're all tucking into braai-ed meat and salads and drinking beer, she turns and says to me, 'Who are you? What do you want here? Why are we having this party?'

Kathy explains, 'It's Chris, Ma, my husband ...'

I'm not at all offended, especially today when, in a few hours time, Nelson Mandela will walk out of prison after 27 years and lead us all down a long road which a few years ago did not even exist on an official South African road map.

Within his first few months of freedom Mandela probably breaks a new record for meeting the most people a man has ever met. He shakes hands with people I wouldn't have shaken hands with myself, like some Coloured leaders who supported the apartheid tri-cameral parliament.

But who am I to talk? A little reciter of poems between all the speeches. Mandela is the future president.

The first person in my circle of friends and comrades to meet Mandela personally is none other than old Bevan, the educationist, who is still pouring whiskies down his throat and breaking a record of his own.

Once more, I suffer the spray as I lean forward to listen.

Bevan is invited to a play at the Market Theatre in Newtown to raise funds for some charitable cause, and he hears Mandela himself might be attending.

Bevan dresses up, trims his beard, drinks a whisky or two and makes his way to the theatre. He takes his seat, a VIP one, and sits down and waits for the action, either for the show to begin or for the possible arrival of Madiba.

Bevan does not wait in vain. Five minutes after he's taken his seat, there's a buzz of excitement at the door. Can it be …? Bevan wonders, craning his neck like everyone else in the auditorium.

'MandelaMandelaMandela,' the buzz electrifies the entire auditorium. And, sure enough, it is the man himself, flanked – no – surrounded – by bodyguards. And there's a standing ovation.

'I'm in the same room as Mandela,' Bevan tells himself, grinning delightedly.

Mandela is led up the aisle and then Bevan sees him being shown to the very row he's sitting in.

'Jislaaik!' Bevan blows whiskily into the air, 'I'm in the same row as the big man.'

But it doesn't end there. Mandela is ushered right up to where Bevan is seated. And Bevan realises he's sitting in the future president's seat!

'Oh, I'm sorry, Mr Mandela, I … I …'

Mandela says in his unique drawl, 'There is no problem, young man, a seat is a seat, you stay right there where you are and we will enjoy the show together.'

What a story!

Another million or so handshakes later, I get to meet Mandela myself. In 1994 he comes to Riverlea on the ANC's election campaign trail. On the stage are Allan Boesak, Trevor Manuel and Mandela himself. And me! My job is to ignite the audience with a poem before the speeches begin.

Riverlea has come out in force, in broken shoes and patched jackets, and missing teeth, smothered in Vaseline and smelling of paraffin and confused about being Coloured. They have come to hear and see Mandela.

After my reading I go back to my seat, which is the furthest away from Mandela. But Manuel taps me on the shoulder and says, 'Chris, Mandela wants to thank you for the poem.'

I go up to Mandela and he shakes my hand warmly and says, 'Thank you, young man.' Riverlea erupts and all I can do is nod and say is, 'Yes, Mr Mandela' and for once I'm glad to have such a rowdy neighbourhood.

After the wedding the Galants go back to Cape Town to live there. In 1992 Kathy, Kevin, Karl and I get on to a train to visit them. And they are doing all right and happy to see us.

One Sunday morning the new Mrs Galant, who is still my old Ouma Ruby, is cooking Sunday lunch in the kitchen. Kathy is helping her and I'm sitting in the lounge with my new grandfather, his sons and one or two neighbours who have popped in to say hullo. We're telling jokes and it's Neville's turn. He's Pa Galant's eldest son, about forty-two years old. His joke is all in Afrikaans and it goes like this:

One day there was Gamat and Abdol. But, I tell you, could these two drink! Every day drinking that soetes (sweet wine). One day Gamat staggers out of the bottle store carrying another bottle of wine under his arm. He bumps right into Father Jacobs.

Father Jacobs: So what's that you got under your arm, Gamat?

Gamat: Wine, Father.

Father Jacobs: But when are you going to stop drinking?

Gamat: Father, as God is my witness, this bottle that I have here in my hand will be the last bottle of wine I ever drink.

Father Jacobs: And you really expect me to believe that?

Gamat: I won't lie to the Almighty God, Father.

Father Jacobs: Oh, and what should I do if I ever see you with a bottle of wine in your hands again?

Gamat: Father, if you see me with a bottle of wine after today, I'll take the cork out and pour it all out right here in front of you.

Father Jacobs: That's a deal.

Well, the next day Father Jacobs just happens to be walking past the very same bottle store when he sees the very same Gamat coming out of the bottlestore with a bottle under his arm.

Father Jacobs: Good afternoon, Gamat.

Gamat: Ooh, Father, you gave me such a *skrik*!

Father Jacobs: So what is that you have under your arm, Gamat?

Gamat: It's a bottle of wine, Father.

Father: And did you not make a promise to me only yesterday?

Gamat: Of course I did, Father.

Father: And what was that promise?

Gamat: That I will throw out my wine right here on this pavement if you ever see me with a bottle of wine again.

Father: Well, I'm waiting.

Gamat: But I can't do that, Father.

Father: And why not?

Gamat: You see, Father, me and Abdol we bought this wine together. Now we agreed that the top half of the wine is his and the bottom half is mine. So now I can't throw out my half without throwing out his half first.

While we're all laughing, Pa is adjusting his hearing-aid. He says, 'My turn, my turn,' and he begins: 'One day there was a man called Gamat and could this man drink? One day he comes out of a bottle store in Athlone with a bottle of wine and he walks right into Father Jacobs ...'

A miracle and a wonder

So one day I'm sitting at home with my two sons and we're waiting for Kathy to come home from work. Kevin is six years old and Karl is a baby a few months old and sitting on my lap.

I put on Paul Simon's 'Graceland' album and we're rocking there in the kitchen and if Kathy doesn't come home soon she's gonna be missing one helluva party.

Paul Simon sings and I sing with him: 'These are the days of miracles and wonder, this is the long-distance call. The way the camera follows us in slo-mo …'

'Daddy, daddy, daddy,' Kevin's tugging at my sleeve.

'What?'

'What's a miracle?'

How do I explain this one? 'If something cannot happen, if it's impossible, but it does happen, that's a miracle.' He's not sure what I mean. He's become a very keen birdwatcher over the last few months so I decide to give him an example with birds in it. 'OK, let's say you wake up tomorrow morning and you look through the window and you're hoping to see just one bird and what do you see …?'

'What, what?'

'You see every kind of bird in the world.'

'Could that ever happen, Daddy?'

'If it did it would be a miracle.'

'Now tell me what's a wonder?'

'A wonder. That's also a miracle, but a small one.' Suddenly I have an idea. 'Hey you know what? You're a miracle, my miracle. Because, you see, I never thought I could have a son one day and then you were born and I said to Mummy, jislaaik, look at him, a miracle!'

He likes my example and he smiles and says, 'So I'm a miracle and Karl's a wonder.'

Miracle. Wonder. Call it what you will. On 27 April 1994 it happens for over 40 million South Africans.

The stories begin again

THIS IS MY STORY. Not all of it, but a large chunk of it, anyway. And to tell my own story I've had to tell you about my family, my friends, the people of Riverlea.

What will they say when they read this?

If they're anything like Vivian Basset, then the answer is: nothing.

Let me tell you what I mean.

After the elections many of my comrades and friends move out of Riverlea. The leafy, formerly white suburbs beckon and they migrate with undue haste.

I decide to stay here. There are so many people in their eighties and nineties who have stories to tell. Stories that need to be told, stories that are a part of our history and which apartheid had made us believe should never be told.

(Who am I fooling? I can't afford those heavy bond repayments.)

But now these people are telling these stories. And they're telling them to me. And they trust me and speak to me easily because I grew up here. I played football in the streets here. I went to school here. I got married here. I was an activist here. And now I even work from home here, as a full-time writer.

So, at least once a week, I take my tape-recorder and I my 90-minute cassette and I go and have a good *skinder* with an old man or woman. And the stories I hear!

The other day I go and interview Mrs Stoltenkamp, who is ninety years old and in a wheelchair. She's hard of hearing so I have to shout a little. Otherwise everything else is fine.

She tells me that when her mother was a little girl in the late 1800s she and her sister became well known far and wide for their fine singing voices. So famous in fact that President Paul Kruger himself used to send for them to come and sing for him at his Presidential home in Pretoria.

'President Paul Kruger, Oom Paul?' He was the president of the old Transvaal republic, who led the *Boers* in battle against the British in the Anglo Boer War in 1899.

'Yes, my son. But my mother was scared to sing in front of him?'

'Why?'

'Because she thought he was ugly.'

She smiles while I have a good laugh.

I say, 'And so, what did your mother do?'

'Well, the president found a good way to solve the problem. He let my aunt sing in front of him but he told my mother it's OK if she stood down the passage where she didn't have to look at him. Then they sang.'

So way back in the late 1800s the president had a stereo system going in his house.

But I was going to tell you about Vivian. He's about three or four years older than I am. When I was in primary school, he was in high school. But by the time I got to high school, he had long since dropped out and gone to work in a factory somewhere. Today he's a taxi driver taking Riverlea commuters to town and back about ten times a day in his minibus.

Even though I work from home these days, once or twice a week I have to go into town on some or other business. I always take a book with me and as soon as I get into a taxi I open it and read. After several years and probably about two dozen books, Vivian turns to me and asks me what he's obviously been wanting to ask for a long time:

'Hey, Chris, have you finished with school?'

I put my book down on my lap. 'Aw, Vivian. I'm 38 years old. Of course I'm finished.'

'Are you at varsity or college or something?'

'No, I'm not?'

'You not studying?' he makes sure.

'No.'

'Then why the hell are you still reading books?'

Glossary

19-voetsak – 19-whatever

aan die vrek – lifeless
aangename kennis – pleased to meet you
amperbaas – almost a master
amperbaasskap – the job of being a master
atchar – a spicy pickle made from vegetables or fruit

babalaas – a hangover
bangbroek – scaredy pants, coward
Boer (plural Boere) (*n* and *adj*) – Afrikaner
boesmanne – bushmen (a derogatory term for Coloureds)
bokkie – little buck, also a term of endearment
boude – thighs

chommies – buddies, chums

Die Jood – The Jew
die tieties het jou groot gemaak – you were raised on these breasts
diezie – to divvy up or share out
dorp – town
duisendpoot – centipede

en hier te lank en daar te kort – talking about this, that and the other

gatjie klip – stone in the hole, a game
goggas – creepy-crawlies
gwara – teasing

heit – hi
hoezit – howzit
hok – cage
Hotnot – a derogatory term for Coloureds
houtkop – wooden head

jags – feverishly randy, desperate for sex
jislaaik – an exclamation of surprise
juffrou – madam

kak – shit
kerksmens – an ardent churchgoer
kirrebekke – a street game
klaar – finish
klein gatjie – small hole
koek – private parts (female)
koeksister – a plaited, doughnut-like confectionery
koezat – to pool your money with a group of friends
kruie – herbs
kwela-kwela – police van

laaitie – a male child, youngster, kid
larney (*n*) – white man, boss, (*adj*) – rich, posh

mealiemeal – maize meal
meneer – sir
mfowethu – brother
moer – hit
morogo – a type of wild spinach

nogal – to boot

Ollie – a children's game, also known as Tag
opstel – essay
ougat – too big for your boots

padkos – food to have on a long journey (food for the road)
pasop man, jou fokken doos – a very vulgar way to tell someone to move out of the way

renoster – rhinoceros

saamgaan? – May I come too?
sambal broek – overlarge pants
sersant – sergeant
shaya – beat up
skelm – a scoundrel

skinder – gossip
skorokoro – jalopy
skrik – fright
smaaks me stukkend – loves me to bits
sommer – just, simply
stokstyf – stiff as a stick
stokvel – an informal savings club
stompie – a cigarette end
streepie – a mouse with a stripe on its back
strokies – cartoons

takkies – flat, soft shoes for sport or casual wear, running shoes
tieping – passed out from having had too much to drink
tieties – breasts

Vader Jakob – Brother Jacob (Frère Jacques)
vang die ding en laat ons klaarkry – catch the thing and let's get it over with
Verwoerd gaan sterwe / wie gaan hom begrawe / sy eie soldate – Verwoerd will die / who will bury him / his own soldiers
vetkoek – fatcake, a deep-fried cake made from unsweetened dough
vlei – stream

wietie – chat, have a discussion, say
woza – come here

yebo – yes (Zulu)